Mass Political Culture Under Stalinism

Olga Velikanova

Mass Political Culture Under Stalinism

Popular Discussion of the Soviet Constitution of 1936

Olga Velikanova
Department of History
University of North Texas
Denton, TX, USA

ISBN 978-3-319-78442-7   ISBN 978-3-319-78443-4 (eBook)
https://doi.org/10.1007/978-3-319-78443-4

Library of Congress Control Number: 2018936593

© The Editor(s) (if applicable) and The Author(s) 2018
This work is subject to copyright. All rights are solely and exclusively licensed by the Publisher, whether the whole or part of the material is concerned, specifically the rights of translation, reprinting, reuse of illustrations, recitation, broadcasting, reproduction on microfilms or in any other physical way, and transmission or information storage and retrieval, electronic adaptation, computer software, or by similar or dissimilar methodology now known or hereafter developed.
The use of general descriptive names, registered names, trademarks, service marks, etc. in this publication does not imply, even in the absence of a specific statement, that such names are exempt from the relevant protective laws and regulations and therefore free for general use.
The publisher, the authors and the editors are safe to assume that the advice and information in this book are believed to be true and accurate at the date of publication. Neither the publisher nor the authors or the editors give a warranty, express or implied, with respect to the material contained herein or for any errors or omissions that may have been made. The publisher remains neutral with regard to jurisdictional claims in published maps and institutional affiliations.

Cover image: © Everett Collection Historical/Alamy Stock Photo
Cover design: Fatima Jamadar

Printed on acid-free paper

This Palgrave Macmillan imprint is published by the registered company Springer International Publishing AG part of Springer Nature
The registered company address is: Gewerbestrasse 11, 6330 Cham, Switzerland

To Maia and Neil

ACKNOWLEDGEMENTS

The work on Mass Political Culture started many years ago when I discovered in the Russian archives bold comments of the Soviet people regarding the Constitution of 1936. I am grateful to the archivists N. I. Abdulaeva at GARF, I. N. Selezneva and G. V. Gorskaia at RGASPI, and G. I. Lysovskaia at TsGAIPD in Saint-Petersburg who helped me search the materials in the Moscow and Saint-Petersburg archives.

I am honored to note for the record that the University of North Texas, its History Department, and my colleagues there generously supported my research with several Faculty Research and Travel grants, a Development Leave award, with valued advice and constant encouragement. For this and so much more I cordially thank my colleagues for making the UNT History Department such a great place to work.

My fellowship at the European University Institute in Florence, Italy, offered a perfect—and perfectly exciting—atmosphere for beginning work on this manuscript. Discussions with students and colleagues there, especially Alexander Etkind and Stephen Smith, helped me to frame my analytical approach. I have never worked so productively as in my office in the medieval monastery that provided inspiration and seclusion for contemplation and writing.

My thoughts and conjectures on the political culture of Soviet society greatly benefited from interviews with Russian historians Arseny Roginsky (Memorial Society, Russia) (deceased) and Anatoly Razumov (Returned Names Center, Saint-Petersburg). I am honored to have had the opportunity to engage in many conversations on politics and culture with Sergey Kovalev, the first Ombudsman of the Russian Federation, and a major contributor to the Article on Rights and Liberties of Man and Citizen of the Constitution of the Russian Federation.

I presented papers on my ongoing research at various international conferences—the Association for Slavic, East European, and Eurasian Studies (US); the British Association for Slavonic and East European Studies (Cambridge, UK); the 24th International Conference of Europeanists (Glasgow); the 14th Annual International Aleksanteri Conference (Helsinki); and several universities. The discussions I had with my colleagues Kirill Alexandrov, Clayton Black, Arch Getty, Lars Lih, Alexander Livshin, Igor Orlov, Richard Sakwa, and Lewis Siegelbaum about various aspects of this study were immensely valuable. I am also appreciative of the anonymous reviewers who read the manuscript or its parts and made insightful suggestions and extremely helpful critiques.

This book would not have been possible without the support of and intellectual inspiration from these many people and institutions.

I want to express my special thanks to people who gave me friendly or professional assistance at different moments of my work on this book, especially Luda Dillon; and Mikhail Iakovlev, my husband and a historian himself. Superb meticulous work on the proofreading of the manuscript was done by Bonnie Lovell and Hailey Stewart.

Last, to John Dillon, who performed a superlative full literary edit on the manuscript, I give particular recognition and deep thanks. *Spasibo!*

The author and the publishers wish to thank the Central State Archives of Documentary Films, Photographs, and Sound Recordings of Saint-Petersburg for permission to reproduce copyright photographs.

Contents

1	Introduction	1
	References	12
2	Sources	15
	References	23

Part I Government Goals for the Constitution Revision and National Discussion

3	The Origins of Constitutional Reform	29
	References	36
4	Moderation in the Policies of the Mid-1930s	37
	References	46
5	Motives for the New Constitution	49
	5.1 *The International Factor*	49
	5.2 *The Ideological Factor*	52
	5.3 *Internal Policies*	62
	References	67

6	Soviet Sociopolitical Mobilizations	71
	6.1 Reporting Campaign in the Soviets	71
	6.2 The Local Cadres: Between a Rock and a Hard Place	74
	6.3 Participation: Managed and Voluntary	78
	6.4 The Soviet Public Sphere in the 1930s	92
	References	96
7	State's Goals for the Nationwide Discussion	99
	References	107

Part II Popular Perceptions of the Constitution

8	The Economic Condition at the Grassroots	111
	References	121
9	Liberal Discourse	123
	9.1 The Judicial Innovations of the Constitution	124
	9.2 The Workings of the Soviets and Electoral Reform	129
	9.3 The Rights of Special Settlers in Light of the Constitution	137
	9.4 Skepticism About Fair Elections	144
	9.5 New Freedoms in the Popular Discourse	149
	References	159
10	Voices Against Liberties	163
	10.1 Religious Liberties: Popular and Government Views	171
	10.2 The Duty to Hate: Brutalization on the Ground	187
	10.3 The Statist Code of Political Culture	191
	10.4 Militarism, Defeatism, and Regimentation	195
	References	199
11	Other Comments and Recommendations	205
	11.1 Demands for Welfare Benefits	205
	11.2 Distrust	212
	References	218

12	Outcome of the Discussion: From Relaxation to Repression	221
	References	232
13	On Russian Political Culture in the Twentieth Century	235
	References	242
14	Conclusion	245
	References	250
Glossary		251
Index		253

List of Figures

Photo 6.1	The students of the Lesgaft State Institute of Physical Education and Sport in Leningrad discussing the draft of the constitution. Photographer unknown. Courtesy of the Central State Archives of Documentary Films, Photographs, and Sound Recordings, Saint-Petersburg (TsGAKFFD SPb)	83
Photo 6.2	Discussion of the constitution. 1936. Photographer unknown. Courtesy of the Central State Archives of Documentary Films, Photographs, and Sound Recordings, Saint-Petersburg (TsGAKFFD SPb)	85
Photo 7.1	Political seminar (*kruzhok*). Note the portrait of Stalin, bust of Lenin, and a slogan "Under the banner of Lenin, under the guidance of Stalin, forward to Communism." Leningrad. 1930s. Photographer unknown. Author's family archive	101
Photo 9.1	Collective farmers of cooperative Zaklinie, Luga *raion*, Leningrad *oblast'*, near the polling station on the day of elections of the Supreme Soviet of the USSR. December 1937. Courtesy of the Central State Archives of Documentary Films, Photographs, and Sound Recordings, Saint-Petersburg (TsGAKFFD SPb)	134
Photo 9.2	Polling station no. 19 in Leningrad, December 1937. The slogan reads "On 12 December 1937 here will take place a secret voting to elect the Supreme Soviet of the USSR." M. P. Yanov. Courtesy of the Central	

	State Archives of Documentary Films, Photographs, and Sound Recordings, Saint-Petersburg (TsGAKFFD SPb)	148
Photo 10.1	Pioneers in gas masks participating in a military training march. Leningrad *oblast'*. 1935. V. Bulla. Courtesy of the Central State Archives of Documentary Films, Photographs, and Sound Recordings, Saint-Petersburg (TsGAKFFD SPb)	196

List of Tables

Table 12.1 Proposed amendments according to article
(table compiled by TsIK summarizing typical comments,
17 November 1936. GARF f. 3316, op. 8, d. 222, l. 160)   224

Table 12.2 Proposed amendments according to chapter
(table compiled by TsIK summarizing typical comments,
17 November 1936. GARF f. 3316, op. 8, d. 222, l. 159)   225

CHAPTER 1

Introduction

When the Soviet Union unexpectedly collapsed in 1991, the world observed the developments, trying to guess where they would lead. The common hope inside and outside the former Soviet Union was that after decades of debilitating socialism, the new countries would rush to real democracy and the free market. Early surveys of public opinion in post-Soviet Russia prompted sociologists' optimistic prognoses (Reisinger 1993, p. 274; Shlapentokh 1998, pp. 28–52). In the turbulent transitional period that followed, the ambivalent political and electoral behavior of the post-Soviet "subjects-turned-citizens" puzzled observers and instigated speculations about the political and cultural traditions of the population and the extent of its democratic political culture. In the 2000s, Russian citizens showed strong support for their president, Vladimir Putin, who, though associated with the country's economic growth, imposed increasingly authoritarian politics, suppressing free media and taming the judicial system. To the dismay of Russian liberals, the high ratings of this former KGB officer and his repetitive reelections to high office demonstrated a political culture that seemed far from the ideals of liberal democracy. The New Russia Barometer studies showed support for the ruling regime in Russia (36–39% in the 1990s and growing in the 2000s to 84%), reflecting economic growth, a preference for stability, and, possibly, acceptance of an authoritarian trend in politics (Rose et al. 2011, p. 77).

Gradually, it became clear that this ambivalent Russian transition was not unique, but paralleled the experience of other countries. In the last decades of the twentieth century various transformations opened the doors for democratization, and many nations, while proclaiming democratic reforms, displayed developments quite different from the Western liberal model. And it happened not only to the majority of newly independent countries in the post-Soviet space—the Russian Federation, Ukraine, Belorussia, Kazakhstan, Kyrgyzstan, Azerbaijan, Uzbekistan, and Georgia. Many other developing countries—Venezuela, Pakistan, and the majority of African countries—evolved into sham democracies, where elections—a cornerstone of democracy—took place but constitutional liberties are praised in theory but violated in practice. Fareed Zakaria defined this phenomenon as the rise of "illiberal democracies"; others have defined it as "nominal" constitutionalism, "managed" democracy, or competitive authoritarianism. Yes, elections take place, but the population too often votes for illiberal policies and authoritarian figures who shape their regimes with weak legislatures and judiciaries which gradually mutate into dictatorships. This perplexing process stimulated new interest in what structures the behavior of citizens and their support for authoritarian or illiberal regimes.

In various specific circumstances, many interrelated factors determine human behavior and the direction of social transformation—economic (both personal and systemic), political, cultural, and demographic (the "youth bulge").[1] Lucien Pye, a proponent of modernization theory, emphasized the emancipatory energies of modernization (among them urbanization, education, mobility, technology) as additional components that determine the outcome of change in authoritarian regimes (Sakwa 2008, p. 456). Other scholars have highlighted that the rapidity of modernization and the catastrophic events of the twentieth century in Russia might have produced conditions unfavorable for the democratic choice. All Russian revolutions—of 1905, 1917, and 1991—asserted modernization and democracy, but the resulting regimes finally stubbornly drifted in an authoritarian direction. Thus, scholars and the educated public are left to ponder whether Russia possesses the cultural conditions for successful democratization or an inherent proclivity for authoritarianism.

---

[1] In 1936, according to Soviet statistics, 46% of the population were under the age of 21. Together with this demographic factor, the mass migration of the population to cities could have influenced the proclivity to radicalism in society.

Is Russian political culture fundamentally unreceptive to democratic institutions? Or did the Soviet modernization project, even in its authoritarian shape, unavoidably mold conditions for democratization and pluralism that also transform social attitudes? This book contributes to these debates by its historical analysis of popular opinions of the Soviet people in the 1930s, reflective of mass political culture.

In explaining the political behavior of the masses, the concept of political culture is instrumental. "Political culture" is defined by the *International Encyclopedia of Social Sciences* as "the set of attitudes, beliefs and sentiments that give order and meaning to a political process and which provide the underlying assumptions and rules that govern behavior in the political system." The political culture of the party elite, especially of Stalin, has received much attention from scholars, mostly because of the more immediate outcomes of such studies in foreign affairs and diplomatic applications and the accessibility of the sources (public pronouncements, for example). (Among many, see Tucker 1972; van Ree 2002.) This elite culture is generally described as rooted in the underground and Civil War experience, with such features as a confrontational Manichean worldview, dogmatic and wishful thinking, and with militant elements rejecting compromise—a culture wracked by fear and suspicion of internal and external plots and enemies (Getty and Naumov 1999, pp. 15–24). Now, the availability of new serial sources makes the study of *mass* political culture in Stalinism possible—not in general suppositions, but documented as a specific belief system in a specific time period.

Interest in the mental and political dispositions of Soviet citizens and the problematic prospects of democratic transformation emerged in the 1970s and understandably increased in the 1990s. But this interest was hardly new. Margaret Mead, for example, studied the mindset of the Soviet people in the 1950s, using the tools of anthropology, and called it authoritarian. Since her study, the historiography debate has evolved from two major positions. One view argues that Russian political culture has a strong authoritarian coloration and is poorly prepared for democratic and liberal development due to the country's historical experience not favorable for liking freedom, affinity for collectivism over individualism, and its dislike of private property (Biryukov and Sergeev 1993; Brown 1989; White 1979 and others). Focusing mostly on the elite and the government's political culture, these historical and cultural determinists emphasized the disposition of Russians for authoritarianism, though such views were sometimes politically motivated.

An alternative view emphasizes the plurality of elements in Russian national traditions, the multidirectional potential of the cultural sphere, and dismantles the theory of autocratic destiny. Richard Sakwa (2008, p. 355), Nicolai Petro (1995), and James Millar (1987) believe that modernization per se organically produces new forces and new attitudes, sometimes even in dying social groups like the nobility or peasantry. Societies develop, though unevenly and at different paces. Even during reactionary or stagnant periods, a democratic potential exists, as, for example, in the "Miraculous Decade" in the 1840s when Russian intelligentsia emerged under the police regime of Nicholas I. After its apex at the beginning of the twentieth century, the civil culture existing outside of officialdom never died, even in the USSR, and was exemplified by antiregime resistance, dissent, a dissident movement, religious opposition, *samizdat* (the clandestine copying of forbidden literature), a subculture of rumors and anecdotes, semiunderground charity, bard songs, and the hiking movement of the 1970s.

A common concern of scholars is that political culture studies sometimes select arbitrary facts from the past and a culture, disregarding the peculiarities of each historical periods, to arrive at their conclusions. The objective of this case study in Soviet political culture is to analyze methodically the corpus of archival sources, never before approached from the angle of political culture, and to place the popular comments and opinions about the constitution into the political, economic, cultural, and social context of the 1930s. The mass political culture of the 1930s can now be documented on a new level of historical, cultural, and methodological knowledge.

Studies of Russian-Soviet society at specific periods, for example at the beginning (Figes and Kolonitsky) and end (Rose, Lukin) of the Soviet period, pointed out the weak basis for liberal democracy in the political culture. Medushevsky and Lewin support this view for the Stalinist period.

Orlando Figes and Boris Kolonitsky reviewed the political symbolism and language of workers and peasants in 1917 and argued "there was no real cultural or social foundation for the liberal conception of democracy in Russia, at least not in the midst of a violent revolution". If the liberal intelligentsia understood democracy in terms of the constitution, parliament, and the rule of law, workers and urbanites rather saw it as synonymous with the power of the common people. During the public debate about democracy in 1917, this notion, in contrast to the liberals' inclusive meaning of democracy, was understood among the masses as the exclusive idea of class conflict. The authors maintain that the discourse of exclusion and dichotomous views, which they observed in revolutionary 1917, had deep roots in Russian culture (Figes and Kolonitsky 1999, pp. 122–3, 189).

The view that the political culture under Stalinism had powerful roots in the traditionalist Russian peasant culture is accepted by many as a given. Moshe Lewin emphasized not only the religious-autocratic traditions of the society–state nexus in establishing Stalin's new autocracy, but also the impact of rural religiosity on polity, however secular and committed to rationalism. Reacting to the tremendous changes around them, the peasant majority transformed and adjusted instructions, propaganda, fashions, and images through specific cultural filters. The pressure of these traditional and peasant grassroots, stated by Lewin as a conservative force, molded polity: "The social matrix was breeding just that: authoritarianism." The historical traditions of state–society relations, plus the homogeneous, commune-focused, illiterate or semiliterate peasantry, as well as the "backslide of 1917–1921" which debilitated the social basis (the peasantry retreated into a more archaic mode and the working class lost "many of its experienced and sophisticated layers"), made Russia strongly conducive and favorable to authoritarianism. Waves of crises brought disorientation, depersonalization, and loss of identity; Bolshevik acculturation was marred by deculturation (the shallowing of the cultural elite) and a cultural "void" when peasants lost their old values but did not acquire new ones quickly enough (Lewin 1985, pp. 274, 304–11, 314). Lewin's last point about the homogeneity and inflexibility of the peasantry was challenged by recent studies of the Peasant Union movement in the first third of the twentieth century, which showed the political and social maturation of the peasantry at its most entrepreneurial part (Seregny 1988; Kurenyshev 2004; Velikanova 2013, pp. 118–59). This growth of bourgeois and civil values in the peasantry cannot now be ignored. The resulting two political cultures—traditional and Bolshevik, according to Lewin—appear more nuanced today. The new complexity and the intricacies of this changing identity was revealed also in the peasant-turned-workers' diaries, notably Andrei Arzhilovsky's.

Since political culture is the product of both collective history and the life histories of individuals, the private experiences described in diaries and personal letters provide deeper insights into the culture. The debates on liberal and illiberal subjectivity introduce an intimate dimension and lifespan temporality to the formation of Soviet political culture. While the political culture concept examines the multitudes, social groups, and formation of collective identity, the cultural trend in historiography and the newly available personal sources stimulate studies of individual subjectivity. Defined as a reflexive self that possesses self-awareness, subjectivity formation and the search for identity were both pursued by individuals and promoted by the state project of the New Soviet Man. In parallel to the dynamics of political and social currents and shifts, the diaries pointedly reveal the dynamics of personal actualization—the process of internalization and negotiation of Stalinist values, sometimes the drift away from liberal personhood to illiberal citizen, as in the case of Nikolai Ustrialov. At a specific moment, for example, in the discussion about the constitution, these social and personal trajectories met and generated a variety of opinions. The constitution was a frame of reference against which individuals tested and shaped their identity. Scholars like Sheila Fitzpatrick found in the Soviet Union of the 1930s a liberal Soviet subject—rational actors, motivated by the pursuit of self-interests, competing with one another for better positions in life. Other scholars like Jochen Hellbeck and Anna Krylova see liberal discourse as culturally alien to the USSR, and socialist subjectivity as mainly illiberal and disinterested in personal autonomy and devaluing of private interests. Studies of political culture and Soviet subjectivity complement and enrich each other.

The much-debated dichotomy of Soviet life and duality of the Soviet subject has a direct connection to the theme of this book. Many authors have commented on that duality: official ideology versus folk beliefs, political ideals versus operative norms of polity, government intentions versus implementation and unexpected results on the ground, democratic elements of political culture versus authoritarian-patriarchal elements. All suggest different interpretations. Recently, this debate incorporated valuable contributions from Michael David-Fox and Andrei Medushevsky: we can gain important insights into the incongruity of constitutional norms against dictatorial reality if we place it in the general context of the historical development of constitutionalism in the twentieth-century Russia. Medushevsky sees a continuity of sham constitutionalism in the Fundamental Law of the Russian Empire of 1906, the Soviet constitutions of 1918, 1924, 1936, 1977, and in the 1993 constitution. Here, he follows Max Weber's view about the token nature of 1906 reform, exemplified in the Duma and seen by Weber more as the product of difficult circumstances and disinterest of the social forces in liberalism rather than the Russian people's "immaturity for constitutional government" (Beetham 1985, pp. 194–8). With its conflict between declaration and practice, Soviet constitutionalism was a continuation of its sham model of the previous period. Medushevsky defines Soviet democracy as nominal constitutionalism with the goal of masking the dictatorship of one party with propagandistic and programming functions rather than promotion of the rule of law. He explains it by the established pattern of society–state relations, characterized by inherent "negation of law in general … as a way of regulation of these relations" and by the pressures of the traditionalist social environment. While focusing on political factors, Medushevsky nevertheless recognizes the important role of culture, with its fusion of modern and traditional elements. Thus he defines "Stalinism as a specific form of totalitarianism evolving and functioning under modernization and resting upon traditional components of Russian monarchic political culture" (Medushevsky 2005, pp. 156, 187, 241).

David-Fox's book brings important ideas to the debates on the dichotomy of Soviet life (David-Fox 2015, pp. 44, 94). He summarizes the debate on modern versus neotraditionalist elements with his thesis about the combination of modern and other features in the Soviet order—either traditional, or peculiarly Russian, or illiberal. It was only with access to the voices of the masses that the problem of the twisted perception of the official message was discovered. David-Fox follows Fitzpatrick, Suny, and Viola, emphasizing the need to distinguish the level of intentionality, with its hyperplanning, from the unexpected consequences and uncontrollable chaos on the ground. Especially stimulating to the argument of my book is his and Evgeny Dobrenko's[2] notion of the ritualistic and performative dimensions of ideology, when citizens show "good behavior," which took precedence over content (Dobrenko 2004; Brooks 2000). Alexei Yurchak reasons that this gap between performance and content widened in the late post-Stalin socialism (Yurchak 2006, pp. 12, 21). As my argument will show, in the 1930s the ideological message of the constitution, alongside ritualistic reactions, was nonetheless embraced by a significant set of participants in the discussion. This is especially true of the new Soviet generation who had not yet

[2] "Ideology as representation" in Dobrenko's term. See Evgeny Dobrenko, "Socialism as Representation and Will" (2004), and his works on socialist realism. The performance culture was also noted by Jeffrey Brooks.

suffered through cycles of failed promises. Many of them believed in the constitution and seriously discussed its content (democracy).

Sociological studies undertaken by Western and Russian scholars evaluate the attitudes of Russian citizens toward democracy during the 1990s and 2000s, serving as a reference point for the characteristics of political culture in the 1930s. But unlike my sources, sociological data is quantitative. One of the most representative surveys was launched in 1992 by Richard Rose and colleagues in Britain and continued for 20 years. Called the New Russia Barometer, the project reports on the failed hopes for democratization and the authoritarian resilience in post-Soviet Russia. The Russian example is representative in relation to the third democratization wave when the introduction of competitive elections often resulted in a transition to hybrid regimes called, in various contexts over time, nominal, sham, illiberal, or totalitarian democracy. Rose reminds us that a legitimate regime is not necessarily democratic. If support is coerced from subjects, political equilibrium between society and the government results in compliance, resigned acceptance, or a show of support, and in perspective—a growing risk of political indifference, skepticism, and dissent. The public can, of course, demonstrate its support for a democratic or undemocratic system. Sociological polls, for example, evidence that while "a big majority of Russians regard democracy as ideal", they increasingly support Putin's undemocratic political practices in the same or larger degree than Europeans support Central and East European democracies (Rose et al. 2011, pp. 3–15). The question of how the general public and the Russian "democrats"[3] see democracy is the subject of continuing examination.

Thus, the view of Russian mass political culture as unfavorable to liberal values dominates in historiography.

In June 1936, the draft of the new Soviet constitution was published for public discussion. It announced that the USSR was approaching a nonantagonistic socialist society and, accordingly, promised to cancel restrictions on voting rights and to introduce universal suffrage, a secret ballot, separation of powers, an open judicial process, and the right of

---

[3] Lukin's qualitative research (2000) on the democratic movement during 1985–1991 concludes that Gorbachev's Russia lacked the necessary cultural preconditions for successful democratization.

the accused to a defense. It declared freedom of the press, the right to assemble, and the inviolability of the individual, housing, and correspondence. In view of the Bolsheviks' previous fixation on class struggle, this democratic impulse was an unexpected swing in the official party line that stirred various comments in a state-sanctioned nationwide discussion, which comprise the key data for this book. Political values and beliefs expressed in the discussion and beyond it will be interpreted in the following analysis.

Historians sometimes express skepticism about attempts to study what people "really" thought in authoritarian regimes because unfree people tend to uncritically accept official truth and are afraid to express oppositional views. This study fully acknowledges this epistemological problem. Its major finding, not yet interpreted and explained in historiography, is a massive rejection by society of the democratic principles of Stalin's "holy" constitution, which people were unafraid to voice. Another finding is the existence of liberal, conciliatory popular discourse present in the intolerant atmosphere of Stalin's dictatorship. A very skeptical and sharp-eyed observer, the British consul in Leningrad, stated in 1934: "Perhaps public opinion has to be studied a little, even here" (Bullard 2000, p. 258).

In historiography, the Constitution of 1936 has been studied mainly from the governmental or judicial perspective—in P. Solomon (1996), K. Petrone (2000), E. Wimberg (1992), A. Getty (1991), and in Soviet works. The former concentrated mostly on the political procedure and circumstances of the Soviet constitution's creation: organization of a commission in February 1935, its composition from the party's top leaders, and the evolution of five drafts of the constitution (Bogatyrenko 1959; Ronin 1957; Tretiakov 1953; Kabanov 1976). Western authors discussing the major reasons for writing the new constitution emphasize the goals of creating a positive image in the international and domestic arenas—that is, a "publicity stunt," and the drive for centralization. The first part of this book explores government motivations for introducing the new constitution, launching the popular discussion, and then the quiet reversing of the constitution's democratic innovations. Newly available documents, including internal correspondence of the leaders, and revelations of recent literature present insights into the authorship of the reform, once ascribed unanimously to Stalin. More, they bring forward the ideological motives, and economic and political context of the reform and disclose the mystery of the zigzagging policy in 1936–1937;

thus, the conventional interpretation of the constitution as a propaganda show mostly for the West no longer encompasses the range of the government's motives.

In opposition to historiography's attention to the political circumstances of the constitution's creation and leadership's debates, my study focuses on society's reactions. In contrast to a structural and institutional perspective, this book offers a cultural approach to complement the historical picture of the period. A few authors have briefly approached the topic of the public's response to the constitution (Siegelbaum and Sokolov 2004; Davies 1997; Goldman 2007). These authors have dealt with the question of popular support, relations between democracy and terror, and Siegelbaum and Sokolov have, in particular, translated key documents on popular perception of the constitution.

A pioneering article by Arch Getty paved the way for further research. This early 1991 article, published before the opening of the archives and the subsequent reconsideration of Soviet history, utilized available archival documents to study the topic. Getty was the first to discuss the goals of the discussion campaign in social scientific rather than ideological terms: sampling of public opinion, mobilization strategy, and channeling of public discontent against local officials (which was emphasized in his subsequent works). Focusing mostly on the government's political intricacies, Getty nevertheless in only four pages formulated the major themes of society's reactions to the constitution in Leningrad and Smolensk, summarized as a massive rejection by the majority of the constitution's liberal innovations. Getty's conclusion: the constitution had not been a democratic farce from the very beginning. The intention of the state had been the democratic and participatory reform of the dictatorship. After experimentation, however, Stalin—frightened by local officials and the peasants' hostility—changed his mind. Consequently, Stalin canceled the democratic and participatory reforms and retreated to a renewal of force (Getty 1991).

This brief but dense article by Getty will serve as the basis for the following study of such crucial topics as the plausibility of democratic reforms and their planned or unpremeditated character, the relationship between democracy and terror, and the role of the all-nation discussion in Stalin's political turnabouts. Both politics and the reactions of society too briefly introduced in the literature deserve a comprehensive analysis using the new level of knowledge and wider range of sources. The novelty of my approach is in the application of political culture methods to the study of society's mindset: how political participation, mass mobilization, the ideal of popular sovereignty, the notion of civil rights, and individualistic values evolved under the peculiar conditions of Stalinism.

The concept of political culture as an integrated system of interrelated beliefs, attitudes, and values is well suited as an investigative tool. The classical typology of political culture suggested by Almond and Verba describes a parochial, subject, and participant culture—each congruent with, respectively, a traditional political structure, a centralized authoritarian structure, and a democratic political structure (Almond and Verba 1965). This categorization does not match exactly the Soviet patterns of thought and beliefs, for what we see in Soviet opinions is a spectrum of features from liberal values to authoritarian features—with a tendency toward a simple, bipolar world, intolerance for minorities, and personification of power. The nature of my source base dictates a different taxonomy. Citizens' comments gravitated to two major categories: first, the comments supporting democratic, civic, moderate, conciliatory, tolerant (of religion, for example) values—in other words, liberal values; and second, those comments supporting affective, militant, intolerant, and restrictive—or antiliberal—values, such as hatred of enemies, love for the supreme power, generalized hostility, and adherence to values perceived as endorsed by the leadership. Also pronounced was a subgroup expressing collectivist and clan values, which in the Russian context can be defined as values associated with traditional peasant societies. Many authors discussed the persistence of archaic Russian practices under Stalinism such as "writing letters to power" as a simplified way to represent the interests, reemergence of the "aristocracy" with a particular status (*nomenklatura*, or "*boyars*" in Getty's expression), and a propensity for collective responsibility (Nérard 2016; Martin 2000; Lewin 1985; Getty 2013). Modern sociological polls often use categories of democratic and traditional political culture.

Whatever classification we follow—classical, sociological, or liberal/illiberal—it is important that no classification implies a homogeneity of political culture. In social reality and on an individual level, there has always been a fusion of different culture types: "The 'citizen' is a particular mix of participant, subject, and parochial orientations, and the civic culture is a particular mix of citizens, subjects, and parochials" (Almond and Verba 1965, p. 19). Additionally, such influences as a process of rapid transition, political instability, and a generational shift, particularly pronounced in the 1930s, contribute to the complexity of political culture at any specific period. "Too violent an attack on parochialism may cause both parochial and subject orientation to decline to apathy and alienation. The results are political fragmentation and national destruction" (Almond and Verba 1965, p. 23). Thus, categorizing discourses as liberal or illiberal, this study always implies a cultural mix following the historiographic descriptions of a "culture in flux" (S. Frank and M. D. Steinberg) and the idea of confused and shifted identities defined as "quicksand society" by Moshe Lewin.

References

Almond, Gabriel A., and Sidney Verba. 1965. *The Civic Culture: Political Attitudes and Democracy in Five Nations*. Boston: Little, Brown.
Beetham, David. 1985. *Max Weber and the Theory of Modern Politics*. Cambridge: Polity.
Biryukov, Nikolai, and Viktor Sergeev. 1993. *Russia's Road to Democracy: Parliament, Communism, and Traditional Culture*. Aldershot: Edward Elgar.
Bogatyrenko, Z. S. 1959. "Obzor dokumental'nykh materialov po istorii sozdaniia konstitutsii SSSR, 1936 g." *Istoricheskii Arkhiv* (2): 197–205.
Brooks, Jeffery. 2000. *Thank You, Comrade Stalin! Soviet Public Culture from Revolution to Cold War*. Princeton, NJ: Princeton University Press.
Brown, Archie. 1989. "Ideology and Political Culture." In *Politics, Society, and Nationality Inside Gorbachev's Russia*, edited by Seweryn Bialer. Boulder, CO: Westview.
Bullard, Reader W. 2000. *Inside Stalin's Russia: The Diaries of Reader Bullard, 1930–1934*. Charlbury: Day Books.
David-Fox, Michael. 2015. *Crossing Borders: Modernity, Ideology, and Culture in Russia and the Soviet Union*. Pittsburgh, PA: University of Pittsburgh Press.
Davies, Sarah. 1997. *Popular Opinion in Stalin's Russia: Terror, Propaganda and Dissent, 1934–1941*. Cambridge: Cambridge University Press.
Dobrenko, Evgeny. 2004. "Socialism as Will and Representation, or What Legacy Are We Rejecting?" *Kritika: Explorations in Russian and Eurasian History* 5 (4): 675–708.
Figes, Orlando, and Boris Kolonitsky. 1999. *Interpreting the Russian Revolution: The Language and Symbols of 1917*. New Haven, CT: Yale University Press.
Getty, J. Arch. 1991. "State and Society Under Stalin: Constitutions and Elections in the 1930s." *Slavic Review* 50 (1): 18–35.
———. 2013. *Practicing Stalinism: Bolsheviks, Boyars, and the Persistence of Tradition*. New Haven, CT: Yale University Press.

Getty, J. Arch., and Oleg V. Naumov. 1999. *The Road to Terror: Stalin and the Self-destruction of the Bolsheviks, 1932–1939*. New Haven, CT: Yale University Press.
Goldman, Wendy Z. 2007. *Terror and Democracy in the Age of Stalin*. Cambridge: Cambridge University Press.
Kabanov, V. V. 1976. "Iz istorii sozdaniia konstitutsii SSSR, 1936 goda." *Istoriia SSSR* (6): 116–27.
Kurenyshev, A. A. 2004. *Vserossiisky Krestiansky Souz, 1905–1930 gg: Mify I real'nost'*. Moscow: Dmitry Bulanin.
Lewin, Moshe. 1985. *The Making of the Soviet System: Essays in the Social History of Interwar Russia*. London: Methuen.
Lukin, Alexander. 2000. *The Political Culture of the Russian "Democrats"*. Oxford: Oxford University Press.
Martin, Terry. 2000. "Modernization or Neo-traditionalism? Ascribed Nationality and Soviet Primordialism." In *Stalinism: New Directions*, edited by Sheila Fitzpatrick, 348–76. London: Routledge.
Medushevsky, Andrei. 2005. *Russian Constitutionalism: History and Contemporary Development*. Hoboken, NJ: Routledge.
Millar, James R., ed. 1987. *Politics, Work and Daily Life in the USSR: A Survey of Former Soviet Citizens*. Cambridge: Cambridge University Press.
Nérard, François-Xavier. 2016. "Stalinism as Traditional Political Culture." *Kritika: Explorations in Russian and Eurasian History* 17 (2): 475–82.
Petro, Nicolai. 1995. *The Rebirth of Russian Democracy: An Interpretation of Political Culture*. Cambridge, MA: Harvard University Press.
Petrone, Karen. 2000. *Life Has Become More Joyous, Comrades: Celebrations in the Time of Stalin*. Bloomington: Indiana University Press.
Reisinger, William M. 1993. "Conclusions: Mass Public Opinion and the Study of Post-Soviet Societies." In *Public Opinion and Regime Change: The New Politics of Post-Soviet Societies*, edited by Arthur H. Miller, William M. Reisinger, and Vicki L. Hesli. Boulder, CO: Westview.
Ronin, S. A. 1957. *Konstitutsiia SSSR, 1936 goda*. Moscow: Gosyurizdat.
Rose, Richard, William Mishler, and Neil Munro. 2011. *Popular Support for an Undemocratic Regime: The Changing Views of Russians*. Cambridge: Cambridge University Press.
Sakwa, Richard. 2008. *Russian Politics and Society*. 3rd ed. London: Routledge.
Seregny, Scott J. 1988. "A Different Type of Peasant Movement: The Peasant Unions in the Russian Revolution of 1905." *Slavic Review* 47 (1): 51–67.
Shlapentokh, V. 1998. "Russian Citizenship: Behavior, Attitudes and Prospects for a Russian Democracy." In *Citizenship and Citizenship Education in a Changing World*, edited by Orit Ichilov, 28–52. London: Woburn.
Siegelbaum, Lewis, and Andrei Sokolov. 2004. *Stalinism as a Way of Life*. New Haven, CT: Yale University Press.

Solomon, Peter H. 1996. *Soviet Criminal Justice Under Stalin.* Cambridge: Cambridge University Press.

Tretiakov, G. F. 1953. "Vsenarodnoe obsuzhdenie proekta Konstitutsii SSSR." *Voprosy Istorii* (9): 97–102.

Tucker, Robert. 1972. *The Soviet Political Mind: Stalinism and Post-Stalin Change.* London: George Allen and Unwin.

van Ree, Erik. 2002. *The Political Thought of Joseph Stalin: A Study in Twentieth-Century Revolutionary Patriotism.* London: Routledge.

Velikanova, Olga. 2013. *Popular Perceptions of Soviet Politics in the 1920s: Disenchantment of the Dreamers.* Basingstoke: Palgrave Macmillan.

White, Stephen. 1979. *Political Culture and Soviet Politics.* London: Macmillan.

Wimberg, Ellen. 1992. "Socialism, Democratism and Criticism: The Soviet Press and the National Discussion of the 1936 Draft Constitution." *Soviet Studies* 44 (2): 313–32.

Yurchak, Alexei. 2006. *Everything Was Forever, Until It Was No More: The Last Soviet Generation.* Princeton, NJ: Princeton University Press.

CHAPTER 2

Sources

Since the beginning of the era of mass politics, modern governments monitored their citizenry's opinions with the purpose of better managing the population. This resulted in the emergence of sociological polls and in the practice of surveillance. Both sociology and surveillance sought to know what people thought, and both tackled the elusive nature of opinions. Even in free democratic countries, the problem of a poll's potential for inaccuracy is serious. A number of theories explain possible errors in polling methodology—pertaining to both the pollsters (who could manipulate answers by wording or the sequencing of questions) and the respondents. Survey results may be affected by response bias (noncandid answers), nonresponse bias (omitting those who refused to answer the poll), media influence, and other factors. Incidents of opinion polling failure are well known in history—for example, in the 1948 and 2016 US presidential elections, in Great Britain's 1970, 1974, and 1992 parliamentary elections, and in the Russian 1993 parliamentary elections with the unexpected success of the nationalists. Still, the potential for inaccuracy does not preclude our using polls as an important instrument for studying society.

This introduction is necessary here to discuss the potential for inaccuracy of opinions articulated and gathered under conditions of, first, dictatorship and fear, second, a time when scientific polls were at best rudimentary, and third, when historians were unable to ask relevant questions, but instead major events usually triggered outpourings of spontaneous or solicited opinions. These conditions, unorthodox in the eyes of modern sociologists, produced a wave of criticism in the historical community when the huge complex of surveillance data became accessible for scholars, first in Germany and later in the 1990s in Russia—especially the reviews (*svodki* and *Stimmungsberichte*) of political moods and opinions compiled by the security police for totalitarian regimes. These reviews were often criticized for bias and unreliability. The brutal reputation of Nazi and Soviet security police institutions probably contributed to the skepticism. Twenty-five years of debates about the limits and potential of the sources produced by the totalitarian regime in Russia resulted in a particular genre of literature regarding the methods of criticism and the usage of such sources, significantly advancing the historical sources studies (*istochnikovedenie*) (Viola 2000; Velikanova 1999; Holquist 1997; Fitzpatrick 2009). Recently, after decades of skepticism and fruitful critical debates, triangulation of all available information on specific cases led more and more historians (for example, R. Davies, Lennart Samuelson, and Vladimir Khaustov) to acknowledge, with reservations, the value of the *svodki* as a historical source to illuminate not only society but also official and institutional views on society. "These NKVD reports, located in the KGB archive, ... typically give accurate accounts of the agricultural situation plus a strong emphasis, as with nearly all NKVD documents, on alleged 'counterrevolutionary' activities" (Davies 2014, p. 317; Berelowitch and Danilov 2012, pp. 278–80).[1] Another example of acknowledgment followed when sources traditionally rejected by scholars as unreliable, such as prisoners' gossip (used by Alexander Solzhenitsyn as a source base for *The Gulag Archipelago*), were later, after juxtaposing them to the archival documents, recognized as accurate (Applebaum 2007, p. xix).

This study is based on various government, personal, and foreign sources, but mainly on archival materials: the transcripts of the Soviet governing bodies and nationwide discussion commentaries. Though the Soviet press presented the campaign profusely, the bulk of popular comments was hidden in the government archives. These depositories contain hundreds of files with transcribed statements from ordinary people, including material from official gatherings, unpublished letters to newspapers, anonymous letters to the authorities, and formal proposals. First,

---

[1] R. W. Davies refers there to the report of the Voronezh NKVD, dated 20 July 1936, about the situation in the *oblast'*.

I used the documents of the Communist Party plenums, the Central Committee records, and the internal correspondence of the leaders to study the goals and political mechanism of the discussion campaign. Second, I studied materials of the Soviet security organs (NKVD), which routinely surveilled the people's political opinions and sent regular secret summaries to high party officials. This Soviet documentation is complemented by British and American intelligence data to gain an alternative perspective. Third, I researched the governing body, called the Presidium of the Central Executive Commission (TsIK), the organizational center of the discussion, which created its own summaries of the comments on the constitution. Fourth, I analyzed the TsIK Commission on Cults' reviews about the reactions of believers and clergy to the constitution.

Each of these state institutions had its own agendas and approaches to collecting and interpreting the information which stamped the structure and nature of the reports. This variety of agendas provides historians the opportunity to compare and objectify their information. Materials of surveillance are a peculiar historical source and require commentary. First, when examining such sources, historians consider the security organs' functions and specific corporate culture that influenced presentation of the collected data. According to John McLaughlin, a former director of the US Central Intelligence Agency, the culture of the intelligence world is marked by skepticism. The duty of analysts is to look for trouble and warn the policymakers of dangers. This encourages a darker view of events in the reports (George and Bruce 2008, p. 73). F. E. Dzerzhinsky, the founder of the Soviet security police, noted a similar tendency in Soviet reports. Correspondingly, the Soviet security organs in their reviews of popular moods focused primarily on anti-Soviet activities and dissent, fulfilling policing and repressive functions. Other agencies reporting on the moods (for instance, the Bolshevik/Communist Party) were inaccurate in providing names of the comments' authors, their positions, factory, military unit, or village. Specifically, the NKVD (People's Commissariat for Internal Affairs) detailed and additionally categorized speakers according to political lines: such as "Trotskyist-Zinovievist," "Socialist–Revolutionary," or kulak, though it did not mean that these people belonged to some organized entity or possessed a wealthy household. Such denominations were usually a kind of political label that characterized the ideal type of enemy in the mind of a compiler. Politicization was a salient characteristic of surveillance summaries enhanced by the task to catalogue unreliable persons and negative dynamics. The NKVD's repressive function was reflected in infrequent short notes after the description of the dissident in summaries: "Arrested."

The way the *svodki* present the people's moods and political attitudes characterizes the NKVD officers' mindset, marked by a specific Manichean caste worldview, the proclivity to see threats everywhere, and the bureaucrats' common desire to match the expectations of the superiors or leaders,[2] to fit the current party line, and to show their own effectiveness. Understanding that NKVD *svodki* have their epistemological limits, I try in this study to counterbalance their bias with documentation of various origins—for example, the intelligence reports of the British Foreign Office and the American intelligence services on the state of affairs in the USSR. In opposition to the negative bias of the NKVD, the party, soviet, or economic bodies' reports often tended to emphasize a more positive picture of society to please the authorities with a representation of successes. Party official P. A. Kulagin was responsible for Leningrad's food supply in 1932. According to the British consul, he said: "'We don't believe as the people in Moscow do, that all is well.' If he is to be believed, many subordinate officials send in favorable reports which they know to be untrue, because they have not the courage to report the fact, so that the Kremlin never really knows what the situation is" (Bullard 2000, p. 116). The best solution in working with the biased sources is to verify the consistency of their findings by using different sets of data. If multiple sources, situations, and geographies produce consistent results, they allow us to make some generalizations.

Another state agency, Presidium TsIK, administered the discussion and, trying to capture the broad range and variety of opinions, required regular reporting from local officials on the course of the campaign. It accumulated information from republics and regions, newspapers and individuals. Between June and November of 1936, TsIK summarized and categorized 43,427 comments—about a quarter of the discussion

---

[2] The instruction to the American intelligence analysts is to identify what the customer (government) needs and deliver the intelligence to satisfy those needs (George and Bruce 2008, p. 2). In Soviet practice, however, it could turn into a dilemma when the government vision of the event did not correspond to reality as it appeared to the analyst. Soviet statisticians in the "repressed" 1937 census paid with their lives for statistics that did not conform to Stalin's views on society.

materials (Siegelbaum and Sokolov 2004, p. 134; GARF f. 3316, op. 8, d. 222, l. 125)[3]—and produced thirteen *svodki* and other documentation, including statistics, which I refer to as "TsIK estimates" in the text. These statistics will be presented here, though the nature of the sources does not allow a quantification of the size of the various political subcultures in the society. Rather, they show a qualitative characterization of diversity within. These statistics, with all their limitations, provide some rationality to the impressions gained from reading comments. In statistical estimates, in addition to TsIK data, I also refer to my sampling of 470 typical comments systemized and summarized by the Gorky *krai* executive committee out of 4000 comments in its 16 October 1936 report to Moscow. The *krai* committee composed a table of comments to the articles of the constitution from various *raiony* (Kulakov et al. 2005, pp. 389–435). I also use here Arch Getty's sampling of original statements from Leningrad (2627 letters) and Smolensk (474 letters) *oblasts* (Getty 1991; Fitzpatrick 1994, p. 353). Regrettably, Getty did not include in his sampling "nonprogrammatic remarks like thanking Stalin," while I sampled from the whole constituency of comments. Lewis Siegelbaum rightly noted that the entire complex of comments—both practical and fantastic—should be considered, not just those directly relevant to the articles of the constitution (Siegelbaum and Sokolov 2004, p. 134). Sometimes, I present absolute numbers of comments from all my research records from various sources: NKVD, TsIK, and regional *svodki*, letters to newspapers, etc. Though out of proportion, these numbers are telling.

Besides the NKVD and TsIK, other offices collected data. The TsIK Commission on Cults produced reviews about the reactions of believers and clergy to the constitution. Reading between the lines of these reports leaves an impression about the authors' acceptance and even defense of their constituency's concerns. Probably their insufficiently harsh position led to the closure of this commission in 1938. Though the TsIK and Cult Commission pursued their own corporate agendas, their *svodki* had no repressive function and sound more evenhanded, presenting both dissent and affirmative discourse. Soviet newspapers (*Pravda, Krestianskaia Gazeta, Izvestia, Kommuna* [Voronezh] used here) regularly published well-filtered and likely edited citizens' comments

---

[3] By 1 November 1936, seven republics reported 94,521 recommendations.

imposing politically correct frames for interpretations, in parallel confidentially submitting to the government reviews of unpublished comments (for example, *Krestianskaia Gazeta*) (Danilov et al. 2002, pp. 795, 804, 819). The confidential lists of questions recorded at the meetings and in seminars and designed for the local party committee only, with their vernacular, naiveté, and harshness, seem more authentic than the standardized lists of suggestions compiled according to template and possibly sanitized by bureaucrats for presentation to Moscow. These documents originated in the state and party offices.

We can compare the summaries compiled by bureaucrats with the first-person documents: diaries and letters to the newspapers and authorities, which are biased too but by other sets of influences. Scholars who work with documents of a personal origin from the Stalin era know that their authors demonstrated unsettled identities, influenced by changes of their status and by the social turmoil: some citizens eagerly internalized official values and made them their own (Lubov' Shtange and diarists introduced by Natalia Kozlova); others were in the process of molding their identities (young diarists like Stepan Podlubny, Leonid Potemkin, Nina Kosterina, and former liberal Nikolai Ustrialov); still others learned to demonstrate outward compliance, publicly obeyed the norms, but kept their agenda or even dissent hidden (Arzhilovsky, Man'kov, Ginzburg, Shaporina). Such fluidity of identity dealt a major complication for the interpreter of their records. Members of all these groups had their own reasons for contributing to the discussion of the constitution—for example, to manifest loyalty. Diaries, however, project an aura of intimacy and sincerity. In the Soviet situation of continued crisis and fluid identity, the motivation for self-expression was much stronger than in political regimes with a long-established system of values. Moreover, some Soviet diarists (Potemkin, Podlubny, Ustrialov), inspired by the idea of a New Man, confess to the continuous efforts of the young and even mature persons to transform themselves into an integral part of the imagined socialist community, thus sacrificing their personal autonomy associated by them with the "petit bourgeois" way of life (Hellbeck 2009, p. 53). This psychological evidence of "flight from autonomy," dissected by scholars of the subjectivity school, adds epistemological depth to the corpus of illiberal comments about the constitution.

Among the sources used here are about 2000 interviews and questionnaires, conducted in 1950–1951 with the Soviet refugees in Europe and the US, known as the Harvard Project on the Soviet Social

System. Among the questions that American interviewers suggested to the refugees was "What impression was made upon you by the Soviet Constitution in 1936?" That is why a plethora of materials can be found there. The worldview of this constituency was wider than of their compatriots in 1936. All correspondents could compare the conditions in the USSR with the European and/or American experience. Considering possible bias, the organizers cannot ignore that refugees probably felt obliged to the country that promised or gave them asylum and wanted to please the Americans and tell them what they thought appropriate; the attempts to measure such "flattery" were undertaken. In addition, these evidences are distanced from the event (the all-nation discussion) and enriched by knowledge of the consequences. Together with an outside perspective, this influenced the refugees' often critical view of Soviet reality recognized by the researchers. It was not rare, however, for respondents to convey views against the political mainstream in the US—for example, praising state control, welfare, and honestly recognizing that they personally benefited from the new liberties in 1936 when children of kulaks obtained access to education. This data allows a comparison and study of the dynamic of the political orientations in the 1930s and 1950s.

Despite the limitations of each particular source, their various types, being juxtaposed, do provide the opportunity for the triangulation of information, and characterize major elements of political culture. The diversity of sources provides as representative a sample of Soviet society as possible, especially when the opinions found in different sources, both personal and official, express the same attitudes. Despite epistemological problems of bias, representativeness of each particular source, veracity of the sources, as well as actual immeasurability, inconsistency, and ambiguity of popular opinions, scholars cannot neglect such enthralling evidence about Soviet society. The lack of ability to quantify data does not refute the importance of popular opinions in the shaping of the Stalinist society.

The puzzling ambiguity and duality of thinking of the Soviet citizen, when sometimes contradictory opinions and combined allegiances coexisted even within one individual, can be explained by the duality of surroundings with the divide between official representation and real experience. The attitudes were determined both by everyday life with its hardships and by the larger declared goal of socialism: the first might provoke criticism, the second—inspiration (Fitzpatrick 2009, pp. 25–6). Nevertheless, such an "irrational" thinking pattern was not a unique Soviet phenomenon; it was quite typical for peasants of any nation with a basically social rather than economic way of reasoning, in which two contradictory opinions may be held simultaneously (Shanin 1971, p. 247). Additionally—to make the task of an analyst even more challenging—any single human could feel inspiration and patriotism one moment and dissatisfaction in another moment, depending on so many variables, including changing social status or such elemental needs as hunger or satiety, as shown by sociologist Pitirim Sorokin (1975).

These difficulties and limitations of the data at hand do preclude making quantitative estimates about the frequency of opinions associated with public opinion studies. But the nature of our sources and the methods used in studies of culture are different from sociological or historical positivist studies. Evaluating the voluminous unstructured data, I will use the qualitative method as an analytical technique to gain insights into cultural practices. This method, categorizing historical and cultural data into patterns in order to make it interpretable, was used primarily in anthropology and ethnography to reach an understanding of what motivates human behavior, but it has recently become more multidisciplinary, moving to history studies (Denzin and Lincoln 2011). Thematic analysis is the most common method used in qualitative research to determine patterns in collected data. Unlike with a sociological survey, the benefit of this method lies in the successful reduction of possible bias imposed or predetermined by a researcher (Boyatzis 1998).

This method won recognition in the fieldwork, for example, conducted by professionals with the task of sociocultural assessment of the local population in support of the International Security Force in Afghanistan. In an attempt to determine the currents of thought and beliefs of the Afghans, professionals departed from traditional survey or interview questions as too often reflecting bias on the part of the researcher, and thus returning expected responses. Instead, the researchers asked extremely open-ended questions, provoking storytelling that encoded values, perceptions, and concerns into the narrative. Overlaying several stories opened the possibility for analysis (Price 2017). Behavioral economists have also responded to surveys' criticism by focusing on field studies rather than lab experiments and sociological data. Unlike conventional economics, which assumes that people are mostly rational and unemotional, behavioral economics takes into consideration how individual behavior is influenced by limited rationality, social preferences, and lack of self-control. Thus, specifics of the sources studied here dictate the use of a combination of analytical methods because an emotional component was part of the constitution discussion comments.

Researchers can apply statistical analysis to validate themes when possible, though quantification is not among the advantages of the qualitative method. Forming a weighted impression is recognized as an analytical tool in qualitative studies when this impression is reported in a structured form. Strong efforts were made here to collect as much representative data as possible to introduce the themes and narratives that characterized the political culture of the Soviet society as enunciated in the constitution discussion.

The term *popular opinion* reflects this uncertainty and is used here to distinguish my subject from well-organized and measurable *public opinion* based on sociological data. Although until now the materials of the nationwide discussion were sometimes unjustifiably undervalued by some historians,[4] appropriate criticism of those materials allows us to study Soviet society in the 1930s and its attitudes toward individualism, pluralism, civil rights; toward violence and compromise; and the level of tolerance that characterized its transition from a traditional society to modernity.

References

Applebaum, Anne. 2007. "Foreword." In *The Gulag Archipelago, 1918–1956: An Experiment in Literary Investigation*, translated by Thomas P. Whitney and Harry Willets. New York: Harper Perennial Modern Classics.

Berelowitch, Alexei, and Victor Danilov, eds. 2012. *Sovetskaia derevnia glazami VChK-OGPU-NKVD: Dokumenty i materialy*. Vol. 4. Moscow: ROSSPEN.

Boyatzis, R. 1998. *Qualitative Information: Thematic Analysis and Code Development*. Thousand Oaks, CA: Sage.

Brandenberger, David. 2011. *Propaganda State in Crisis: Soviet Ideology, Indoctrination, and Terror Under Stalin, 1927–1941*. New Haven: Yale University Press.

Bullard, Reader W. 2000. *Inside Stalin's Russia: The Diaries of Reader Bullard, 1930–1934*. Charlbury: Day Books.

---

[4] I. B. Orlov and E. O. Dolgova wrote: "Many citizens of the USSR did not notice the introduction of the constitution"; Medushevsky and Brandenberger, in relevant studies, almost ignored the 1936 discussion (Orlov and Dolgova 2008, p. 150; Medushevsky 2005; Brandenberger 2011).

Danilov, Viktor Petrovich, Roberta Thompson Manning, and Lynne Viola. 2002. *Tragediia sovestskoi derevni: kollektivizatsiia I raskulachivanie: Dokumenty i materialy.* Vol. 4. Moscow: ROSSPEN.
Davies, R. W. 2014. *The Industrialisation of Soviet Russia, Volume 6, The Years of Progress: The Soviet Economy, 1934–1936.* London: Palgrave Macmillan.
Denzin, Norman, and Yvonna Lincoln. 2011. *The SAGE Handbook of Qualitative Research.* Thousand Oaks, CA: Sage.
Fitzpatrick, Sheila. 1994. *Stalin's Peasants: Resistance and Survival in the Russian Village After Collectivization.* Oxford: Oxford University Press.
———. 2009. "Popular Opinion in Russia Under Prewar Stalinism." In *Popular Opinion in Totalitarian Regimes: Fascism, Nazism, and Communism*, edited by Paul Corner, 17–32. Oxford: Oxford University Press.
George, Roger Z., and James B. Bruce, eds. 2008. *Analyzing Intelligence: Origins, Obstacles, and Innovations.* Washington, DC: Georgetown University Press.
Getty, A. 1991. "State and Society Under Stalin: Constitutions and Elections in the 1930s." *Slavic Review* 50 (1): 18–35.
Gosudarstvenny Arkhiv Rossiiskoi Federatsii (GARF) [State Archives of Russian Federation].
Hellbeck, Jochen. 2009. "Liberation from Autonomy: Mapping Self-understandings in Stalin's Time." In *Popular Opinion in Totalitarian Regimes: Fascism, Nazism, and Communism*, edited by Paul Corner, 49–63. Oxford: Oxford University Press.
Holquist, Peter. 1997. "'Information Is the Alpha and Omega of Our Work': Bolshevik Surveillance in Its Pan-European Context." *The Journal of Modern History* 69 (3): 415–50.
Kulakov, A. A., V. V. Smirnov, and L. P. Kolodnikova, eds. 2005. *Obshchestvo I vlast': Rossiiskaia provintsiia.* Vol. 2. Moscow: Institute Rossiiskoi Istorii RAN.
Medushevsky, Andrei. 2005. *Russian Constitutionalism: History and Contemporary Development.* Hoboken, NJ: Routledge.
Orlov, I. B., and E. O. Dolgova. 2008. *Politicheskaia kul'tura rossiian v XX veke: Preemstvennost' I razryvy.* Sergiev Posad: SPGI.
Price, Brian R. 2017. "Notes on My Mixed Methods Approach to Rapid Assessment." Unpublished Manuscript.
Shanin, Teodor, ed. 1971. *Peasants and Peasant Societies: Selected Readings.* Harmondsworth: Penguin Books.
Siegelbaum, Lewis, and Andrei Sokolov. 2004. *Stalinism as a Way of Life.* New Haven, CT: Yale University Press.
Sorokin, Pitirim A. 1975. *Hunger as a Factor in Human Affairs*, translated by Elena Sorokin. Gainesville: University of Florida Press.

Velikanova, Olga. 1999. "Berichte zur Stimmungslage: Zur den Quellen politischer Beobachtung der Bevolkerung in der Sowjetunion." *Jahrbucher fur Geschichte Osteuropas* 47 (2): 227–43.

Viola, Lynne. 2000. "Popular Resistance in the Stalinist 1930s: Soliloquy of a Devil's Advocate." *Kritika: Explorations in Russian and Eurasian History* 1 (1): 45–69.

PART I

Government Goals for the Constitution Revision and National Discussion

CHAPTER 3

The Origins of Constitutional Reform

Internal communications of the high Communist Party officials brings us new knowledge about the authorship, intraparty machinery, and initial goals of the constitutional reform. Historical writings are unanimous in ascribing the initiative to Stalin. Newly discovered archival documents, however, allow us to see how the idea was born: it emerged as early as 1933 from the suggestion of A. S. Yenukidze, the secretary of the Central Executive Committee (TsIK) of the USSR, about election reform.

Avel Safronovich Yenukidze (1877–1937) was an old party member. Born in the Transcaucasia, he had friendly personal relations with Stalin and Ordzhonikidze and belonged to "Stalin's close circle." In the midst of internal debate about constitutional reform, on 3 March 1935 the Politburo dismissed Yenukidze from his position as the secretary of the TsIK during the course of the so-called Kremlin Affair involving Kremlin employees (January–April 1935); nevertheless, he remained a member of the constitutional commission elected on 8 February. At the June 1935 Central Committee (CC) Plenum, he was expelled from the party, a year later restored, but finally arrested on 11 February 1937 and shot in October 1937 (Khlevniuk 2010, pp. 252–6).

As early as 25 May 1933, Yenukidze sent a note on behalf of the party group of the TsIK secretariat to the CC in which he called for changes to election procedure in the coming 1934 soviet election campaign. He used several arguments to rationalize a more inclusive election law. The first point he made was the successful accomplishment of collectivization, which according to Yenukidze by itself made peasants socialist and loyal ("turned peasants into a real and strong foundation for Soviet power") and enhanced their cultural level and political consciousness. It seems he sincerely believed in the tenet of communist ideology, that the collectivist life of the *kolkhoz* immediately alters the individualistic and petit bourgeois mentality ascribed to peasants by the Marxists. Another argument of Yenukidze was the growth of proletarian elements in the countryside as a result of the introduction of machine-tractor stations (MTS) and state farms, which helped Sovietize villages. Inspired by collectivization and social changes, he suggested that, first, the voters in the villages in future elections would be organized according to their work units (brigade, *kolkhoz*) rather than by territorial unit (village) and, second, the representation of workers and villagers in the soviet congresses would now be equal.[1] He attached a draft of the TsIK decree, which ended with suggestions to introduce the changes into the constitution.

> In connection with the successful collectivization of 65 per cent of the peasant population of the USSR and a significant organizational and economic strengthening of the collective farms, which turned members into a real and strong foundation of Soviet power, and taking into account the huge growth of the peasants' cultural level and increase of proletarian elements in the countryside (workers of state farms, MTS, mining industry, etc.), the TsIK decrees ... (4) introducing the changes into the constitution of the USSR and Union republics. (RGASPI f. 667, op. 1, d. 10, ll. 15–21, 22–4)

Thus, the crucial motive for the Yenukidze initiative was a transformation in agriculture. This vision was shared by those at the top, as we can see from various documents—for example, from the secret CC All-Union Communist Party (VKPb) instruction two weeks earlier of 8 May 1933, signed by Stalin and Molotov, ordering an end to mass repressions in the countryside: "These three years of struggle led to a defeat of our class enemies in the countryside and to a final establishment of soviet socialist positions in the village" (Kulakov et al. 2005, p. 152). This vision

---

[1] According to the previous constitution, one delegate represented 25,000 workers and one delegate 125,000 peasants. Through the 1920s, the peasantry persistently demanded equality.

of a new condition in villages reflected also the CC decision in 1934 to reformulate the Kolkhoz Statute from 1930. The new version was adopted in 1935.

Yenukidze's note caused no known immediate consequences. For a year, between May 1933 and 1934, the idea of the changes in election law did not go any further. In his speech at the 17th Party Congress in January 1934 about future soviet elections, Yenukidze repeated his appraisal of changes in the villages after collectivization—a more organized and cultural peasantry, the growth of proletarian elements—but now he did not connect these changes with the need for election reform and only expressed his belief that elections in the fall would be a success ("17th Congress of VKPb" 1934). Again, on 22 May 1934, he approved the detailed plan, obviously compiled by someone else, of how to prepare for the upcoming soviet elections. Among other points, this plan suggested organizing the report and accounting campaign and inspection (*proverka*) of the soviets' work to enhance soviet democracy (RGASPI f. 667, op. 1, d. 10, ll. 25–8). The plan was realized later in 1936 and turned into a purge. Though the plan included the revision of the election instructions and publication of the election law, it did not talk about reform. It still discussed the cataloguing of the disenfranchised constituency.

Nevertheless, internal consultations about election reform probably took place, as we can see from a letter that Yenukidze, again on behalf of the TsIK party group, directed to the Politburo a few days later—on 29 May 1934. It concerned the calling of the 7th Congress of Soviets in January 1935 and included "Constitutional questions" as number 6 on the agenda. The analogous statement was sent to the Politburo by TsIK chair M. I. Kalinin. Probably on 10 May, the question was discussed with Stalin and the members of the government, when both Yenukidze and Kalinin visited Stalin's study in the Kremlin (Zhukov 2009, p. 63). On 25 June 1934, the congressional agenda was approved by Stalin, who edited number 6 to read "Report on constitutional questions." In August 1934, Stalin requested a copy of the 1924 USSR Constitution (Khromov 2009, p. 42). Oral consultations continued and resulted in Yenukidze's next note to the CC on 10 January 1935, which opened with a reference to Stalin's instructions: "Following your instructions, about the appropriateness and timeliness of the transfer to direct elections to soviet power organs (from the level of *raion* executive committees to TsIK USSR), I am presenting to the CC the following note: 'On the changes to the election procedure to the government organs'." In the following draft decree for the upcoming 7th Congress of Soviets, Yenukidze developed his previous arguments about changes in the social forces in the USSR. He made another step forward and suggested the transition to "direct and open [*sic*] elections" with the equal representation for the urban and rural population (RGASPI f. 82, op. 2, d. 249, ll. 12–3). The draft decree suggested: "working out and establishing the order of elections and incorporating appropriate changes to the constitution of the USSR." Internal communication between Yenukidze, Kalinin, and Stalin, which took place over almost nineteen months, evidences the gradual evolution of the idea and sincere concern about democratic progress as the participants understood it.

This note provoked the first of Stalin's documented reactions on the issue: his letter to the Politburo, Yenukidze, and Zhdanov from 25 January 1935:

> Circulating Yenukidze's note, I want to make the following comments. In my opinion, the question about the constitution of the USSR is much more complicated than it seems at first glance. First, the election system should be changed—not only to eliminate multistep elections. It should be also changed in relation to the replacement of open voting with <u>secret</u> [Stalin's underlining] voting. In this matter, we can and should go all the way, without stopping halfway. The conditions and balance of forces in our country make it politically beneficial for us [to do so]. Plus, it goes without saying, the reform is necessary in view of the interests of the international revolutionary movement, as this reform will play the role of a strong weapon (*orudiia*) striking international fascism. Second, we should keep in mind that the USSR constitution was created for the most part in 1918,[2] during the period of civil war and War Communism, when we had no modern industry, when individual farming dominated our agriculture, when collective farms and state farms were at the beginning, … when small and large capitalists represented an important factor of our economy, … when socialist property had not yet become a foundation of our economy as in the last two to three years. It's clear that a constitution created under different conditions does not conform to today's circumstances and today's needs. Respectively, we need to make such changes in the articles,

---

[2] The USSR was created in 1922 and its constitution was adopted in 1924. Stalin probably meant the election system established in 1918 and not addressed and respectively not modified by the Constitution of 1924.

formulas, and definitions that will make the constitution conform to current conditions. Thus, we need to introduce the changes to the constitution in two directions: (a) to improve its election system; (b) to conform it to a socioeconomic foundation. I suggest:

1. In one–two days after the opening of the 7th Congress of Soviets to summon the Plenum of the VKP(b) CC and make a decision about necessary changes in the constitution of the USSR.
2. To authorize one of the VKP(b) Politburo members (comrade Molotov, for example) to deliver a reasoned suggestion at the 7th Congress of Soviets on behalf of VKP(b) CC: (a) to approve the VKP(b) CC decision about the changes in the constitution of the USSR; (b) to authorize the TsIK USSR to create a constitutional commission for working on the appropriate amendments to the constitution to be approved by the following TsIK USSR session and in the future to elect the organs of government according to the new election system. Stalin (RGASPI f. 71, op. 10, d. 130, ll. 13–15; f. 17, op. 3, d. 958, l. 38; f. 82, op. 2, d. 249, ll. 1–3; f. 558, op. 1, d. 3275, l. 12).[3]

This letter suggested a considerable enlargement of the initial amendments' idea for a greater reform.

All Russian scholars attribute the beginning of the constitutional reform to this letter and personally to Stalin. Close reading of the documents does not support their assertions. Surprisingly, scholars ignore Stalin's reference to Yenukidze at the beginning of the letter. But Yenukidze's aforementioned two notes discovered in the archives correct this assertion. Not accidentally, Stalin in his letter proposed that V. M. Molotov would make a report to the 7th Congress of Soviets. This new name in our story was probably Stalin's reaction to the denunciation he received from his close relative A. S. Svanidze at the beginning of January: that Yenukidze was involved in an antigovernment conspiracy, later called the Kremlin Affair. Yenukidze's gradual dismissal began, though it did not bury the idea of reform. Yenukidze still introduced it to the Congress on 5 February and became a member of the constitutional commission, but Stalin's suspicions put Yenukidze away: it was

---

[3] Minutes 20, Politburo decisions from 4 to 30 January 1935.

Molotov who made reports on 28 January and 6 February and became a main speaker on this subject. The suggestions about "the amendments to the constitution in the direction of democratization of the election system"—in Stalin's formula, equal, direct, and secret voting (the latter corrected and emphasized by Stalin twice in Yenukidze's drafts)—were approved by the Politburo on 30 January, then at the CC Plenum on 1 February, and finally at the 7th Congress of Soviets on 6 February ("Decree of the 7th Congress of Soviets"; RGASPI f. 17, op. 2, d. 537, l. 7). The decision of the CC Plenum continued: "(b) To bring the constitution's definition of the socioeconomic foundation into conformity with the current balance of class forces in the country: defeat of kulaks, victory of the *kolkhoz* system, establishment of socialist property as a foundation of the Soviet system. To authorize the commission of Stalin, Molotov, Kalinin, Kaganovich, and Yenukidze to draft the project of the 7th Congress of Soviets' decision." The commission was organized and announced in the newspapers (*Pravda* 7, 8 February 1935). The decisive turn, however, from the amendments to the entirely new constitution took place only at the June 1935 CC Plenum. The grand project was launched.

In the sequence of exchanges on the subject, we can decode the main reasons as they evolved in the minds of the leaders. In his report to the 7th Congress of Soviets, Molotov repeated Stalin's two motives: internal and external. He rationalized the changes in the constitution by the new balance of classes in the city and countryside, but he also brought forward the international factor: "First, the balance of classes has changed in our country since 1918 and especially after the victory of the socialist public property principles in the city and countryside. Second, it's time when we can expand soviet democracy in full and change our election system … [while] in some countries the fascist transformation goes full speed toward terroristic methods of rule" (RGASPI, f. 82, op. 2, d. 247, ll. 26–45). Then Molotov discussed in his report the key elements of election reforms—to make elections direct and secret, to equalize rural and urban voters, and—a new thing!—to cancel disfranchisement: "The USSR comes close to the complete cancellation of all restrictions of universal voting rights." According to Molotov, in 1934, the *lishentsy* (disenfranchised) comprised 2.5%, or more than two million out of ninety-one million voters. He also emphasized one more reason for reform: "Secret voting … will strongly hit bureaucratic elements and will be a good shake-up for them … motivating them to subjugate the work of their offices to the workers' and peasants' [will]" (RGASPI f. 82, op. 2, d. 247, l. 29).[4] Besides social and international reasons, two new factors came forward here: the suggestion of universal voting and the intended targets of the election reform—the "bureaucratic elements." Thus, the leaders outlined the rationale for the reform. So far, in the internal exchange, we see no hints of a hidden agenda in the minds of the leaders involved in the discussion, but a straightforward belief in socialist progress in the country.

The genesis of the idea of *election* reform, which turned to *constitutional* reform, shows that the originator was not Stalin but, as early as 1933, A. Yenukidze. If Stalin were a background author of the idea, it would hardly have taken so long—almost two years—to begin discussing the idea. Only in January 1935 did Stalin actively join the debate and take the lead, while Yenukidze was dismissed and later repressed. Molotov became a main speaker about the election reform, but the real vehicle was Stalin: he was an active chair of the constitution committee, gave instructions, guided the debates, and edited the text. He appropriated and developed the idea, eliminating its author. Y. Zhukov recognizes Yenukidze's role in constitution reform, but the historian is so much attached to the idea of Stalin's authorship of "democratic reform" that without convincing evidence he presents Yenukidze (and some other party officials) as being antagonistic toward Stalin's reforms, allegedly because of the TsIK secretary's devotion to the ideals of the world communist revolution and his opposition to a moderation course (Zhukov 2003, p. 46; 2009, p. 106). Relying on the interrogation material—very dubious in its nature due to the violent methods used in the process—Zhukov asserts in his books that A. Yenukidze, resisting democratization, organized a plot to overthrow the Soviet government. Uncritical use of the sources and the omission in his research of Yenukidze's collection (fond 667) in the RGASPI led Zhukov to his conclusions in Stalin's favor.

The second revelation from Yenukidze's story is that the core drive for the grand initiative was a reform of the election system generated by an idealistic understanding of the new social conditions prevailing in the countryside after collectivization. As soon as elections were under the jurisdiction of the constitution, in 1933–1934, this initiative first

---

[4] Molotov's report at the 7th Congress of Soviets, 6 February 1935.

emerged as the partial amendments to the current constitution of 1924 and then grew into a grand project—a new Soviet constitution. This centrality of election reform in the origins of the endeavor shifts our understanding of the functions of the entire constitutional project.

References

"Decree of the 7th Congress of Soviets." 6 February 1935. *Constitution of Russian Federation.* http://constitution.garant.ru/history/ussr-rsfsr/1924/postanovleniya/3946696/. Accessed April 5, 2017.

Khlevniuk, Oleg. 2010. *Khoziain: Stalin i utverzhdenie stalinskoi diktatury.* Moscow: ROSSPEN.

Khromov, S. S. 2009. *Po stranitsam lichnogo arkhiva Stalina.* Moscow: MGU.

Kulakov, A. A., V. V. Smirnov, and L. P. Kolodnikova, eds. 2005. *Obshchestvo I vlast': Rossiiskaia provintsiai.* Vol. 2. Moscow: Institute Rossiiskoi Istorii RAN.

Rossiisky Gosudarstvenny Archiv Sotsial'noy Politicheskoy Istorii (RGASPI) [Russian State Archives of Social and Political History].

"17th Congress of VKPb." Verbatim Report. 28 January 1934. *Khronos.* http://www.hrono.ru/dokum/1934vkpb17/5_2.php. Accessed July 11, 2016.

Zhukov, Yury. 2003. *Inoi Stalin. Politicheskie reformy v SSSR v 1933–1937 godah.* Moscow: Vagrius. http://www.litmir.me/br/?b=93055&p=26. Accessed July 12, 2016.

———. 2009. *Narodnaia Imperia Stalina.* Moscow: Eksmo.

CHAPTER 4

Moderation in the Policies of the Mid-1930s

The initiative to reform the constitution was part of a larger discourse—a range of tendencies in 1933–1936 seen as moderating in political, economic, judicial, and ideological developments, including the trend for more legality. This chapter discusses a number of political changes that have allowed scholars to define this period as one of regime consolidation, or to speak about the relaxation of harsh policies and even the attempt at democratic reforms planned by Stalin. As the Soviet leaders did not overtly announce the beginning of a policy of conciliation and democratic reforms (unless we see such an announcement in the claim of the victory of socialism at the 17th Party Congress), the evaluation of this conciliatory trend and its place in the general course of politics remains a matter of interpretation.

As early as 1946 Nicholas Timasheff, in *The Great Retreat*, evaluated cultural, social, and ideological changes in the mid-1930s as a government retreat from socialist ideals in order to earn popular support and stabilize society (Timasheff 1946). For him the Soviet Constitution of 1936 was only window dressing. Recent studies do not see a refutation of socialism by the government during this period, but rather a kind of relaxation due to a perceived attainment of the new socialist order. While Terry Martin emphasizes a turn to traditionalist values, David Hoffmann and Matthew Lenoe see the politics in the official culture discussed by Timasheff—a return to family, promotion of patriotism, departure from the world revolution maxim—as pragmatic, a selective use of traditional institutions and culture for modern mobilizational purposes (Martin 2001, p. 415; Hoffmann 2004; Lenoe 2004).

The relative moderation could be perceived by historians as a conscious policy. However, very contradictory and inconsistent developments of the mid-1930s, together with few forced concessions to reality, continued to include repressions. This period represented a typical pattern of duality in Stalinist politics, when informal norms and practices coexisted with and often dominated over formal legal structures. The political system was permeated by this duality: when legal reform in 1934–1936 coexisted with the continuation of extralegal practices; when freedom of conscience declared in all Soviet constitutions coexisted with religious persecutions; when the legal norms established in the constitutions and authorized by government bodies existed in parallel with numerous (often secret to the public) instructions, directives, decrees issued by various other organs—the NKVD, the party—that degraded or modified the letter of the law; when the pretended power system of the soviets was paralleled by the real power of the party. The gap between the utopian project and Russian realities produced this duality and zig-zags in policies: (1) the introduction of the New Economic Policy in 1921 (tactical retreat); (2) its cancellation in 1928 (resuming socialism program); (3) Stalin's article "Dizziness from Successes" in 1930 (recovery tactic); (4) the German–Soviet Nonaggression Pact of 1939 (situational maneuver), and others. Such changes were provoked by the incompatibility of utopian ambitions with the pressure of reality, the resistance of human nature, and aggravated by voluntarism,[1] maladministration, the dogmatism of the leadership, and the breakneck speed of transformation.

The policymakers were led by the vision of a great goal—the socialist ideal—yet at the same time they had to cope with the imperfections they saw on the ground—a backward population, unmanageable local officials, a threatening foreign environment. The moderate tendencies can be explained on two causational levels: first, as a reactive, ad hoc politics, an adjustment after extraordinary excesses; and second, on the level of metadiscourse, as a relaxation motivated by the advent of socialism. While some moderation steps were programmatic—policies benefiting the youth, or the introduction of a constitution—other politics

---

[1] The doctrine that the will is a fundamental factor in the individual or the universe.

were situational—directed toward recovery and the correction of earlier mistakes and excesses. The constitution, especially its section on election reform, belonged to a metanarrative of socialism achieved; it was a continuation of the socialist program, not a change of political course.

Historians see the signs of relaxation in economic life, in repression, and in political concessions projected in Stalin's famous mottos: "Life has become better; life has become more cheerful!" and "A son is not accountable for his father." Almost all concessions were, however, forced, contingent, or half-hearted, correcting the consequences of previous policies. Because of depleted resources, the targets and pace of the second Five-Year Plan (1933–1937) had been reduced, accompanied finally, after a decade of neglect, by moderate investments in consumer goods production. The good harvest of 1933 and the end of the perilous famine allowed the country to draw an economic breath. The end of rationing after six years, and the permission of free bread trade in 1935, offered an important though faltering easing of life. Free bread trade, however, was actually suspended during the procurement campaign in the fall and was accompanied by the "purges of class-alien, speculative, and theft-prone elements" in the procurement apparat (at grain elevators, delivery points) and again in the summer of 1936 when the NKVD prohibited bread, grain and flour trade by collective farms and individuals (Danilov et al. 2002, pp. 468–9, 560, 794).[2] Alongside a few financial incentives, labor experienced new pressures to raise productivity per worker. Also dedicated to increasing production, the official introduction of Stakhanov's movement in August 1935 gave rise to work norms hated on the shop floor. Workers complained they could not perform the hard physical work because they were underfed (Bullard 2000, p. 52). The predictable consequences of Stakhanovism were disruptions in the economic process and new tensions among the workers, who perceived the new norms as exploitation.

The regime made several adjustments to the harsh repressions, as reflected in the 8 May 1933 decision to partially discharge the prisons and reverse the 7 August 1932 law on the theft of socialist property. This correction was caused by the crisis (not the first one) in the overcrowded punitive system and the lack of a workforce in agriculture—for example, in Ukraine, decimated by famine (Romanets' 2014, p. 204; Ellis 2009,

---

[2] NKVD circulars 19 April 1935; 5 August 1935; 20 June 1936.

pp. 345–6). While a couple of decrees on 30 June 1931 and in May 1934 restored the civil rights of certain categories of kulaks, the deportees were still restricted in mobility, without permission to return home from exile (Wheatcroft 2002, p. 122). Another decision made by the Central Committee (CC) in December 1935 allowed kulaks and their children to join collective farms, annulling the ban from 1930, but the fact that that decision was not made public evidenced inconsistency (Fitzpatrick 1994, pp. 240, 365). Another "softening" step was a Politburo permission from 9 February 1936 for exiled specialists to work in their profession in their place of exile and for their children to get an education (Khaustov et al. 2003, p. 721).

Several concessions were made to the young generation. It was in December 1935 at the all-Union meeting of operators of combines that Stalin announced his famous dictum, "A son does not answer for his father," which sounded like an invalidation of the previously incurable social origin label and inspired hope in many children of repressed or ostracized parents. The decisions about the younger generation were strategic. Officialdom saw the generation that entered life after the Revolution and comprised 43% of the population as a new breed of man uncontaminated by the bourgeois past and as a reservoir of loyalty. During tumultuous events of discontinuity, as with the October Revolution, the process of socialization was organic in the youth, but much more problematic in adults, who needed resocialization (Rose et al. 2011, p. 8). The Bolsheviks understood this very well when, during the cultural revolution, they exploited tensions and turned the new generation of professionals against the older specialists educated under the tsarist regime. A foreign observer, Dr. Rajchman, reported in 1936 on "the preponderance of young people over old … and the increasing influence in social and political life of the young generation" (British F.O. 371, 1936, vol. 20351, p. 75). Aiming to split the oppressed population, a common practice of Stalinists, the regime made several gestures in favor of youth—for example, separating young from old in the special settlements by pseudo-privileges such as permission to celebrate the October Revolution holidays. In March 1933, kulaks' children received voting rights; in December 1935, a government decree waived restrictions based on social origin for admission to higher education institutions. These concessions reflected the party leaders' belief that the new socialist environment played a primary role in a person's political development. The artificially widened gap between older and younger generations contributed to the schism in Stalin's society and social tensions.

In 1935, the terms of kulaks exiled in 1930, who numbered about a million special settlers, came to an end. On 28 July 1935, the Politburo cleared criminal records from those collective farmers who were sentenced to less than five years (excluding counterrevolutionary crimes), effectively completing their terms. As a result, by March 1936, 557,964 collective farmers were rehabilitated in the USSR, and beyond that— 212,199 peasants in Ukraine in 1934 (Danilov et al. 2002, pp. 553, 721). Though the removal of criminal records from former convicts formally meant the restoration of all civil rights and eligibility for passports, in real life they continued to bear the label of "unreliable elements" and often became the first targets in the mass operations that soon followed (Romanets' 2014, p. 210). A general decision about the deportees' return was not adopted, but separate individual petitions had been approved, and in February 1936 exile for the children of the disenfranchised was canceled (Khlevniuk 2010, p. 246). In another step, 54,000 of the local officials who "sabotaged" procurement in 1932–1934 were liberated according to the Politburo decision of 10 August 1935. Following the 1 February 1933 decree, on 16 January 1936 the Politburo decided to revise the cases of those convicted under the infamous decree of 7 August 1932 of death for the theft of socialist (state) property. As a result, by 20 July 1936, 115,000 cases had been reviewed and 37,425 people (32%) were liberated (Khlevniuk 2010, p. 243).

An important step to a social truce was the April 1936 removal of previous restrictions from Cossacks that allowed them to serve in the Red Army. The Cossacks explained the concessions as a way to ready soldiers for service in a future war. They said that the Soviet government began trusting the Cossacks because, after years of repressions, "no more Cossacks remained in the *stanitsy* (villages)—all [have been] exiled and convicted ... there are more new settlers (*inogorodnie*) now in the villages" (Danilov et al. 2002, pp. 752–3). This logic probably ruled throughout the government. Another compromise was the new Kolkhoz Statute adopted in February 1935 giving permission for collective farmers to cultivate small private plots of land. Stalin played the role of a benevolent father when he personally defended the idea of a plot and its large size at the 7th Congress of Soviets. It was exemplary, not obligatory, and left final approval to the collective farm according to local conditions (Fitzpatrick 1994, 126–7). This concession, though it was presented as a gift to the population, was a silent recognition of the inability of the collective farm system to meet the food needs of the country.

The turn to more legality was an attempt to regularize and control the arbitrariness that reigned during the collectivization process. This turn included the establishment of the USSR Procuracy in 1933 and reorganization of the legal agencies in 1935–1936 with the aim of building a strong, centralized state after the previous trend of simplifying judicial procedure and extralegality. Thus, on 10 July 1931, the Politburo forbade the arrest of Communists and *spetsy* (professionals) without permission of the CC and required all death sentences passed by the OGPU Collegium to be affirmed by the CC (Wheatcroft 2002, p. 123). On 8 May 1933, Stalin and Molotov secretly mandated to OGPU and party-state officials that a new procurator agency would monitor repression (Kulakov et al. 2005, pp. 152–6). Next, the decree from 17 June 1935 confirmed the procurator sanction and stated that arrests of party members, professionals, and officials needed approval from the appropriate ministers and party committees (Khlevniuk 2010, p. 242). Neglected during the Great Terror, the procuracy powers were restored in November 1938 by L. P. Beria's order.

More emphasis on legality could be seen in the attempts to enhance the desperately low qualifications of the legal corps. The press broadcast the calls of L. M. Kaganovich and G. G. Yagoda to develop the legal consciousness (*pravosoznanie*) in the population. The reorganization of the OGPU into the NKVD in 1934 pursued the same goal of centralizing violence and making the institution look slightly more constitutional. However, in support of the expanding number of tasks given to the political police, the headcount of State Administration for State Security NKVD personnel grew by 47.3% to 25,573 between 1931 and 1935 (Shearer and Khaustov 2015, p. 118). After the massive extralegal measures taken during the process of collectivization and industrialization, "some kind of 'constitutionality' was needed to regularize, to consolidate ... to ensure a ruly and predictable working of the responsible institutions" (Lewin 1985, pp. 282–3).

The low tide in Stalinist policies during 1933–1936, with the constitution as its component, did not mean the end of repression and mobilization as a mode of administration. The emerging forces interested in stability and legality coexisted with the old revolutionary habits and practices. Institutional rivalry between the USSR Procuracy headed by Andrei Vyshinsky and the Commissariat of Justice led by Nikolai Krylenko contributed to gyrations in policy (Solomon 1996, pp. 153–73). A shift in sentencing from extralegal agencies to legal structures starting in July 1931 was interrupted by the rise in extralegality in the winter of 1932–1933, associated with the famine: troikas (emergency-style three-member boards) were introduced in Ukraine in November 1932, in Belorussia in February 1933, in West Siberia in March 1933, and in Leningrad in April 1933. In periodic mass police sweeps that purged the cities of criminals, homeless children, the disenfranchised, and other marginal groups, *troikas* were also used. Nevertheless, from the second half of 1931 to 1936, the overall level of mass killing by the security agency regressed from 20,201 in 1930 to only 1118 in 1936 (Wheatcroft 2002, p. 125). On 7 May 1933, the Politburo forbade the *troikas* from imposing death penalties (this right resumed in the Great Terror); the next day Stalin and Molotov issued secret instructions against disorderly mass arrests by *troikas* and for reducing the prison population from 800,000 to 400,000 (Kulakov et al. 2005, pp. 152–6; Shearer and Khaustov 2015, pp. 143–7).[3] But between 1932 and 1935, the prison and camp population grew again by 210.9% to 1,251,501 persons (Khaustov et al. 2003, p. 748). The steps undertaken pursued the goal of control and centralization rather than mercy and humanity, as can be seen in the rhetoric of the instructions, which used expressions such as "mass disorderly arrests," "excesses (*razgul*)," "strict control by appropriate organs," "rationalization," "organization," and finally an angry note: "Anybody who is not too lazy, and who, as a matter of fact, has no right to arrest, makes arrests."

The moment of relaxation in the evolution of Stalinism included the new mass operations launched: the exile of 11,000 "former people" and "oppositionists" from Leningrad in the spring of 1935; "unreliable elements" from the western border[4]; and criminals, hooligans, and "socially

---

[3] Instruction to all party and soviet officials and all organs of OGPU, the court, and Procuracy about changing the work methods in the countryside.

[4] In the mass operations of cleansing the border area, more than 134,000 people were deported in the first half of 1935 in Western Ukraine, Leningrad *oblast'*, Karelia, North Caucasus, Azerbaijan, West Siberia, and Azov-Chernomorskii *krai*. Seventy percent of the targets were kulaks and *lishentsy*, but they also included Poles, Germans, Finns, Estonians, and Latvians. Social origin and status were a reason for arrests, exile, and discrimination at the workplace.

harmful elements" from the major cities (Danilov et al. 2002, pp. 387–8, 417, 550, 339, 508–9, 550–1). As David Shearer claimed, the regime "reduced level of mass repression in rural areas [now Sovietized in view of Stalinists—OV] only to intensify operations ... in urban and other areas," cleansing multitudes of people marginalized by the regime's disruptive policies, thus correcting results of excesses. In the spring of 1936, a new round of repressions took place in the Comintern and against Trotskyist-Zinovievite oppositionists. These purges targeted not only criminals and oppositionists but also certain categories of the population. Victims of the collectivization and famine, despite enforcement of the passport system and the residence registration law, migrated en masse to cities, turned to begging and criminality, and destabilized the social order and infrastructure. With the "social defense campaigns" of the mid-1930s, when hundreds of thousands of people were deported from cities and other strategic areas (Shearer 2009, pp. 10–11; Hagenloh 2009), the picture of moderation as a conscious policy is not so convincing. Arrest, deportation, and exile remained the well-used tools of the state administration in the mid-1930s—the "stick" in the classic combination of "the carrot and the stick." "There was, therefore, no 'relaxation' of repression in the mid-1930s, as was once commonly argued. Rather, its nature changed" (Priestland 2010, pp. 1553–5).

During the Great Terror itself, the government continued adjusting and correcting the consequences of previous repressive policies. The campaigns of "the strengthening of socialist legality" and "the reconciliation with convicted socially allies" were conducted: for example, on 23 October 1937, the Politburo ordered an all-Union Procurator inspection of criminal cases of the *kolkhoz* and village soviets' officials going back to 1934. Another Politburo order followed to end the cases and liberate collective farmers charged with minor crimes. As a result, the cases of 1,176,000 persons were revised: 107,000 cases ended; 480,000 people rehabilitated; and 23,000 liberated. Another decree from 10 November 1937 denounced the discrimination of young people purged from the education institutions due to connections with the convicted. In January 1938, the Politburo disapproved the dismissal of relatives of the counterrevolutionary "criminals" from jobs; after the CC Plenum decree "about the mistaken expulsion of the communists," a number were readmitted to the party (Khlevniuk 2010, pp. 317, 389–90). Of course, the apocalyptic scale of simultaneous repressions and the massive number of shootings does not allow us to see described concessions as moderation politics, but rather as measures of adjustment. Episodes of concessions in 1937–1938 (if realized) argue against the amplification of similar steps in 1933–1936 as political reform.

Described concessions in the mid-1930s gave historians a reason to interpret them as relative liberalization and explain it by the positive tendency of economic development and by international and political factors. There is no consensus on the nature of this process; uncertainty is expressed by marking "moderation" with quotation or question marks (Harris 2016, pp. 101, 139–40). Most historians interpret these political adjustments on the ground as part of the plan for restoring social stability inside, and a positive image of the USSR outside its borders, as well as the balancing of forces in the upper echelons of Soviet power. Historians interpret it as a change of political course (Khlevniuk 2010, pp. 220, 231) or as Stalin's intent to introduce democratic and participatory reform (Getty 1991, pp. 34–35; Fitzpatrick 1994, p. 281). The terms democratization, program, and reform, however, are overstated, as they presuppose some intention and even design. Such design would undoubtedly be somehow discussed in the Kremlin and recorded, but we lack such evidence. There are no records because relaxation was implied by default, a self-evident product of the completion of Lenin's plan of socialism-building.[5] The leaders remained the Marxists-Leninists, thinking in big terms of socialism. The victory of socialism announced at the 17th Party Congress *implied without saying* that excessive pressure was now unnecessary. "As a result of our success in the countryside (defeat of class enemies) the time had come when we are no longer in need of mass repression."[6] The next chapter suggests a more feasible interpretation that government expectations (not plans) of relaxation (not reform) belonged to a master narrative of socialism's victory through the Five-Year Plan and elimination of "enemies." As Stalinists maneuvered between paradigmal expectations of a triumphant socialism and realpolitik on the ground, they failed to pursue a coherent policy.

---

[5] The plan included industrialization, collectivization, and cultural revolution.
[6] Politburo decree of 10 May 1933.

References

British Foreign Office–Russia Correspondence, 1781–1945. 1975. Wilmington, DE: Scholarly Resources.
Bullard, Reader W. 2000. *Inside Stalin's Russia: The Diaries of Reader Bullard, 1930–1934*. Charlbury, UK: Day Books.
Danilov, Viktor, Roberta Thompson Manning, and Lynne Viola, eds. 2002. *Tragediia sovestskoi derevni: Kollektivizatsiia I raskulachivanie; Dokumenty i materialy*. Vol. 4. Moscow: ROSSPEN.
Ellis, Evdokia. 2009. "Svidetelei net: Vospominania." In *Rossiiskaia i sovetskaia derevnia pervoi poloviny XX veka glazami krestian*, edited by N. F. Gritsenko, 345–6. Moscow: Russkii Put'.
Fitzpatrick, Sheila. 1994. *Stalin's Peasants: Resistance and Survival in the Russian Village After Collectivization*. Oxford: Oxford University Press.
Getty, J. Arch. 1991. "State and Society Under Stalin: Constitutions and Elections in the 1930s." *Slavic Review* 50 (1): 18–35.
Hagenloh, Paul. 2009. *Stalin's Police: Public Order and Mass Repression in the USSR, 1926–1941*. Baltimore: Johns Hopkins University Press.
Harris, James. 2016. *The Great Fear: Stalin's Terror of the 1930s*. Oxford: Oxford University Press.
Hoffmann, David L. 2004. "Was There a 'Great Retreat' from Soviet Socialism? Stalinist Culture Reconsidered." *Kritika: Explorations in Russian and Eurasian History* 5 (4): 651–74.
Khaustov, V. N., V. P. Naumov, and N. S. Plotnikova, eds. 2003. *Lubianka. Stalin I VChK-GPU-OGPU-NKVD. 1922–1936*. Moscow: Demokratia.
Khlevniuk, O. V. 2010. *Khoziain: Stalin i utverzhdenie stalinskoi diktatury*. Moscow: ROSSPEN.
Kulakov, A. A., V. V. Smirnov, and L. P. Kolodnikova, eds. 2005. *Obshchestvo I vlast': Rossiiskaia provintsiia*. Vol. 2. Moscow: Institute Rossiiskoi Istorii RAN.
Lenoe, Matthew E. 2004. "In Defense of Timasheff's 'Great Retreat.'" *Kritika: Explorations in Russian and Eurasian History* 5 (4): 721–30.
Lewin, Moshe. 1985. *The Making of the Soviet System: Essays in the Social History of Interwar Russia*. London: Methuen.
Martin, Terry. 2001. *The Affirmative Action Empire: Nations and Nationalism in the Soviet Union, 1923–1939*. Ithaca, NY: Cornell University Press.
Priestland, David. 2010. Review of *Policing Stalin's Socialism: Repression and Social Order in the Soviet Union, 1924–1953*, by David R. Shearer and *Stalin's Police: Public Order and Mass Repression in the USSR, 1926–1941*, by Paul Hagenloh. *The American Historical Review* 115 (5): 1553–5.
Romanets', N. 2014. "The Campaign of 1934–1936 to Remove Criminal Records of Peasants Convicted in the Period of 'Great Fracture': The Purpose

and Methods of Implementation" [Kampania po schodo sniatia sudimosti s selian zasuzhdennykh u period 'velikogo perelomu': meta ta sposobi realiztsii]. *Z archiviv VChK–GPU–NKVD–KGB* 2 (43): 204. Kiev.

Rose, Richard, William Mishler, and Neil Munro. 2011. *Popular Support for an Undemocratic Regime: The Changing Views of Russians.* Cambridge: Cambridge University Press.

Shearer, David R. 2009. *Policing Stalin's Socialism: Repression and Social Order in the Soviet Union, 1924–1953.* New Haven, CT: Yale University Press.

Shearer, David, and Vladimir Khaustov. 2015. *Stalin and the Lubianka: A Documentary History of the Political Police and Security Organs in the Soviet Union, 1922–1953.* New Haven, CT: Yale University Press.

Solomon, Peter H. 1996. *Soviet Criminal Justice Under Stalin.* Cambridge: Cambridge University Press.

Timasheff, Nicholas. 1946. *The Great Retreat: The Growth and Decline of Communism in Russia.* New York: E. P. Dutton.

Wheatcroft, S. 2002. "Towards Explaining the Changing Levels of Stalinist Repression in the 1930s: Mass Killing." In *Challenging Traditional Views of Russian History*, edited by S. Wheatcroft, 112–46. London: Palgrave Macmillan.

CHAPTER 5

Motives for the New Constitution

5.1 The International Factor

The newly available archival documents about the early stage of the constitutional reform are especially helpful in understanding its major motives, both domestic and international.

The conventional explanation stresses that the Constitution of 1936 was designed primarily for external use: to impress the West and the European public, who observed the growing fascism and economic crisis, with the alternative of socialism, and to enhance the Soviet Union's reputation among Western democracies so it could attract allies. During the preparation of the draft, the texts of foreign constitutions were studied and discussed as models by the members of the constitution commission; in public communications, however, they constantly depreciated their applicability by contrasting socialist democracy (real) with bourgeois democracy (fake). In its coverage of the constitution, *Pravda* continuously presented the reactions of the foreign public, both officials and workers, and of foreign Communists, who never failed to emphasize the leading role of the USSR in the promotion of democracy. Such coverage reflected the party leadership's expectations and goals.

The constitution offered a kind of democratic self-representation in a divided world, and without a doubt, it impressed many. Faced with the spread of fascism and the aggressiveness of militarists, Japan's occupation of Manchuria in 1931, and especially Hitler's victory in Germany in 1933, the USSR was moved to reconsider its foreign relations and particularly to seek new allies. It joined the League of Nations in 1934. In the Communist International, the popular antifascist-front tactic was adopted in the summer of 1935, and in the diplomatic sphere, the construction of "collective security" was premeditated to oppose the aggressive intentions of Nazi Germany and Fascist Italy. The reputation of the USSR was not democratic: "The idea that Stalin had created a despotic form of personal rule became firmly established in 1936" in Western countries and even in Communist circles (Rees 2014, pp. 130–1). Seeking allies in Europe, Stalin aimed to soften and liberalize the image of the USSR to the world. It was advantageous to confirm the Soviet Union's devotion to the principles of democracy while he urged Communist parties in Europe to cooperate with Socialist parties and "bourgeois democracy" against fascism. The case to impress the world with the Soviet variant of democracy presented itself at the International Exhibition in Paris in 1937. A special stand displayed the adoption of the Soviet constitution with its provisions guaranteeing full employment, free education, and medical care to citizens.

Among other motives, the USSR's international image was certainly present in the minds of its leaders in 1935 when they discussed the revision of the constitution. It is often considered the major factor in Stalin's drive for the liberalization of policies (Khlevniuk and Favorov 2015, p. 135). True, the leadership repeated this point about international prestige, but mostly as secondary to domestic goals. In Stalin's working note to the Politburo about changes to the constitution and elections from 25 January 1935, we read: "Besides (!), the reform is necessary in view of the interests of the international revolutionary movement, as this reform will play the role of a strong weapon against international fascism" (RGASPI, f. 17, op. 163, d. 1052, l. 153). In August 1934, and again at the 7th Congress of Soviets in February 1935, Molotov justified the campaign for "revolutionary legality" similarly, as a method of raising the authority of the party "not only within, but also (!) outside the boundaries of the Soviet Union" (RGASPI, f. 17, op. 165, d. 47, l. 164).

It was not the first time that international considerations influenced the introduction of a charter. In 1905, besides revolutionary society, empty coffers and pressure from foreign bankers—who promised a desperately needed loan to the tsarist government on the condition of parliamentary reform—were brought to bear on the tsar to introduce parliament and a token constitution (Beetham 1985, p. 193). In 1936, interest in an alliance with Western democracies, as well as the interests of the Comintern, again contributed to constitutional reform. A positive outside image of the USSR—which positioned itself as "a torch of freedom for the toilers of the world"—was a permanent concern of the leadership during these years and the constitution was a tool to manipulate both Soviet and world public opinion. The invitation to visit the USSR to Western leftist writers—Lion Feuchtwanger, Romain Rolland, Bernard Shaw, André Gide—and their consequent writings served this goal (except Gide's book).

The Soviet diplomats in Washington reviewed the American press in June and July and reported a generally trusting reaction to the constitution in the US. The American press noted the omission of the world revolution goal in the new charter, unlike in the 1918 Soviet constitution. Though diplomats could tailor their reports to satisfy the expectations in the Kremlin, they described skeptical "wait and see" views in the US: "Voluntary self-restriction of the dictatorship is unprecedented in history ... The immutability of the one-party system restricts the scale of reform." On the basis of only one such diplomat's report from June–July 1936, A. N. Medushevsky reached a conclusion about an extremely effective constitution propaganda trick, "which built a positive image of Stalinism in the West for a long period" (Medushevsky 2016, pp. 122–38). If American reception was positive, it was cautious and short-term. In contrast, British diplomats were unconvinced by the reform.

By August 1936, the international image of a democratic USSR, which Stalin desired to project to the outside world, was opportunistically sacrificed in favor of the hard "necessities" of home security, as Stalin viewed them. The show trial of the Zinovievists and Trotskyists was staged in Moscow and garnered international resonance. News about show trials in the USSR and then cancelled contested elections to the Supreme Council in October 1937 discredited Stalin's regime in the eyes of European public opinion and disqualified attempts of the left to cooperate within the framework of the popular front's politics (Vatlin 2009, p. 362). Some leftist authors who visited the USSR, such as Lion Feuchtwanger and Romein Rolland, acknowledged later in their private correspondence that they did not know what to say to the public in their countries nor how to "defend socialism" when news about arrests in the USSR in 1937 reached a Western audience (Artamonova 2016).

As we learned that the constitution project originated in election reform (with mostly domestic implications) and that international prestige was easily sacrificed in favor of Stalin's fear of the "fifth column" inside, the government's international image concerns, although still valid, diminished from their dominant place among the range of motives for the constitution's revision. International factors involving the long-term goal of global socialism and the leaders' perception of a foreign threat provided a context, or precondition in Getty's categorization, for politics on the ground. A. Getty sees precondition as "a long-term situation that creates an environment in which major events can take place," or possibilities. Utilizing Lawrence Stone's approach to the English Revolution (Stone 1972), Getty presents the leadership's perceptions of the "unexpected dangers posed by the new constitution" in elections as precipitants or medium-term events that create a probability. Triggers, immediate short-term events or situations, such as personal decisions, turn a probability into a certainty (Getty 2013b, pp. 217–8). This theory of "multilayered" historical causes helps to understand the different degrees of influence of international, ideological, and political factors in the constitution's revision. Implementation of the socialist project as speculative and detached from reality, especially in Russian conditions, too often caused unexpected or unintended, unwanted results on the grounds that required adjustments, which in turn produced multidirectional politics (as in a turn to legality and simultaneous extralegal practice; see Chapters 4 and 9). The ideological factor discussed next also belonged to category of preconditions or context in the constitution's revision.

5.2 The Ideological Factor

Among the motivations for introducing the constitution, the ideological factor played an important role, evident not only in propaganda but also in the leaders' beliefs and practical steps.

The first constitution of 1918 promoted the goal of "the complete elimination of society division into classes." When Stalin launched a "socialist offensive" according to his understanding of Marxism, he established a grand goal for the country and promised the achievement of socialism and prosperity as the result of a Five-Year Plan. The Constitution of 1936 was designed to finalize this ideological program. Now that we have access to the personal correspondence and working transcripts of the Soviet leaders, we can explore their deeper motivations. In the mid-1930s, in various settings, Yenukidze, Molotov, and Stalin declared repeatedly that the goals of the great socialist offensive had been largely achieved. They saw the victory of socialism in the economy and in changes to the social and class structure. According to Marxian theory, changes in the base (relations of production) almost automatically shape the superstructure (ideas, values, beliefs, religion, education—in general, culture). The superstructure grows out of the base. The 17th party conference in February 1932 formulated the political task for the second Five-Year Plan (1933–1937)—to do away with the capitalist elements and class divisions in society and to mold all laborers into conscious and active citizens. This dictum was widely popularized. When in the summer of 1933 the anniversary of the first Soviet constitution was celebrated, Leningrad workers, after a long day's work, had to listen to the usual sloganeering speeches of the day. Chief among them was that by the end of the second Five-Year Plan the classless state must be established and all bourgeois classes eliminated (Bullard 2000, p. 211).

The vision of a new quality of social relations showed a swing from class discourse to the supranational discourse of *narod* (people). The official rhetoric of class gradually changed, reflecting the collapse of a coherent class structure as a result of Stalin's revolution from above (Viola 2009, p. 368). David Brandenberger identified the shift in Soviet propaganda of that time; it moved from referring to the workers as Soviet society's vanguard *class* to a different vision: "now the Russian people were assuming the mantle of its vanguard *nation*" (Brandenberger 2002, p. 44). The discourse of class receded gradually, replaced by the discourse of nationality in the second part of the 1930s, and then by the sermonizing construction of the supranationality of the *Soviet people*, implying socialist, integrational, and imperial connotations. In this larger context, the discourse of class, social origin, and disenfranchisement waned in expectation of the advent of a harmonious Soviet unity where "the boundaries between classes and nationalities erode."

The new socialist society should be inhabited by New Men and Women. The newspapers inflated achievements of the Stakhanovites as evidence that "the socialist personality had come into being". A young, loyal intelligentsia emerged. Literacy was declared universal. Collective labor at special settlements, collective farms and construction sites, like the Belomor Canal, reshaped criminals and kulaks into useful socialist citizens. Socialist realism in literature and art exhibited the hero-models to emulate. Writers engineered new Soviet souls. "Former people," transformed by the nature of the socialist environment, "renounced their past and proved their allegiance to the Soviet cause in deeds and words"

(Fritzsche and Hellbeck 2009, p. 320). A writer, A. M. Gorky, upon returning to the Soviet Union from emigration in 1932, claimed amazement at how the Soviet population had changed after the Revolution: the masses had acquired political consciousness. According to official discourse, the Soviet new personality—hardworking, devoted to socialism, educated, and elevating the collective good above the individual good—became a reality, though not *yet* a mass phenomenon.

Declarations that "socialism, the first phase of communism, had been realized in general" in the USSR were announced at the 17th Party Congress in 1934, deemed "victorious" because of that achievement. Then more such deliberations were made at the 7th Congress of the Communist International in July–August 1935, where the result of the construction of socialism in the USSR and its international meaning in the context of the world revolution was discussed. These public statements aimed to project to citizens and foreigners how strong and successful the USSR was. Of course it was a public relations mantra, but not only that. Internal communications convey how seriously the leaders took this dictum. Addressing the party elite at the Central Committee (CC) Plenum on 1 June 1935, Stalin said: "The project of constitution will be a kind of codex of the main achievements of workers and peasants in our country, index of achievements for which people fought and which means the victory of socialism" (RGASPI f. 558, op. 11, d. 1119, ll. 8–10). And again in a personal letter to Molotov on 26 September 1935: "What I think about the constitution, we should not mix it with the party program. It [the constitution] should contain what has already been achieved. While the [party] program should contain what we are struggling to achieve" (RGASPI f. 558, op. 1, d. 5388, ll. 209–10 [underlining in original]; Kosheleva et al. 1995, pp. 253–4). David Hoffmann stated: "Privately as well as publicly Party leaders stressed the attainment of socialism and the 'new order of classes' as the reason for a new constitution" (Hoffmann 2011, pp. 13–4, 286; 2004, pp. 661, 672). The importance of this ideological factor was mirrored in a work by an exiled former member of the Politburo, L. Trotsky's "The Revolution Betrayed" in August 1936, which countered the assertion that socialism had been achieved in Russia.

This allows us to suggest strongly that the "victory of socialism" maxim had not only propagandistic usage but also expressed the Bolsheviks' fundamental belief, with their overestimation of human agency in structuring history and dogmatic understanding of Marxism, and, as such, their slavish proclivity for wishful thinking. The idea of building socialism worked as an engine in all policies, though these policies often generated unforeseen threats.

It seems Stalin firmly believed in the power of words and their potential to shape reality, called by Sarah Davies and James Harris his logocentrism. In the 1920s, it was a common belief that one can change a person's mind by using the right words—the idea that "language can serve as the ultimate vehicle for the kind of transformation sought by revolution" (Clark 1998, p. 208; Laursen 2007, p. 492). The successor of the Enlightenment, Stalin believed that words of education and propaganda, whether party propaganda or "kulak agitation," were omnipotent in their ability to change personality and its psychology. Consequently, he saw rival ideologies and texts as "equivalent to political rebellion" (Getty 1991, p. 20). Desired norms were imposed on society by the state via rhetorical tools like assigning names ("socialism," "kulak," "enemy of the people"), monopolizing the power of naming and producing political ideas (Bourdieu 1991, pp. 166, 168), or inculcating speech, behavior, and thinking patterns and enforcing state agenda. Discursive strategies structured social reality by encouraging language patterns in line with official ideology, such as "achievements of socialism," and discouraging "wrong" patterns. The words "famine," "repressions," and "peasants' revolts" were excluded from the official public agenda and therefore hidden, becoming "nonexistent," replaced by "food difficulties" and "kulak sabotage." Evgeny Dobrenko describes socialism as a pure representation, tracing Russian preoccupation with the theatricalization of reality back to the eighteenth century. He extensively cites Merab Mamardashvili, who called this phenomenon "logocracy," with "the magical mindset where it was thought that words constituted reality itself … If something has no name … we cannot grasp it" (Dobrenko 2004, pp. 680, 690–2, 703).

Was the motto proclaiming the attainment of socialism just a marketing trick? With the exception of Medushevsky, modern historical writings depart from the view of the constitution campaign as a planned "conscious trick" to deceive the population (Medushevsky 2016, p. 122). An increasing number of historians addressing various policies have shown that there was a surprisingly small gap between Stalin's words and his deeds. Many Stalinists "believed much of what they said" (Getty and Naumov 1999, pp. 22, 26; Davies and Harris 2014, p. 11; Naiman 2002, p. 299; Gaddis 1994, p. 14; Harris 2016, p. 108). So the constitution, with its claims of victory was a desideratum, but the leaders—in our case, Yenukidze, Molotov, and Stalin—believed in its reality. They were "prisoners" of the ideological construction they created, the distorted information they received, and of their perceptions and beliefs: they did not want to see the real, contradicting conditions.

According to Lenin's and Stalin's adaptation of Marx's theory, the major steps on the way to socialism were elimination of the market, introduction of planning and welfare, industrialization and technology, collectivized and mechanized agriculture, reeducation and enlightening of the population. Beside economic benchmarks, social and cultural accomplishments were constantly at the forefront of party propaganda, epitomized in the cultural revolution drive inter alia. *Pravda's* editorial in June 1936 highlighted the success of the reeducation process conducted by the Bolshevik party in relation to the former exploiting classes and intelligentsia during the years of revolution and especially the Five-Year Plans: "Socialist labor like cleansing rain washed and is washing away from the people of the Soviet country the scum of bourgeois psychology and morals, bourgeois values and beliefs." "Nineteen years of revolution became a purging fresh wind for our motherland." Among other attainments, Molotov saw in decreasing vodka consumption[1] the emergence of New Men and the rise of the cultural level of the workers (*Pravda* 13 June 1936; 7 July 1936; 15 January 1936).

An important ideologeme of a successful transformation was Friendship of the Peoples. A propagandistic press campaign was launched by Stalin in December 1935 which celebrated Soviet patriotism and "the interethnic cooperation and racial harmony purportedly made possible by socialism" (Brandenberger 2002, pp. 43, 45; Martin 2001, p. 441). It made possible the fusion of nationalities into a supreme form of unity—a single Soviet people (narod) free of national prejudices, based on "the brotherly cooperation of peoples," as Stalin emphasized in his speech introducing the constitution. Collectivization transformed agriculture and peasants, their petit bourgeois way of thinking, and their relation to the means of production. As participants in collective labor, they were acquiring a socialist consciousness. Industrialization created a large working class. The old technical intelligentsia, distrusted and persecuted after the Shakhty trial (1928), partially renewed by a freshly

---

[1] In 1936, consumption of state-produced vodka was at 3.6 liters per head of population per year, compared to 8.1 liters before the war (Fitzpatrick 1994, p. 361).

educated cohort of specialists, sided now with socialism and represented no threat, as was announced by Stalin in his speech "New Conditions" in 1931 (Hoffmann 2004). As soon as these transformations were more or less accomplished in the USSR, the Bolsheviks believed that society was approaching a "promised land"—if only a few enemies would not hinder the construction of socialism. "Communists believed that the classless society of the future was guaranteed by the long-term movement of history" (Smith 2016, p. 9).

This ideology factor has often been interpreted in the literature as mostly a public relations tool. Historians and the public tended to seek the hidden agenda behind Soviet politicians' public statements. The available documents show, however, Stalin and his cronies as true believers in what they said publicly about the goals of the constitution. Two main arguments helped me in assessing the "genuineness" of Stalin's beliefs. One is based on evidence and another is based on the absence of evidence. The evidence is textual: Stalin's communications with his close associates, never meant to be publicized, repeatedly affirm their belief in the achievements of socialism. It is highly improbable that Stalinists systematically lied to themselves and to one another in private exchanges. This suggests that we have access to Stalin's genuine thought process. The absence of evidence is that sources do not show Stalin saying or writing "I believe one thing, but to the public we will assert the opposite." Both in official discourse and in informal exchanges with the colleagues, Stalin straightforwardly repeated the same ideas. The documents available to historians give no textual evidence of a hidden agenda on the declared goals of the constitution and elections.

Not only their words but also real political steps in this direction show the leaders' sincere belief in the success of socialism in the USSR: enfranchisement of former enemies, confirmation of the right of republics to exit the Soviet Union, significant though not universal expansion of the welfare measures announced by the constitution, and the support of peasants in the famine looming in 1936. In contrast to the 1932 famine, authorities in 1936 did not employ the idea of punishing the peasantry for sabotage of state procurements (Osokina 2001, pp. 161–2). The authorities now viewed peasants as successfully collectivized and socialist, with enemies (kulaks) eradicated. Therefore, food aid was provided to the starving countryside. Granting voting rights to former "enemies" in the middle of a tempest about "wrecking" and "vigilance" has no explanation other than ideological considerations about the new socialist condition of the society. Expansion of the welfare policy also reflected the Stalinists' understanding of progress to socialism as a result of the elimination of hostile capitalist elements (Hoffmann 2011, pp. 62, 286). Thus, in their wishful thinking and desire to see their program fulfilled and socialism accomplished, Bolsheviks closed their eyes to real conditions, and celebrated this achievement by the constitution, which formally announced the victory.

We can see from another document that Stalinists were sincere in their belief that now a turn to more democracy was suitable—N. Bukharin's death letter to Stalin. Having been arrested on 27 February 1937, the candidate to the CC wrote this letter in prison on 10 December 1937, seeking to save his life. Isolated since February, he tried to understand the situation. "(4) I have formed, more or less, the following conception of what is going on [in our country]: there is some great and bold political idea of a general purge. [It is] (a) connected with the prewar situation and (b) connected with the transition to democracy. This purge encompasses (a) the guilty (b) persons under suspicion, and (c) persons potentially under suspicion." (Bukharin 1937). He was a member of the constitution commission and knew the deep background of this project. His death letter implies that the transition to democracy, at least before the plenum, was taken seriously and meant as reality, not a trick. He explained the repressions of which he became a victim as a preelection excision of potential enemies. According to the letter, there were no plans for a mass repression campaign before the plenum as far as Bukharin knew.

The phenomenon of socialist realism helps us to understand the position of party leaders. By depicting how life ought to be, the constitution, in the same way as socialist realism art and literature, claimed it not merely reflected reality but transformed it. Art and the constitution in the same way focused only on the desired socialist elements of life, providing a pattern to emulate and laws to follow. Socialism was here "in principle" (a Russian expression), and minor imperfections would soon be corrected or *purged* (!). A dogmatic and simplistic understanding of Marx's tenets[2] and a distorted picture of the first Five-Year Plan's results allowed Stalin to announce the triumph of socialism in the USSR,

---

[2] Apocryphal sources say that in the 1920s, I. E. Sten (1899–1937), a knowledgeable Marxist, lectured Stalin on Marxist philosophy. Somebody asked him, "How is Stalin as a student?" Sten answered, "A bit dumb" (Chudakov 2012, p. 145; Borev 1990, pp. 42–3).

so much awaited by the exhausted population seeking realization of the promises. The prescribed reconciliation of classes—the major message of election reform—fitted the eschatological ideal of socialism as a conflict-free state that party leaders took so seriously they dared granting universal secret suffrage. Now that all classes (peasants and workers) in Stalin's and Yenukidze's view had become socialist and friendly, the government could enfranchise remaining former enemies (kulaks, priests, and a few others), expand the welfare measures, and even offer help to socialist peasants coping with the famine. The Stalinist vision of attained socialism and transformed peasants explains why the idea of election reform with the enfranchisement of former enemies ascended, but later, when abstraction (harmonious society) showed its discord with reality (warnings about hidden enemies and resistance of the party barons discussed in Chapter 10), the most daring part of the constitutional reform—contested elections—was castrated and the constitution *became* a sham.

A review of *Pravda* in June–July 1936 can help us to see how this major ideological trope of socialism's success was realized by propaganda. Coverage of the new constitution project started after the June CC Plenum and gained new impetus after publication of the draft on 12 June. Newspaper articles devoted to freedom of speech and assembly, or about the Supreme Soviet structure and its functions, educated the readers in the constitution's principles. These publications of the first days and weeks of the all-nation discussion were crucial as they framed the agenda and presented "a normative standard" for the public. The rhetoric of the reports about popular reactions, including letters presented as original, matched very closely the vocabulary and imagery of the editorials and Molotov's and Kalinin's speeches. The main party organ presented official discourse even when it pretended to speak peasant parlance (for example, *"trudovaia spinushka kretianina"*) in published comments that bore a clear mark of editing. These comments from workers and *kolkhozniks* selected for publications, if true, demonstrated that letter writers had successfully learned the new speech. Acquisition of a new political language was a condition of belonging to Soviet society and often a key to promotion and even survival. Both published popular comments and official articles in the pages of *Pravda* shared vocabulary, jargon, metaphors, and main topics. Until 6 August, when the Troskyist-Zinovievists' trial materials appeared for the first time in the summer and distracted the public's attention, seven narratives dominated in the constitution materials in the newspaper.

The main story discussed ad infinitum by the mouthpiece of the party was the achievements of the USSR which proved the fulfillment of socialism: full employment, equality of women, an end to national and racial prejudices and tensions, and free education. The accomplishments embodied in the constitution should inspire the populace to raise the productivity and harvest—the second theme. "The leader of the Moscow Bolsheviks [N. S. Khrushchev] called the workers of the Moscow plant named after Vladimir Iljich to respond to Stalin's constitution with the new rise of the Stakhanov movement, with higher productivity and over-fulfillment of the industrial plan." The letter authors eagerly answered these requirements: "The constitution called us to more enthusiasm and more energy to work better. I promise to keep the leadership in the tractor brigades' competition" (*Pravda* 6 July 1936; 13 June 1936). In *Pravda*'s rhetoric, the accomplishments of socialism were presented as a gift of government to the population with an expectation of the return gift—the rise of productivity.

Next, almost every personal comment, and also officials' speeches, started with a historical or biographical introduction that contrasted the prerevolutionary dark past with the current happy and prosperous life. Such paragraphs about the dark past were an indispensable part of the typical Soviet complaints described by Matthew Lenoe. Stories about the hard life before the Revolution turned complaints into "'ritualized discourse' through which realms of politics, economics, and law are navigated and negotiated," in Nancy Ries' (1997) words. The comments of the disfranchised reflected the same pattern: a progression from the kulak past to light and consciousness, then finally, due to the constitution, to full citizenship.

> I became a full citizen. My father was a kulak, a village miller ... I also was involved in my father's business. In 1929 I was deported to the Vishera camps where I worked almost four years. I was liberated early and went to my native Orel. However, I failed to find a job because of my social origin and my camp record. So, I applied to the NKVD and worked as a volunteer [*volnonaemnyi*] on the canal Volga–Moskva ... Now I am a shock worker ... After reading the constitution draft, I feel great enthusiasm. Now the constitution gives any citizen of the Soviet country, despite his past, the rights of labor, rest, and education! ... I decided—after finishing

the canal, I will go to engineering school. Any citizen will gladly sacrifice his life for the defense of our country! (*Pravda* 13 June 1936)

This darkening of the past helped citizens to see the present joyfully, thus constructing memory and manipulating the perception of the present. The official grim picture of the past stood in sharp contrast to a vernacular narrative common to the older generation that incessantly compared the current hardships with their prerevolutionary lives of relative wealth (Koval' 2009, p. 238).

The comments of these former outcasts often culminated in hysterical praise of Stalin intended to demonstrate their loyalty and secure their newly obtained places in the community. "Thank you, comrade Stalin" was the fourth most persistent theme in the discussion materials in the pages of *Pravda*. Next came references to the international community, which, in Stalinists' eyes, either ignored the Soviet constitution or greeted its democratic character. Usage of the phrase "*primer* (model) to all toiling humankind" revealed the missionary symbolism in the ideology of the Bolsheviks, who viewed themselves as destined to bring harmony to all humanity. It supports the idea that the international factor was an important motivation in the constitution's introduction. The outside perspective was verbalized in another narrative found in the pages of newspapers—expressions of readiness to defend the socialist achievements proclaimed in the constitution. This topic was raised by military men and even more often by civilians—for example, by a worker at the Verkh-Isetsky plant, Alexei Tretiakov. A collective letter from the 89th Aviation Squadron warned that "our enemies prepare for war and invent the satanic means of humans' annihilation." They titled their letter "We have everything to defend the new Constitution" and specified how—by more perfect and more diverse weapons, including new planes, tanks, artillery, U-boats, and chemical weapons (*Pravda* 13 June 1936; 6 July 1936). Last among the most influential narratives were calls to raise the level of vigilance toward enemies, who, though reeducated, could remain hostile—like the priests, for example. *Pravda* was a party bullhorn that translated ideological tenets for the masses and framed the agenda, telling the public what to think.

5.3 Internal Policies

As always in history, various reasons stimulated constitutional reform. It did not intend to put limitations on the government, as the Western notion of "constitutionalism" implies. Its functions were different. I argue here that among other political motives was the managerial goal of improving the effectiveness of government through a new election law—to use democratic procedures to motivate, revitalize, and purge the sluggish local elites.

Discussing the government's motives for the constitution, historians suggest ideological and international factors, along with the restoration of social stability and political legitimacy (Chapter 7) that had been undermined by the social catastrophes of the first Five-Year Plan period (Khlevniuk 2010, pp. 241–9; Hoffmann 2003, pp. 147–55; Zhukov 2009; Siegelbaum and Sokolov 2004). They propose several internal political factors that motivated authorities. Yury Zhukov, in his highly biased and publicity-seeking writings, presents Stalin as the initiator and planner of democratic reform, opposed in his efforts by high officials—"fundamentalists"—who conspired against him and thus pushed the general secretary to resort to repressions—for example, in the case of Yenukidze. Sheila Fitzpatrick suggests that "there had been a genuine impulse towards democratization at an earlier point, but this impulse had disappeared almost completely ... by ... the February–March Plenum [of 1937] and the program went through out of inertia. ... If this was indeed an experiment in soviet democracy, it was stillborn" (Fitzpatrick 1994, p. 281). Arch Getty also sees the concessions as an attempt at democratic reform, with the strategic goal of broadening the social base of the dictatorship by expanding participation and political education but without truly democratizing it (Getty 1991, pp. 33–4).

Recently, Arch Getty, in his book, and Wendy Goldman examine Stalin's use of the new constitution as a weapon in his struggle with the regional elites. Wendy Goldman supports the idea that one of the goals of election reform was a struggle by the center for control over the local cadres, who often prioritized clan-network interests and showed laxity or arbitrariness, inertia or excesses in implementing Moscow's policies (including the discussion of the constitution) (Getty 2013a, p. 206). As Goldman concludes, Stalin's democracy was not only a way to increase popular support but also to ensure a more thorough purge of regional elites while also invigorating the rank and file, and, I might add, the whole political system, which worked ineffectively (Goldman 2007, p. 111; Siegelbaum and Sokolov 2004, p. 130). If the regime felt impotent in its effort to successfully control the apparatus from the center, it saw a possible option to involve control from below, exploiting the lingering energies of civil war and mass discontent.

Wendy Goldman successfully resolves the epistemological paradox of democracy and terror, which did not conflict in the "political psychology of Stalin." She discusses two election campaigns—in the unions and in the party—in 1937, which ran in line with the new constitution rules and led to a significant rotation of the cadres there. The report campaign in the soviets in 1936, which merged with the constitution discussion, was of the same kind and will be deliberated in Chapter 6. Democratic mobilization of the masses was used to keep in check soviet and party officials, who were, when necessary, labeled as wreckers or red tape bureaucrats. These four political campaigns were presented by the government as socialist democracy in action, as popular sovereignty and criticism from below. Ultimately, the primary function of democracy is "1. to check arbitrary rulers, 2. to replace arbitrary rules with just and rational ones, and 3. to obtain a share for the underlying population in the making of rules" (Moore 1993, p. 414). The campaign around the constitution (among other goals) belonged to this pattern of mobilization that pressed the public to act and dismiss ineffective officials. By what means? By voting them out. Why did dismissals turn to massive arrests? In the warlike atmosphere, with a black-and-white vision of the world, the bureaucrats who deserved dismissal turned into enemies of the people. The campaign stirred up and exploited the social hatred of the lower classes for "party bureaucrats." It was easy to manipulate the poorly educated, miserable, frightened masses, brainwashed by class ideology, divided by the recent experience of civil war, by stirring their dark emotions and channeling them to appropriate targets. In a fractured society, "democracy became the means to a more thorough repression" (Goldman 2007, pp. 128, 134).

In the democratic election campaigns (in the party, unions, and to the Supreme Soviet in 1937), the campaign of popular criticism against local officials, inspired from above, was accompanied by a violent wave of denunciations from below, generated by the pursuit of pure ideological motives, by understanding of civic duty, and by various personal interests: self-protection, social hatred, and settlement of old scores. These denunciations were invited as a kind of "popular monitoring of bureaucracy" and, as such, Fitzpatrick sees them as "a form of democratic political participation" (Fitzpatrick 1997, p. 87). In the specific warlike cultural and political environment, democracy became "a double-edged sword" leading to repressions against the targets of criticism and condemnations.

Both Goldman and Getty concentrate mostly on the utilitarian goal of democracy, embodied in a new election law—to use the democratic election procedure to purge the slothful local elites. Even without the new law, however, the masses were successfully egged on the party and soviet bureaucracy through the current campaigns of hunting the wreckers and raising revolutionary vigilance. The details of the initiation of a new campaign supports the argument that the new election law and the constitution as a banner of democracy had much wider functions beyond the purges—but also had ideological, international, managerial, and legitimizing goals.

Let us take a close look at the motive behind Stalin's frustration with the undergovernment. He repeatedly expressed his discontent with the poor performance of the apparatus both publicly and privately. According to Erik van Ree, who analyzed the political thought of Stalin, the efficient functioning of the Soviet state and economy together with state power were uppermost in Stalin's mind. He was a true believer in Marxism, with its tenets of class struggle, and in the specific contemporary need for total unity and a strong state under socialism. Habitually ascribing apparatus malfunction primarily to "sabotage" of local barons, Stalin saw the rotation of cadres by free elections as an instrument to reenergize the soviet and party system and to enhance the management of the huge country. He declared this in several statements directed to both outsiders and insiders, and, according to van Ree, Stalin took his publicly avowed doctrines seriously. In a conversation that lasted three and a half hours, he told American journalist Roy Howard, "Our new electoral system will tighten up all institutions and organizations and compel them to improve their work. ... Universal, equal, direct and secret elections will be a whip in the hands of the population against idle power organs" (*Pravda* 5 March 1936). If this interview can be read as self-representation to the potential Western allies, Stalin's speech to the CC February–March Plenum in 1937 was directed at the selected party elite. There he repeated this motive: the need to rotate the cadres and purge ineffective ones and "pour fresh forces waiting to be promoted in the ranks of the apparat" (Stalin 2004, p. 107). It was Stalin's strategy to replace the old guard distrusted by him with the young upstarts dependent on and loyal to him personally. Vyacheslav Molotov emphasized the same goal several times at the earlier stages of reform, "Elections will hit the [inefficient] bureaucratic elements as a useful shake-up. ... This [election] system makes it easy to promote new forces to replace backward bureaucratic elements" (*Pravda* 6 February 1935; 30 November 1936).

Pravda repeatedly conveyed this message to slow-thinking officials: "The future elections [according to Stalin's constitution] will be a serious test. It will weed out those who are unable to work in a new way." "Those chairs of city and village executive soviet committees that won't change their work style and fail to win the trust of the population, they won't be reelected. They should remember that elections according to the new constitution will be radically different. This change is not yet internalized by many. They should ponder now about that. They should enhance the soviet work drastically." (*Pravda* 5 November 1936; 28 November 1936). Facing the problem of an undergovernment inherent in a huge and backward country, aggravated by the low quality of management on all levels, Stalin tried to cure it by hypercentralization, the increasing use of force (Viola 2009, pp. 372–3), by the education of the cadres (for example, party and judicial), and in 1936–1937 by controlled democracy as an instrument to make the state apparatus more efficient, organized, and obedient.

These managerial considerations in the constitution's democratization impulse (which in no way means to justify the brutal purges) becomes even more pronounced if we consider two other parallel campaigns of the period: that of the soviets' accounts [*otchet*] about their work to the voters in the summer and fall 1936 and the verification of party documents. These two campaigns were both of a cataloging, mobilizing, invigorating and purging nature. Verification [*proverka*] started in May 1935 as a clerical rectification of party documentation and turned into a mix of a routine purge of "inactive and morally corrupt members" and a special operation of the NKVD directed against local, unreliable nomenclature members. In 1935, a total of 263,885 members, which comprised 9.1 or 11.1% of party membership, had been expelled and 15,218 arrested; in 1936, 134,000 were excluded.[3] Reflecting violent Stalinist

---

[3] Khlevniuk cites 301,000 excluded and 30,600 members readmitted in 1935. The purge continued in 1937 when on 22 May and 8 June, the Politburo ordered into exile all those

modus operandi, those expelled were too often automatically dismissed from their jobs, deprived of their apartments, and expelled from the universities (Getty 1991, pp. 198, 232, 275; Khlevniuk 2010, pp. 235–6; Khaustov and Samuelson 2010, p. 61). Goals were not clearly conveyed by the center nor understood at the bottom. Reluctant to purge their own apparatus, local officials, as Getty showed, very often "deflected the purge downward to the rank and file" (Getty 1991, p. 274). The campaign went awry and Stalin was dissatisfied with the results, because the high regional officials successfully escaped the net. The June 1936 CC Plenum "denounced careless mass expulsions from the party" and suggested prompt consideration of the appeals and rehabilitation. In 1936, 37,000 were readmitted to the party (30,600 in 1935), but purges continued: 13,372 members were expelled from the party between June 1936 and February 1937 (Getty 1991, pp. 242–3, 275; Khlevniuk 2010, p. 236).[4] It was reported that in many places there were more expelled party members than active ones: for example, in Kyrgyzstan, the party organizations shrank from 14,000 to 6000 members (Schloegel 2012, pp. 195–6). The party purge and the following rehabilitation was Stalin's typical political about-face, showing the limits of his control in center–periphery relations.

The statement of the Moscow party organization published in *Pravda* just after the June 1936 CC Plenum revealed anxiety, servility, and confusion: "We should successfully finish verification of party documents, cleansing from the party damned enemies of socialism, Trotskyists, Zinovievists, and double-dealers who had not yet been uncovered during the campaign … We are guided by the CC and comrade Stalin's instructions about having a careful attitude toward those expelled from the party, though deprived of the name of Communist, but still working honestly as a Soviet citizen" (*Pravda* 11 June 1936). The disconcerted apparatchiks tried desperately to comply with the contradictory directives. The secretary of the Leningrad party organization, A. I. Ugarov, rightly saw the result of "verification" in a reshuffling of the cadres and promotion of new people to the administration (*Pravda* 3 November 1936).

---

previously purged party members who belonged earlier to the party opposition, together with their families from six cities: Moscow, Leningrad, Kiev, Rostov, Taganrog, and Sochi.

[4] For documents from the June Plenum, see Getty (1991, pp. 231–8).

CC Plenums in June and December 1936, and a secret CC letter to party committees on 29 July, again and again expressed the dissatisfaction of the center with ineffective, lackluster, politically unreliable and unvigilant regional party leaders (Goldman 2007, pp. 65, 67, 72, 86, 91, 95, 120). The 29 July CC letter on the eve of the Moscow show trial of Trotskyists and Zinovievists called for raising Bolshevik revolutionary vigilance and unmasking enemies in the party (*Izvestia TsK KPSS* 1989, pp. 100–15; Getty 1999, pp. 250–5; Goldman 2007, pp. 70–2). This "checking and rechecking" of party cadres paralleled purges of other groups and culminated in the Great Terror.

These campaigns—verification of party members, constitutional election reform, reporting in the soviets—were significantly motivated by Stalin's striving for control and the logic of centralization. Among other motives for attacking the cadres—their incompetence, intraparty conflicts, center–periphery tensions, corruption, Stalin's fear of conspiracies—the efforts to enhance managerial effectiveness could not be neglected. This managerial concern was evident in the logic of another reform—the reorganization of the judicial system, which started in 1936 and included a "review" of legal cadres and their reeducation. Seeking to centralize, to improve the international and internal image of the Soviet justice, the leaders could have considered the actual effectiveness of the system (Solomon 1996, pp. 179, 183, 400–2).

While permitting some democracy in the constitution, the leaders intended to keep their hands on the levers to control it and make it a useful weapon, first to discipline the slow and unreliable party barons, to add competition element in the promotion and election of cadres, and, finally, to win over the world and domestic public opinion.

Internal working party transcripts speak against depreciating the managerial goal as mere rhetoric.

REFERENCES

Artamonova, Zhanna. 2016. "Kamenev i Zinoviev na pervom Moskovskom protsesse." 4 September 2016, *Echo Moscow*. http://echo.msk.ru/programs/cenapobedy/1829252-echo/. Accessed December 12, 2016.

Beetham, David. 1985. *Max Weber and the Theory of Modern Politics*. Cambridge, UK: Polity.

Borev, Yuri. 1990. "Staliniada." *Pod'iom* (1): 42–3.
Bourdieu, Pierre. 1991. *Language and Symbolic Power*. Cambridge, MA: Harvard University Press.
Brandenberger, David. 2002. *National Bolshevism: Stalinist Mass Culture and the Formation of Modern Russian National Identity, 1931–1956*. Cambridge, MA: Harvard University Press.
Bukharin, Nikolai. 1937. The Last Letter to Stalin. http://stalinism.ru/dokumentyi/768-predsmertnoe-pismo-buharina.html. Accessed September 18, 2017.
Bullard, Reader W. 2000. *Inside Stalin's Russia: The Diaries of Reader Bullard, 1930–1934*. Charlbury, UK: Day Books.
Chudakov, Alexander. 2012. *Lozhitsia mgla na starye stupeni*. Moscow: Vremya.
Clark, Katerina. 1998. *A Crucible of Cultural Revolution*. Cambridge, MA: Harvard University Press.
Davies, Sarah, and James R. Harris. 2014. *Stalin's World: Dictating the Soviet Order*. New Haven, CT: Yale University Press.
Dobrenko, Evgeny. 2004. "Socialism as Will and Representation, or What Legacy Are We Rejecting?" *Kritika: Explorations in Russian and Eurasian History* 5 (4): 675–708.
Fitzpatrick, Sheila. 1994. *Stalin's Peasants: Resistance and Survival in the Russian Village After Collectivization*. Oxford: Oxford University Press.
———. 1997. "Signals from Below: Soviet Letters of Denunciation of the 1930s." In *Accusatory Practices: Denunciation in Modern European History, 1789–1989*, edited by Sheila Fitzpatrick and Robert Gellately, 85–119. Chicago: University of Chicago Press.
Fritzsche, Peter, and Jochen Hellbeck. 2009. "The New Man in Stalinist Russia and Nazi Germany." In *Beyond Totalitarianism. Stalinism and Nazism Compared*, edited by Michael Geyer and Shelia Fitzpatrick, 302–42. Cambridge: Cambridge University Press.
Gaddis, John L. 1994. *We Know Now: Rethinking Cold War History*. Oxford: Oxford University Press.
Getty, A. 1991. "State and Society Under Stalin: Constitutions and Elections in the 1930s." *Slavic Review* 50 (1): 18–35.
———. 2013a. *Practicing Stalinism: Bolsheviks, Boyars, and the Persistence of Tradition*. New Haven, CT: Yale University Press.
———. 2013b. "Pre-election Fever: The Origins of the 1937 Mass Operations." In *The Anatomy of Terror. Political Violence Under Stalin*, edited by J. Harris, 216–35. Oxford: Oxford University Press.
Getty, A., and Oleg V. Naumov. 1999. *The Road to Terror: Stalin and the Self-destruction of the Bolsheviks, 1932–1939*. New Haven, CT: Yale University Press.

Goldman, Wendy Z. 2007. *Terror and Democracy in the Age of Stalin.* Cambridge: Cambridge University Press.
Harris, James. 2016. *The Great Fear: Stalin's Terror of the 1930s.* Oxford: Oxford University Press.
Hoffmann, David L. 2003. *Stalinist Values: The Cultural Norms of Soviet Modernity, 1917–1941.* Ithaca, NY: Cornell University Press.
———. 2004. "Was There a 'Great Retreat' from Soviet Socialism? Stalinist Culture Reconsidered." *Kritika: Explorations in Russian and Eurasian History* 5 (4): 651–74.
———. 2011. *Cultivating the Masses: Modern State Practices and Soviet Socialism, 1914–1939.* Ithaca, NY: Cornell University Press.
Khaustov, V., and L. Samuelson. 2010. *Stalin, NKVD I repressii, 1936–1938 gg.* Moscow: ROSSPEN.
Khlevniuk, Oleg. 2010. *Khoziain: Stalin i utyerzhdenie stalinskoi diktatury.* Moscow: ROSSPEN.
Khlevniuk, O. V., and N. S. Favorov. 2015. *Stalin: New Biography of a Dictator.* New Haven, CT: Yale University Press.
Kosheleva, L., V. Lel'chuk, V. Naumov, O. Naumov, L. Rogovaia, and O. Khlevniuk, eds. 1995. *Pis'ma I. V. Stalina V. M. Molotovu, 1925–1936 gg. Sbornik Dokumentov.* Moscow: Molodaia Gvardiia.
Koval', N. 2009. "Put' k nishchete: Vospominania." In *Rossiiskaia i sovetskaia derevnia pervoi poloviny XX veka glazami krestian*, edited by N. F. Gritsenko, 233–43. Moscow: Russkii Put'.
Laursen, Eric. 2007. "Bad Words Are Not Allowed! Language and Transformation in Mikhail Bulgakov's Heart of a Dog." *Slavic and East European Journal* 51 (3): 491–513.
Martin, Terry. 2001. *The Affirmative Action Empire: Nations and Nationalism in the Soviet Union, 1923–1939.* Ithaca, NY: Cornell University Press.
Medushevsky, A. N. 2016. "Kak Stalinu udalos' obmanut' Zapad: Priniatie Konstitutsii 1936 goda s pozitii politicheskogo piara." *Otechestvennye nauki i sovremennost'* 3: 122–38.
Moore, Barrington. 1993. *Social Origins of Dictatorship and Democracy: Lord and Peasant in the Making of the Modern World.* Boston: Beacon Press.
Naiman, Eric. 2002. "Discourse Made Flesh: Healing and Terror in the Construction of Soviet Subjectivity." In *Language and Revolution: Making of Modern Political Identities*, edited by Igal Halfin, 243–69. London: F. Cass.
Osokina, Elena. 2001. *Our Daily Bread: Socialist Distribution and the Art of Survival in Stalin's Russia, 1927–1941.* Armonk, NY: E. Sharpe.
Rees, Tim. 2014. "1936." In *The Oxford Handbook of the History of Communism*, edited by Stephen Smith, 125–39. Oxford: Oxford University Press.

Ries, Nancy. 1997. *Russian Talk: Culture and Conversation During Perestroika*. Ithaca, NY: Cornell University Press.

Rossiisky Gosudarstvenny Archiv Sotsial'noi Politicheskoi Istorii (RGASPI) [Russian State Archives of Social and Political History].

Schloegel, Karl. 2012. *Moscow, 1937*. Cambridge: Polity Press.

Secret Central Committee letter to party organizations from 29 July 1936 "Concerning the terroristic activity of the Trotskyist-Zinovievist counterrevolutionary bloc." *Izvestiia TsK KPSS*, 1989 (8), 100–15.

Siegelbaum, Lewis, and Andrei Sokolov. 2004. *Stalinism as a Way of Life*. New Haven, CT: Yale University Press.

Smith, S. A. 2016. "History of the Future. Imagining the Communist Future: The Soviet and Chinese Cases Compared." In *The Palgrave Handbook of the Mass Dictatorship*, edited by P. Corner and J.-H. Lim, 9–21. Basingstoke, UK: Palgrave Macmillan.

Solomon, Peter H. 1996. *Soviet Criminal Justice Under Stalin*. Cambridge: Cambridge University Press.

Stalin, I. V. 2004. "Speech at the February–March CC VKP(b) Plenum." In *Lubianka: Stalin i Glavnoe Upravlenie Gosbezopasnosti NKVD, 1937–1938*, edited by V. N. Khaustov et al. pp. 95–109. Moscow: ROSSPEN.

Stone, Lawrence. 1972. *The Causes of the English Revolution: 1529–1642*. London: Routledge & Kegan Paul.

Vatlin, Alexandr. 2009. *Komintern: Idei, Reshenia, Sud'by*. Moscow: ROSSPEN.

Viola, Lynne. 2009. "Stalinism and the 1930s." In *A Companion in Russian History*, edited by Abbot Gleason, 368–85. West Sussex, UK: Wiley-Blackwell.

Zhukov, Yury. 2009. *Narodnaia Imperia Stalina*. Moscow: Eksmo.

CHAPTER 6

Soviet Sociopolitical Mobilizations

6.1 Reporting Campaign in the Soviets

Let us turn now to one more mobilization campaign. While the party document verification shifted to the purging of cadres, the managerial function was also pronounced in another campaign—the reporting (*otchet*) campaign in the soviets, which ran simultaneously and in practice merged with the referendum in the summer and fall of 1936 (GARF f. 17, op. 120, d. 232, l. 473). The nationwide campaign of reports in the soviets was Yenukidze's idea from 1934, intended as a tool to enhance soviet democracy on the eve of the coming elections (RGASPI f. 667, op. 1, d. 10, ll. 25–8; Kukushkin and Timofeev 2004, p. 68). Though now Yenukidze was in disgrace, his idea was realized. The Central Executive Committee (TsIK) Presidium initiated the assessment (*proverka*) of soviets at all levels on 2 August, instructing the chairs to organize the accounts of soviets to the electors, subject them to criticism, and elect the deputies to the *raion*, *krai*, and all-Union congresses. This reporting campaign, scrutinizing the soviet functionaries, was seen as a preparation for future soviet elections according to the new rules of the constitution and a tool to revive the soviets' activity. In this chapter we will see how reports in the soviets amalgamated with the constitution discussion and converged on the question of new election rules.

The ineffectiveness of the soviet system grew as soon as the party-state enhanced its control over the soviets. In response to this ineptness, attempts to revitalize the soviets were periodically undertaken—for example, between 1924 and 1926—with the goal of expanding *party* influence in the countryside. As a matter of course, soviets failed to implement voters' requests (*nakazy*) and to report on the work to the voters (TsGAIPD SPb, f. 24, op. 2v, d. 1755, ll. 118, 136–7, 140–1). The soviets' reporting campaign started in August 1936, one more attempt by the central authorities to energize the soviets, which the party itself had emasculated.

The nationwide discussion of the constitution was launched according to the Presidium TsIK decree of 11 June 1936. Together with organizing meetings and circles to discuss and study the constitution, this part of the campaign involved collecting and accumulating popular comments. It was the duty of party organizers and chairs of the soviets to compile regular reports and send them to the TsIK. Because of the customary dull reactions of local cadres, the center was compelled to push and pull them, for many years a common practice in relations between central and local authorities—nothing new. Following the decree, the TsIK chair, Mikhail Kalinin, sent telegrams to the chairs of all-level soviets demanding regular ten-day reports about the course of the discussion and summaries of popular suggestions (GARF f. 3316, op. 8, d. 222, l. 33). He directed the local cadres to connect the discussion of the new charter with the improvement of the soviets' work. In parallel with the July Central Committee (CC) letter to the *party* committees mobilizing them to search for the enemies in their ranks, two weeks later, in a 14 August telegram, Kalinin expressed dissatisfaction with the poor work of *soviets* on reporting the discussion. He instructed regional officials that discussion of the new constitution and its innovations should "revive and improve the working of the soviets and executive committees." The TsIK chair criticized local workers and urged them to work hard: "Many soviets are not promoting the nationwide discussion … (1) The chairs of soviets and executive committees are personally responsible for the organization [of the discussion]. (2) They should organize the regular recording and summation of all materials … and amendments … The chairmen of soviets and executive committees [*ispolkoms*] are obliged to ensure a genuine discussion of the draft Constitution by all citizens …" (GARF f. 3316, op. 8, d. 222, ll. 33–4, 36; Getty 2013, p. 210). Just as the party committees showed a reluctance to hunt for enemies in their own ranks (Goldman 2007, pp. 86–91), local soviets too—after the initial stir in June and July and now busy with the harvest while facing impending famine and flight from the collective farms—were slow in organizing discussions and reporting. They seemed not to care about improving their work: "Self-criticism of the drawbacks in the soviets' work is not sufficient," as *Pravda* stressed. "The conversation about the constitution project by itself will expose backward and inactive leaders unsuited for administrative work" (*Pravda* 17 June 1936).

Annoyed with the soviets' sloth, the TsIK on 12 September gathered the Presidium and heard reports from several regions about the progress of the discussion campaign. Once again the TsIK insisted on regular reports on the course of the discussion and now stressed the task of criticizing and dismissing the bureaucrats in the soviets. It offered a template to follow: "3. During the discussion [of the constitution], initiate a critique of soviets' work. Bring examples. 4. Examples of revocations of deputies for bad work or other depravities. 5. Examples of class enemies' attacks" (GARF f. 3316, op. 8, d. 222, ll. 38–9). The template worked as a political filter that not only structured reports but also framed the discourse at the meetings as well as the behavior of the organizers. As TsIK instructions disclosed, the discussion of constitutional and electoral reform was seen as a tool to direct popular discontent against local officials and their mismanagement. But when the center pushed local officials again and again to continue with new rounds of the discussion—tasking them with either improving their work or self-purging inefficient cadres—they often refused to understand their task. The chair of the Gorky *krai* soviet executive committee did not call for purges when in September 1936 he instructed the local soviets on the reporting campaign in light of the constitution (Kulakov et al. 2005, pp. 381–6).

Emissaries went to the provinces to ensure the locals understood and fulfilled the instructions. The TsIK instructor Babintsev went to the Belorussian Orshansk and Borisov districts and discovered that the "big failure in the organization of the all-Union discussion was that the soviets and *ispolkomy* did not direct the discussion toward a critique of weaknesses in the soviets' and deputies' work. There were only three cases of revocation of deputies during the discussion of the constitution in the village soviets in the Borisov district." Emphasizing first the purging function, Babintsev only subsequently reported another failure—in organizing the cataloging of the popular comments. "M. I. Kalinin's telegram did not cause a change in the work" (GARF f. 3316, op. 8,

d. 222, ll. 44, 51–2; *Pravda* 13 September 1936).[1] The same failure "to direct the critique to the shortcomings of soviets and deputies" was observed in the Pavlovsky soviet, Gorky *krai*, where not a single revocation took place. *Pravda* reported that the workers warned the chair of the Vorsmensky soviet in Gorky *krai*, who ignored their requests: "If you do not fulfill our request, we'll vote for your dismissal." The central newspaper of the Communist Party quoted Stalin: "The criteria applied by the millions of electors to the candidates will be high. They will dismiss the ineffective, cross them off the lists, and instead nominate the best candidates" (*Pravda* 19 and 25 September 1936). In due course, representatives of the *raion* soviets sought a critique of *village* soviets at the meetings, thus, in Getty's words, "deflecting the fire to lower levels."

6.2 The Local Cadres: Between a Rock and a Hard Place

As we see, two campaigns in the fall of 1936—the reporting of the soviets and the discussion of the constitution—merged and, according to Moscow's instructions, targeted the regional soviet apparat. The apathy of regional powers was understandable: they felt the campaigns were directed against them. Responding to the pressure from Moscow, they reported pro forma to the TsIK about the meetings, criticism, and, as required, listed a few cases of revoking deputies, mostly for mismanagement, embezzlement, and drunkenness (GARF f. 3316, op. 8, d. 222, ll. 51–2, 136, 138; Getty and Naumov 1999, p. 229). The national *Krestianskaia Gazeta* and the local Voronezh newspaper *Kommuna* used the same standard streamlined formulas: "Discussion of the constitution project was accompanied by a critique of the soviets and *ispolkomy* work and revocation of incompetent officials," though without the numbers and names of the dismissed deputies. Avoiding the encouragement of criticism required from above, the soviet workers often limited the meetings to simply reading the constitution's articles.

In the cultural and political climate of the 1930s, the situation facing local officials and propagandists of the constitution was often dangerous. It was true that many mid-level officials and cultural workers often did not understand the complexities of the constitution and were

---

[1] *Pravda* published a brief by Babintsev speaking only about poor reporting in Belorussia.

not equipped with adequate knowledge to explain the document to the common people. But their poor performance was not only the result of ignorance, poor education, and a reluctance to self-purge. As Karen Petrone justly noted, behind their "slothfulness" was their inability to deal with the grand contradiction between the constitution and everyday practice, which inevitably produced inconvenient questions from the audience that the unfortunate cadres could not answer. "How is it possible to combine vigilance and freedom of speech, press, assembly? After all, any counterrevolutionary scum will try to use these freedoms against the socialist state. Now it won't be possible to stop them of speaking at a meeting or put them behind the bars." "According to the constitution would they close the churches without the consent of the believers?" "How to understand the ban on arrests [without procurator warrant], though what we see now is quite opposite [that is, an increase in arrests]" (TsGAIPD SPb f. 24, op. 2v, d. 2059, l. 128; Kulakov et al. 2005, p. 442). Moreover, *any* answer could lead the functionaries to serious trouble in the fraught atmosphere of the search for enemies. To avoid possible dangers, some organizers forbade any questions at the meetings. Executives or propagandists expected punishment for not promoting the new official course, but likewise explaining and realizing the new freedoms to their logical ends could cause them trouble. How could they answer a question about freedom of speech: "Does it mean that all citizens may speak what they think [now]?" Petrone described the case of a rehearsal for the elections to the Supreme Soviet organized by a reading room attendant, who was finally blamed in deprecating the scale of the event (Kulakov et al. 2005, p. 442; Petrone 2000, pp. 199–200). The reason for the officials' apathy was that they felt the threat from below that new freedoms and the coming elections could bring to their own positions of power. Encouraging the people to realize their rights according to the constitution and to dismiss the unproductive bureaucrats from their offices would be to chop off the branch on which they sat.

It was a difficult task for everybody—officials and participants—to find a safe way between the officially declared norms to be imitated and the unwritten norms according to which the society and power really operated. For the participants, certain behaviors—nonattendance, lack of comments or criticism—could have dangerous consequences too. When the newspapers invited criticism from below, the worker Arzhilovsky wrote in his diary: "A new phrase has appeared in our lexicon 'Carelessness—the disease of idiots' [he cites Stalin—OV]. The newspapers push people in a new direction—to criticize, to be more active. A completely new, unusual campaign in the spirit of the latest Constitution." He was skeptical: "They can find subversive meaning in the most well-intentioned criticism" (Garros et al. 1997, pp. 127, 156). He was right to be cautious: persecution often followed such critiques. On 9 October, when the *raion* soviet reported its work at the "Krasnoe Sormovo" plant meeting in Gorky, four communists criticized the work of the soviet. The next day, they were summoned to appear before the chair of the soviet, Kalagaev, who threatened them with repression. The *raion* party secretary supported the attack and issued the communists with a formal reprimand (*vygovor*) (Berelowitch and Danilov 2012, p. 346). For ordinary people, the safest way to behave when pressed to speak was to pronounce their loyalty.

Obedience did not guarantee safety, however, as the orders to be fulfilled often contradicted each other, the party line oscillated, and local administrators faced threats both from above and below. So all handled the challenges as best they could. The Chechen-Ingush *oblast'* did its best to respond to the instructions and showed high rates of revocation: in the Gudermess *raion*, 62 members of the soviet were revoked and replaced by outstanding *kolkhozniks*. In the Levokumsk *raion*, 50% of members were revoked (Berelowitch and Danilov 2012, pp. 346–54). As many as 559 deputies were recalled for poor work in the Gorky *oblast'*, 18.2% of deputies in Uzbekistan, and 15% in Georgia (GARF f. 17, op. 120, d. 232, l. 46; Kulakov et al. 2005, p. 204; *Pravda* 1 November 1936; *Kommuna* [Voronezh] 17 October 1936). In sum, during the campaign, 80% of all soviets and about 85% of all deputies reported their work to the electors; 21 *krai* and *oblast'* of the Russian Federation revoked 14,953 deputies; almost one-third of soviets experienced rotation (GARF f. 3316, op. 41, d. 105, l. 1; op. 8, d. 222, l. 125; Danilov et al. 2002, p. 536).

The episode with Kalinin's instruction and official inspection was a common practice. In September 1936, simultaneous with Babintsev's commission, the Moscow party committee sent one of its secretaries, S. Z. Korytnyi, to investigate the results of the verification of party documents in the districts. Furious about the sluggishness of Taganka district officials who ignored the denunciations of some cadres, he pressed party committees: "If one of these people is an enemy, then your dawdling is a crime." Thus, the CC pushed the regional committees, which in turn pushed the district committees below, to take a political action—to purge (Goldman 2007, pp. 86–92).

These three initiatives—verification of party documents, accounts in the soviets, and discussion of the constitution—all declared the goal of improving the workings of the system. They pressed the voters, the local soviets, and the *partkomy* to expel idle, ineffective, or politically unreliable cadres. It was a part of the Soviet ethos—the involvement of the masses in policing the new socialist society with denunciation as the duty of all loyal citizens. The press encouraged the rank and file to guard against bureaucratization, to denounce "enemies," and to report any ineptitude or wrongdoing. Party leaders "couched these ... measures in the language of antibureaucratization, socialist revival, and mass control from below, appeals with strong popular resonance ... The slogans of repression were intimately intertwined with those of democracy" (Goldman 2007, pp. 7–8). Under pressure and threats from above, the tepid reaction at the bottom gradually acquired momentum and turned into an orgy of denunciations and charges that worked as proof of loyalty. This mobilization element of the purges, expressed in the term "vigilance," was crucial in the mechanics of power, as the CC instructed: "Each of our attacks should be politically prepared in advance, in order that every attack be supported by mass actions of the peasantry" (Kulakov et al. 2005, p. 154).[2]

Electoral reform and the channeling of people's anger against the bureaucracy attempted to purge and revive the local state apparatus—using both democratic rotation and repressions. Getty sees electoral reform and the repressions that followed as a sally in the center–periphery struggle, referring to Stalin's own words: "Elections will be a whip in the hands of the population against officials in the organs of power who work badly" (Getty 2013, p. 207). How did it work?

Quite representative of this trend was a series of 30 rural show trials of local authorities in the fall of 1937, described by Fitzpatrick. There, regional and village officials were blamed for failing to meet not the state but the peasants' needs; they were charged with abuse of power, the imposition of impossibly high grain procurements and arbitrary fines camouflaged as "taxation" or "state loans," suppressing *kolkhoz* democracy, allowing famine-hit collective farmers to depart for the towns in 1936,

[2] Secret party CC and Council of People's Commissars (SNK) instruction from 8 May 1933.

or admitting returned kulaks back into the *kolkhoz*—thus "reconciling with class enemies." The fact that it had then been the official policy of integrating former kulaks was never mentioned (Fitzpatrick 1994, pp. 297–307). The party promoted controlled democracy and show trials on the shop floor to fight arbitrariness, corruption, and incompetence, as well as lack of zeal and disobedience. What was the result? Sheila Fitzpatrick believes that it was relatively effective: peasants vented their hatred and "were increasing their influence over the selection and removal of kolkhoz chairmen" (Fitzpatrick 1994, p. 310).

The campaigns of 1936 all declared the goal of improving the workings of the political system. The state manipulated the discussion of the constitution, channeling it in the desired direction, inter alia to incite the population against the bureaucracy.

6.3 Participation: Managed and Voluntary

The key mobilization events around the constitution were the publication of the draft in newspapers on 12 June, meetings at enterprises and companies, rounds of study of the text in seminars (*kruzhki*), and the Extraordinary 8th Congress of Soviets that opened on 25 November in Moscow. The culmination of the Congress was Stalin's speech (*doklad*) about the constitution draft, broadcast by radio across the USSR.

Historians usually emphasize the compulsory character of participation in Soviet mobilizations. Political scientists in the 1980s concluded that Soviet-style participation was primarily ritualistic for both the rulers and the citizens, as it had no impact on the government's decisions but instead fulfilled functions of promoting loyalty and integration. Even then, however, some authors recognized that meaningful participation did take place, but often in nonprescribed ways (Difranceisco and Gitelman 1984, pp. 603, 607). Later cultural, anthropological, and subjectivity studies questioned the view of political participation as only masquerade: they drew a more nuanced picture. To scholarly debate about resistance and mimicry practices, subjectivity studies introduced practices of ideology acquisition and conscious building of the Soviet identity (Kotkin 1997). Alexei Yurchak shifts the emphasis from the constative dimension of the voting ritual (is there one or several candidates?) to the performative dimension: participating in ritualistic acts reproduced oneself as a "normal" Soviet person within the system of relations (Yurchak 2005, pp. 16, 23, 25). In the state's determination to control both the behavior and thinking of its citizens, Serhy Yekelchyk (2014) also observe more emphasis on the form of participation (totality, in the case of the constitution campaign), rather than on content. Regardless, the party-state could not monitor citizens' beliefs as effectively as their attendance at the meetings. Describing various forms of participation and their motivations, I argue below that even against a backdrop of reported mass passivity, absenteeism, and control of the public sphere, with its orchestrated speeches, rituals and enthusiasm, there was a measure of autonomous expression during the campaign—both public and concealed. In the 1930s, the first Soviet generation had not yet exhausted its reserves of trust and enthusiasm. The older generation had not withdrawn from the discussion, as they had not yet taken state-mandated discourse for granted; for the people, the meanings of authoritative discourse had not yet petrified as they would in late Stalinism. All of these left the opportunity for meaningful participation, negotiation, and interested contribution to the discussion.

The characteristic feature of these events was the emergency mode of mobilization typical of all Soviet interwar politics. The Bolsheviks, who opposed the whole world with their socialist project, understood even after the end of the Civil War their position as one of permanent emergency, which legitimized in peacetime the wartime practices such as mobilizations, the suspension of law, mass operations, expropriations, hostage-taking, deportations, and concentration camps. The sign of such an emergency mode was mass meetings at night: Stalin's speech on the constitution started at 5 p.m. on 25 November in Moscow and was broadcast live in Vladivostok at midnight on 26 November (a seven-hour time difference). Newspapers reported that citizens of the Soviet Far East did not sleep that night and for the first time listened to the voice of the beloved leader at their enterprises, on the streets, or at home (Bullard 2000).[3] Leningrad and Kiev workers listened to the text of the constitution broadcast on the radio at 11 p.m. This was not a unique case. The announcement of the new state loan campaign was broadcast by radio at 7 p.m. on 1 July 1936 and was immediately followed by meetings at factories and plants. At 11 p.m., the evening shift workers, instead of going home to sleep, demonstrated their enthusiasm at the conference halls by publicly lending their monthly salary to the state. Komsomol meetings

---

[3] Loudspeakers on the streets worked all day long in the 1930s and became the background noise of the epoch.

were sometimes convoked on state holidays—during workers' private time. Obviously, on the workshop floor this night-mode was a way for party organizers to demonstrate their zeal in mobilization. In more general cultural terms, it was a dramatic intrusion of state politics into the private sphere and into personal, even intimate, time. Such a style corresponded to the pattern of warlike relations between the Soviet state and society and to the Bolsheviks' paroxysmal attempts to secure control over society.

In the 1920s and 1930s, the government dealt with any crisis as if it were still engaged in a military operation and reproduced a permanent state of emergency (fearing foreign intervention at almost any moment), as evidenced by regular war scares, the most significant in 1923 and 1927. Mass mobilizations belong to those wartime methods with which the state managed society in peacetime—expropriations, surveillance, cataloging, and finally extralegality and mass repressions. In the atmosphere of a besieged fortress, an important function of all mobilization campaigns was the overstraining of all resources, including human, and the directing of them toward the grand goal of building a strong socialist state in the shortest possible time. John Scott, a young American who worked in Magnitogorsk as a welder in the 1930s, wrote, "Ever since 1931 or thereabouts, the Soviet Union has been at war and the people have been sweating, shedding blood and tears. People were wounded and killed, women and children froze to death, millions starved, thousands were court-martialed and shot in the campaigns of collectivization and industrialization. I would wager that Russia's battle of ferrous metallurgy alone involved more casualties than the battle of the Marne. All during the thirties the Russian people were at war" (Scott 1989, p. 5).

The core requirement of all mobilizations was active political participation. Active, informed, and responsible citizen participation in civic affairs is a prerequisite of democracy (Almond and Verba 1989, p. 9). In Russia, mass participation saw its high point in 1917 during elections to the Constituent Assembly. While volunteerism is assumed to be a feature of democracy, a specific mode of participation was formed in the USSR under conditions of pressure and manipulation. Effective mass participation in decision-making changed its character during the 1920s, being gradually restricted and subdued by the party as soon as democratic bodies, such as soviets, unions, and factory committees, were deprived of decision-making power. The new system of party–society relations was established: a public display of support for the regime in exchange for certain rewards and privileges (Pirani 2008, pp. 95–6). Finally, the decade saw a drop in election turnout (especially in 1922–1924), the growth of absenteeism, the decline of village self-government, closing of public associations and implanting of state-controlled entities instead. When political participation took a resistant or independent-from-the-state form—such as workers' strikes, the Peasant Union movement, or the unfavorable results of elections (for the Bolsheviks) to the soviets in 1927 (which were finally canceled)—such political activity was crushed or otherwise strangled, either by repression or by the establishment of controlled proxies like the Committees of Mutual Help in the villages, the Renovation branch in the Orthodox Church, or, in a cultural dimension, the manufacturing of pseudo-folklore. In the 1930s, when public associations came under state control, some islands of grassroots politics remained alive, though in limited semiunderground forms.

When the draft of the constitution was published on 12 June for the all-nation discussion, citizens were already well trained in the Soviet mode of participation. According to the Soviet ethos, every true Soviet citizen, a New Man and Woman, should "demonstrate activeness or civic participation"; nonparticipation was a sign of disloyalty (Alexopoulos 2006, p. 523). Pressure from above intertwined with tactics of social mimicry and conformism at the bottom. The workers and peasants learned the rules of everyday political life and accepted their duty to partake in mass Soviet social events. Together with various personal interests and obedience, we will see as a motive active citizens' commitment to contribute to decision-making.

Who were the authors of the comments in the discussion? Determining which social, age, gender, and ethnic groups they belonged to is not easy. The positions of the authors were not always specified in the TsIK or OGPU reports and were absent from scarce statistics, though usually identified in the letters. Fluidity of social identity in this period contributed to the ambiguity—represented, for example, in the social status of the diarist Andrei Arzhilovsky, a peasant, prisoner, and worker. There is an impression that the majority of comments came from peasants, reflecting their preeminence in the population and their political awakening in the 1920s through to the beginning of the 1930s. Next, the intelligentsia and employees were a well-represented group. Though the workers were more literate than the peasants, they were a smaller group, and many fewer comments came from the factories and plants. Such distribution of social positions among those who contributed to the discussion confirms, first, the state of the declassing of workers during the 1920s, and second, the fusion of peasants into the working class in the 1930s and the poor qualifications and marginal consciousness of these new workers. A worker at the Putilov plant in Leningrad complained in 1930 that "there are no more high qualified workers—where had they gone?" (Shaporina 2012, p. 94). This social process was called the "peasantization" of cities by David Hoffmann and the "archaization" of culture by Moshe Lewin.

We can also hear the women's voices, though not many: housewives, for example, demanded the right to nominate candidates to the soviets. Female collective farmers were well represented in the pages of the newspapers, clearly following a politically correct balance of images, but much fewer were found in NKVD or TsIK *svodki*. Very few voices of Soviet nationalities found their way to the reports, with the exception of Ukrainians. National issues are almost absent from the *svodki*, except for some discontent against the right of the republics to exit the Soviet Union granted in the constitution.[4] The dominant commentators were male Russians and, secondarily, the Ukrainians.

With our focus on the lower strata population unaffiliated with the regime, we cannot forget the articulate group of activists (*aktiv*) whose voices impressed the chart of popular opinions—the party, soviet, and trade union members, Komsomol, a new elite of nominees (*vydvizhentsy*), administrative apparatus, the Godless League (at least 3.5 million), demobilized Red Army soldiers, and cultural mediators like the worker and peasant correspondents. These groups profited from the social changes and consciously participated and managed the discussion. The number of such *aktiv* was said in March 1939 to comprise 5 million (Barber 1990, p. 10). We will see that their comments could favor the new constitution but also reject the new liberties granted to the perceived enemies.

The obligatory nature of political participation in the USSR makes it difficult to evaluate its civic potential. The campaign of official solicitation in the press and the open pressure from party organizers at public meetings took various forms. The practice of locking the factory gates

---

[4] Nationality issues are excluded from this study.

Photo 6.1 The students of the Lesgaft State Institute of Physical Education and Sport in Leningrad discussing the draft of the constitution. Photographer unknown. Courtesy of the Central State Archives of Documentary Films, Photographs, and Sound Recordings, Saint-Petersburg (TsGAKFFD SPb)

to keep people in the conference hall after work hours was very common (Kozlov 1992, p. 274) (Photo 6.1). A diary describes a street scene from 30 August 1937 in Krasnodar :

> A girl leaps out past the checkpoint at the entrance of the Chapaev factory and takes off running down the street, lickety-split. The guard rushes after her, yelling at the top of his voice: "I'll show you how to run away from a lecture!" But the "criminal" Klochkova escaped. The guard Zheltobryushenko gave up the chase and returned to "take up his post" again, closing and locking the front door behind him. Zheltobryushenko has been given unambiguous instructions by Ivankin, the cultural director: "Keep people in!" It's not the first time the factory has used this method to achieve "100 percent attendance" at lectures and meetings. (Garros et al. 1997, p. 40)

The most inventive party organizers resorted to tricks to secure full attendance. In Kabardino-Balkarian autonomous *oblast'*, the public went to the cinema, but instead of watching a movie they were pressed to discuss the constitution. Those who protested and demanded their money back were detained by the NKVD at 1 o'clock in the morning after the movie was finally shown (RGASPI f. 17, op. 120, d. 232, l. 78; Siegelbaum and Sokolov 2004, pp. 128–9). A. Arzhilovsky described a typical meeting:

Ordzhonikidze[5] died. ... There was an assembly at the factory. ... It was deadly dull, it dragged on and on, and the speakers had to be forced to go on stage. They elect the Presidium for the meeting. The audience is restless and noisy, and at first you can't hear the speaker. ... The speech ends. The director addresses the audience: "Who will be speaking next, comrades?" Dead silence. "No volunteers?" the director insists, and a threatening tone creeps into his voice. Eventually one party member, then another, forced out a few words proposing that the factory, to commemorate the death of the staunch Bolshevik, should increase its productivity, and so on. They speak without emotion, without inspiration, following a memorized formula. Seshukov, the cultural director, a special settler, also says a few words about saving the Socialist Kopecks, the Socialist Boards. This particular speaker would have gone on and on, right up to [saving] the Socialist Nails.[6] All of them talked about our "obligation." ... It came down to concrete proposals. The director solicited specific suggestions ... Ultimately the specific details were dragged out of us by force: in January we gave 113.4 per cent [rise of productivity]; in February we need to give no less than 115. (Garros et al. 1997, p. 147)

The task of the organizers—keeping people in and pressing them to discuss the constitution—was not easy in the cities and even more difficult in the villages, which faced a new wave of hunger in the summer of 1936 and massive flight from the *kolkhozes*. "A kolkhoznik is not up to discussing the constitution because he is almost starving," as a rural organizer explained the low attendance (Berelowitch and Danilov 2012, p. 345). A student said in a postwar interview, "We found all the propaganda very dull and the worst lessons in school were the lessons on the constitution. They talked so much and so frequently about the constitution that nobody listened, and they just sat back with their ears closed, and as a result most of the children could not even memorize the numbers of the articles of the constitution and the text, although they had been over it a hundred times" (HPSSS Schedule A, Vol. 11, Case 143, p. 30; Schedule A, Vol. 36, Case 431, p. 17). Almost 20% of the respondents in the Harvard Project, however, cited the agitation

---

[5] G. K. Ordzhonikidze, member of the Politburo, minister of heavy industry. Committed suicide in February 1937.

[6] Arzhilovsky is sarcastic here, referring to the Soviet campaign to fight the waste of resources.

Photo 6.2 Discussion of the constitution. 1936. Photographer unknown. Courtesy of the Central State Archives of Documentary Films, Photographs, and Sound Recordings, Saint-Petersburg (TsGAKFFD SPb)

meetings to be an important source of news—after the newspapers, word of mouth, and radio (Inkeles and Bauer 1959, p. 163).

Political participation for ordinary people in Stalin's USSR meant a sham display of loyalty, playing by the rules of the game, a ritual of conformity (Photo 6.2). Participation, however, also provided a vent for discontent and a channel of communication to the rulers. Despite the pressure and the imposition of a grand normative agenda through newspapers, even in these unfree conditions, outbursts of unorthodox comments often took place at the meetings and seminars, alongside the politically correct speeches,[7] against, for example, collective farms, poverty, and the arbitrariness of the bureaucrats (RGASPI f. 17, op. 120,

---

[7] Just one example: "I, a holder of a state order, A. A. Gavrilov, have read the draft of the Constitution. All its articles I approve with the great joy. ... Many thanks go to our great party and government, to the leader of the people, comrade Stalin, for liberation from the yoke of capitalism!" (Danilov et al. 2002, pp. 804–5).

d. 232, l. 52). People used the constitution discussion meetings as a venue to voice their grievances and discontent. At the discussion meeting in Kistendei *raion*, Saratov *krai*, collective farmer K. P. Levin recommended elimination of the *kolkhozes*, payment of a salary to peasants instead of "workdays",[8] and to allow the private trade of grain. In Karamysh *raion*, Saratov *krai*, the deputy chair of the village soviet, Shatalin, said at the meeting, "All Soviet power is built on a lie. The Communists deceive peasants and levy unbearable taxes." Both were arrested. The democratic nature of the constitution opened the window for the public expression of opinions incompatible with the dictatorial regime—such as support for equality of rights, and freedom of religion and associations. At another meeting, the deputy chair of the *kolkhoz* in the village of Nevezhkino, Fimushkin, suggested organizing Peasant Unions. "But the Soviet government would not permit this. If you demand it—they will imprison you. Here is freedom of speech for you!" (TsGAIPD SPb f. 24, op. 2v, d. 1860, ll. 7–8).[9]

During the discussion, NKVD officer Lupekin summarized the state of mind and the "counterrevolutionary" demands of residents in Leningrad *oblast'*, including leaders of the *kolkhozes* and village soviets: "1. Peasants' jealousy of workers. 2. Defeatist mood. 3. Demands to stop state management of *kolkhoz* life and for liberation from the state's procurement obligations. 4. Rumors that the constitution is a lie. 5. Demands to return exiled kulaks and their possessions and property. 6. Demands to open all churches and to ban antireligious propaganda. Anti-Semitic feeling" (Berelowitch and Danilov 2012, p. 355). The surveillance bodies in their *svodki* reproduced their black-and-white, conspiratorial political imagination, which needs clarification to make sense. Translated from corporate OGPU jargon, "jealousy" meant peasants' demands for the full rights possessed by city workers. "Defeatism" meant the anticipation of war as liberation from the Bolsheviks. Next came anti-*kolkhoz* protests. Demands for religious freedom corresponded to the new constitution, although they were called "counterrevolutionary" by Lupekin. As especially dangerous, Lupekin noted in his *svodka*, was the peasants' agitation for their integration into the political organization

---

[8] A measure of labor in the collective farms included monetary and in-kind portions.

[9] Top Secret. Main Administration of State Security (GUGB). Special information about negative comments during the course of the report campaign in the soviets and discussion on the USSR constitution draft in Saratov *krai*. 15 November 1936.

to oppose the state "because the state did not care about us." It was exactly the freedom of political associations declared in the constitution. An information summary by comrade Lupekin actually reflected the typical demands common for all regions of the country and that were repeated endlessly in numerous documents of various origins.

Labeling these demands as "counterrevolutionary" tells us much about the inertia of the apparatus and its resistance to the enforced agenda of liberties. Moreover, local officials' denigration of popular approval for the constitution's liberties (especially in relation to former enemies—clergy, individual farmers, and kulaks) exemplifies the dichotomy of Soviet life. The constitution embodied the discursive dimension of new official norms, encouraging patterns of thinking and speech—"achievements of socialism," "fraternity of peoples," "life became joyful," "all paths are open for youth," and so forth. These formulas imposed a new representation of the social environment or, in other words, constructed a social reality. To survive and to be successful, people had to learn these speech patterns—how and where to "speak Bolshevik." This normative language and behavior in line with official ideology (joyful demonstrations, political participation, and elections) permanently conflicted with the everyday dimension and its naked realities, where common sense ruled, like food lines and the threat of arrest. Like many commoners, the officials instinctively felt that the political ideals of legality and liberalism were very different from the powerful operating norms of a polity—extralegality, intolerance, aggressiveness, personal connections, patron–client relations—particularly as these norms had just recently been endorsed in official discourse (for example, "enemies are everywhere").[10] The idea of looming socialism inspired and consoled the majority, yet they had to live their earthly life according to its informal rules. It was a specific skill—choosing the right register, either representation according to ideological norms or action according to operational (by default) norms. Liubov' Shaporina offers a vision of this dichotomy when she noted in her diary the inconsistency of the grim, gray faces of the crowd on Nevsky Prospect and the joyful songs on the radio. "Noise, the crowds of ragged, yellow, emaciated, embittered people; frenetic loudspeakers on the corners, ignored by everybody, deafen … the crowd by joyful fox-trots and Roma songs … and [are] installed purposefully to confuse and disorient the people"

---

[10] See discussion of the dichotomist nature of Soviet life in Yurchak (2005, pp. 8–29).

(Shaporina 2012, pp. 92, 182).[11] The enforced agenda encouraged one kind of speech pattern and discouraged other patterns, thus covering up real events (famine, arrests, peasants' revolts), making them taboo and nonexistent. Conflicting formal and informal norms made the Soviet people swing like a pendulum to survive (Kotkin 1997)—for example, within the framework of the invited criticism narrative.

The critique, solicited in the party, soviet, and constitution campaigns, implied some limits: it channeled popular dissatisfaction to specific targets, like local "bureaucrats," but of course not the higher-ups in the Kremlin, and not Soviet policies. Despite solicitation, complaints about the misery of life, lawfulness, oppression, arbitrariness, or statements of disbelief were often followed by repression. Those who did not understand these limits to the criticism might pay with their freedom or life. A respondent of the Harvard Project recalled: "In 1936 there was a meeting about the constitution ... The school director led the meeting. My father said there, 'All this is a lie.' Three months later he was called to the NKVD, then ... they came, searched our home, and took my father ... Then came the trial—it was conducted by the *troika* [extralegal court commission]; six witnesses were present. The director of the school chose them. Father was convicted according to the paragraph 58 [of Criminal Code]—six years in jail and three years of deprivation of civil rights" (HPSSS Schedule B, Vol. 16, Case 358, p. 3). This story and pronouncements by *kolkhozniks* Levin, Shatalin, and Fimushkin show that despite the arrests, unconventional opinions were voiced publicly, even at official meetings, not to mention during informal conversations eavesdropped on and registered by the NKVD.

Besides the controlled venues, another medium—unorganized individual recommendations in personal, group, or anonymous letters to the leaders, TsIK, and newspapers—provided an outlet for more independent and authentic views. Among the comments cataloged by TsIK, individual recommendations comprised 13.5%, or up to 25% according to other estimates (GARF f. 3316, op. 8, d. 222, l. 125; RGASPI f. 5, op. 1, d. 232, l. 53; Berkhin 1972). My impression from their vernacular is that unorganized individual comments in general are more authentic, spontaneous, and personalized than speeches at the manipulated public meetings, which were bloated with clichés, suggesting that people were

---

[11] Entries from 1930 and 1934.

not only pressed to participate but also volunteered. Not only personal interests but also civic virtues and the desire to contribute to decision-making were well articulated in the individual letters. A collective farmer, F. M. Pilindina, from Bogucharsky *raion*, Voronezh *oblast'*, was obviously moved by civic feeling when she wrote to the newspaper:

> Maybe some people are timid to write, but I will write the truth, everyone's opinion. All praise Soviet power that it seized all property from the landowners; all express gratitude for the Soviet government's position against the war, but [in reality] all are discontented with the *kolkhoz*; all sit hungry in the corners, afraid to speak ... Even I see that people do not want to work in the *kolkhoz*; why does the editorial board not hear this? I hear the talk among the people, but at the meetings they are afraid to tell, that ... we are working and working in the *kolkhoz* but have nothing to eat. (RGASPI f. 5, op. 1, d. 232, l. 83)

This compendium of recommendations from outside the mass meetings, besides other possible motives, represented political awareness and the elements of civic consciousness on the part of the population. Evidence of informed and responsible citizen participation in civic affairs found confirmation in the writings of the subjectivity school, which approaches Stalinist society from another perspective—focusing on the personal trajectory of ideology acquisition. The authors discuss that the Soviet regime's claims, incorporating the individual lives of the citizens into a larger continuum of a historical fight for socialism, became attractive to many people. Ideas of self-perfection, social activism, and self-expression found resonance in the souls of the younger generation and inspired romantics from other groups, more so as the state provided rewards and incentives. The constitution depicted the desirable goal that was just around the corner. Participation in the construction of socialism gave self-validation, meaning, and historical purpose to the lives of common people (Hellbeck 2009) deprived of the prospect of religious salvation by the Communist-atheists.

Questions at the meetings and seminars recorded by organizers were another medium that represented this spontaneous primary level of popular understanding of the constitution, and were a form of political participation. Leningrad workers asked, "Is it secrecy of correspondence when the post office opens the letters, especially coming from abroad?" "As soon as we expand the Soviet democracy in full, could we grant an amnesty to the White Guard emigrants?"[12] "Will freedom of press and assembly be expanded to everybody?" "Will religious processions on the streets be permitted?" To such difficult questions the lecturer answered: "This is a dark issue. Nobody can explain this" (TsGAIPD SPb f. 24, op. 2, d. 2059, ll. 47–8, 61, 63). Those lecturers who recorded the questions would probably have refrained from censoring them, aware of the possible informers also reporting on the meeting. A village schoolteacher later recalled:

> The villagers were keen to argue, but soon they found out that what was wanted was not their opinion, but their acceptance of the agitator's opinion. I remember well such meetings, where papers were read and interpreted for the people. At first, there were many questions coming from the listeners, but later a rule was introduced, according to which all questioners had to be recorded in the minutes of the meeting. This discouraged further discussion and questions. Attendance at such meetings was compulsory. I myself remember going to such information meetings at the time the new constitution was discussed. People were very eager to learn all the details as to how the new electoral law would operate and were obviously pleased when it was pointed out that from now on they themselves could nominate several candidates through the various organizations. I can never forget the feeling of general disappointment when, after the meeting, the agitator suggested that we should nominate Stalin. The 1936 Constitution turned out to be a complete fake. It promised some changes, but none were enacted in fact. (HPSSS Schedule A, Vol. 34, Case 494, p. 28)

Another initiative at the grassroots level after the draft publication was the infrequent, spontaneous informal gatherings of believers, peasants, and intelligentsia who discussed the constitution's innovations and possible implications for their fate—for example, the meeting of 50 priests in Belgorod and 13 priests with 40 activists in Leningrad *oblast'*. Local officials and the NKVD reported these unauthorized, though totally constitutional, gatherings with great suspicion, mostly as anti-Soviet collusions (GARF f. 5263, op. 1, d. 32, l. 8; Berelowitch and Danilov 2012, p. 284). By virtue of its protective function, the NKVD saw any political activity beyond the official limits as a threat to the regime. How intimately the constitution impressed many citizens we see from the diaries; not only

---

[12] The White Guard military fled abroad after the civil war.

the elite—Mikhail Prishvin, Kornei Chukovsky, Georgy Mirsky, Nikolai Ustrialov, Vladimir Vernadsky, and Lubov' Shtange—but also a peasant, Andrei Arzhilovsky, and schoolgirls Nina Kosterina and Nina Lugovskaia discussed it. As soon as the constitution expanded benefits and rights, it received interested attention from peasants, especially from groups previously discriminated against. It also challenged common political practices and inspired new hopes, thus securing interest and curiosity, at least in the first months.

Despite involuntary participation, numerous statements about everyday hardships and arbitrariness at the heavily controlled meetings, the large corpus of individual reactions (diaries, letters), and the fact of spontaneous gatherings of citizens—all demonstrated voluntary political engagement. In the documentation that the campaign left to historians, we hear much more than the voices of passive recipients, supplicants and obedient subjects. Numerous nonconformist comments, including those rejecting either *kolkhozes* or democratic innovations, speak not only of discontent but also of the genuine interest of *citizens*. Political participation can take various forms in history—in democratic countries more effective forms than in authoritarian regimes. Comments show the plurality and diversity of beliefs and behavior behind the official façade of monolithic consensus. Among a variety of possible motives for participation—genuine enthusiasm, obedience, self-preservation, pragmatic career motives, display of loyalty, desire to join the mainstream, or spontaneous outburst of discontent—some citizens were stimulated by the civic values of self-realization, political engagement, and the desire to contribute to governing usually associated with conscious responsible citizenship.

The participants who contributed to the discussion accepted this format enthusiastically as it provided one more channel to raise and negotiate their concerns with officials. Moreover, it seemed to grant them the status of citizens, in opposition to the "supplicant" posture, traditional for the old path of letter writing to those in power. Citizen status granted the participants the right to speak with the government as equals, to correct the law and even criticize, if not the regime itself, its bureaucrats. Worth mentioning here is the great share of peasant voices who demonstrated once again that they could behave not like subjects but citizens who relied on law, rights, and liberties.

While letter writing per se is often referred to in the literature as a traditional peasant practice of communicating grievances about the "boyars" to the monarch, the rise of epistolary activity in the

USSR[13]—letters, complaints, denunciations—can stimulate us to read this practice in terms of the modernization of society. Besides a growing literacy, the scale of letter writing characterized the new quality of communication and the need for civil and creative self-expression. In this way, the common people, though hardly literate, internalized the emancipating impulse of the Revolution that now gave them the right to express themselves (also in diaries and amateur poetry) and to speak for their rights and citizenship (Hellbeck 1996, p. 83). Overall, the peasants' aspirations to convey their opinions to the powerful manifested an emerging sense of belonging to the polity—a trait of modern identity. Certainly, we cannot ignore the fact that a significant share of this communication was parochial by nature, requesting welfare or individual benefits. The increase in Soviet citizens' epistolary activity was, of course, a consequence of their limited options to influence decision-making (Fitzpatrick 1994, pp. 16, 259; 1996). It also reflected the atomization of society when individual or anonymous forms of expression (letter writing) predominated over collective actions.

Both peasants and workers eagerly accepted the duty associated in official discourse with citizenship—the duty to report inefficiencies of the system and corrupt bureaucrats. The peculiar Soviet understanding of such duty finally generated a flood of denunciations—both disinterested (guided by ideological or civic motives) and interested (settling personal scores), as Fitzpatrick distinguished—another form of political participation.

6.4 The Soviet Public Sphere in the 1930s

The constitution campaign belonged to an officially constructed public sphere aimed at homogenizing society along socialist lines and creating a New Soviet Man and Woman. Found in the niches of institutionalized ideology were alternative public spheres (Rittersporn et al. 2003, pp. 423–52). Many nonconformist comments indicated the existence of such alternative public spaces.

Soviet public spaces seem nonexistent from the perspective of the normative liberal model of the public sphere. According to theory, the important conditions of liberal culture are market competition,

---

[13] *Krestianskaia Gazeta*, between 1923 and 1933, received 5 million letters.

and the existence of a public and private sphere. At a first glance, none seemed to exist in the Stalinist USSR. But with a second look at the society, we find a "gray" market and citizens competing for their positions and place in life, and also networks of independent critical communications. Even in authoritarian states, public spaces, as nongovernment communicative structures facilitating a dialogue about matters of general concern, can emerge as the result of autonomous social development, sometimes in a subversive underground (Osterhammel 2014, pp. 596–7). Notwithstanding conformism, some autonomy and private and public spheres continued to exist. People discussed political events and expressed independent opinions in spite of their awareness of surveillance and the threat of arrest. They acted according to their own views and understanding—for example, protesting, migrating, reopening churches without permission, or demanding the sanction of a procurator during an arrest, following the letter of the constitution (see Chapter 9).

Under specific conditions, the public spaces could take a variety of forms: in the Soviet case, for example, self-organization in the form of religious communities; the charity network of the old intelligentsia helping political prisoners; Cossack choirs[14]; or the world of rumors, ditties, and anecdotes. Even endless critical talks in the food queues could signal an underground fire of autonomous expression. The network of religious communities surrounding priests or the "church twenty" (*dvadtsatka*) committees was the most influential public sphere infrastructure, akin to passive-resistance communities, which were perceived as a threat by the dictatorship. Between 1918 and 1932, several religious-enlightenment fraternities and semilegal religious-philosophical circles existed in Leningrad, the most well known being the Alexandro-Nevsky fraternity. It united mostly the laity—young people and intellectuals. The fraternities were crushed in 1932 (Shkarovsky 2003). Religious discourse in the discussion will be covered in Chapter 10.

With the appearance of political inmates in the USSR, a few charitable activities lingered, helping families of the repressed. Pompolit, the officially registered organization of E. P. Peshkov, the first wife of the

---

[14] The NKVD reported: "In the Cossack village Novomysskaia … Merkulov recruited only *Whiteguardists* and church people into the Cossack choir. He states: 'You should learn how to live with this pack of robbers [Communists] and how to cope with this iron heel. I conduct the choir, dance, I perform as a Soviet person, but inside I tremble from malice'" (Berelowitch and Danilov 2012, p. 319).

writer M. Gorky, functioned in Moscow to help political prisoners from 1922 to 1938. Peshkov used her personal connections with the chiefs of security police—F. Dzerzhinsky and then R. Menzhinsky—to provide limited support for prisoners and exiles, and information to their relatives (Markov 1978). A less organized form was a network of the intelligentsia that provided often anonymous donations to the relatives of the repressed or people in need—a kind of "clandestine society." The poets Anna Akhmatova, Osip Mandelstam, his widow, and the writer Mikhail Zoschenko—cut by officialdom from any employment or sources of income—lived on such impersonal donations for several years.

Formal charity was forbidden by the Soviet government. The Catholic clergy group of 19 was arrested in April 1936 in Kiev for collecting donations for those convicted of counterrevolutionary crimes. Stalin's resolution: "Exile them to camp for 5 years" (Khaustov 2003, p. 752). Informal charity united people with similar views and values, but not only among the intelligentsia. Such activities existed in other groups— of criminals (*obschak*), Old Believers, Jews, and other national communities—an indication of clandestine self-organization. After the war, this tradition engendered both A. Sakharov's fund to help the children of political prisoners and A. Solzhenitsyn's fund. When we read the diaries of Shaporina, Prishvin, engineer Popov (1998), and the memoirs of Nadezhda Mandelstam, we see the "islands of separateness" in the totalitarian environment: not only the "private sphere" that engineer Popov fenced around his life, but a community of like-minded persons surrounding Liubov' Shaporina or Nadezhda Mandelstam, who spoke their own language, shared values, and lived according to certain moral norms—decency, honor, mercy, and dignity—very different from the official Soviet norms. Though these people usually saw through Communist politics and barely took part in the mobilization "games" of writing to newspapers, the voices of this liberal subculture were still heard in the discussion—for example, in the suggestion of engineer Glebov from Leningrad, who recommended allowing the political parties to prevent discontent from going underground (RGASPI f. 17, op. 120, d. 232, l. 52).

Another unofficial system of communication was a world of rumors that played an important role in the countryside (in parallel with the anecdote culture in the urban world). Influential narratives in the 1930s included apocalyptic views of Communists and collective farms as a sign of the doom, "Bartholomew night" anticipations of a massacre of the Communists and activists, expectations of foreign intervention as a liberation, and so forth. Uncensored ditties (*chastushki*) were another form of popular autonomous expression. Officials called this "hidden transcript" practice "kulaks' agitprop" (propaganda) and took it very seriously. They used a tactic of creating proxy folklore by urging folk bards to manufacture songs and tales glorifying the new age, its leaders, and constitution (Miller 1991; Piaskovsky 1930; Azadovsky 1934). Half of the respondents of the Harvard Project mentioned word of mouth as a source of information, with two out of three persons in this constituency citing it as the "most important" (Inkeles and Bauer 1959, p. 164). The underworld of rumors in the political and cultural context of Stalinism served as a surrogate public space, uncontrollable by the official world and opposed to the "staged public sphere."

The informal exchange of ideas in society was vivid and vibrant enough for Sheila Fitzpatrick to conclude: "We have found a public, though not one of Western 'bourgeois' type, and this public has its opinion even if this opinion is elaborated and exchanged not in a coffee house but over the bottle of vodka split three ways between strangers in a stairwell." Sarah Davies recognized "a remarkably efficient unofficial network of information and ideas" in the Soviet Union and rich alternative discourses—for example, religious or nationalist (Fitzpatrick 2008, pp. 24–5; Davies 1997, p. 183). While the state controlled channels of public communication, surrogate means of communication lingered.

To challenge the notion of social atomization in totalitarian regimes suggested by Hanna Arendt, Sheila Fitzpatrick found new social bonds in place of those weakened or destroyed by the government—for example, those of kin, class, or milieu. New bonds of the stigmatized, strengthened by practices of exclusion, intensified existing bonds in the workplace, networks of contacts based on reciprocal favors, patron–client networks, and collectives of "politicals" among the convict population. These horizontal ties helped Soviet citizens to survive. Evidence of new bonds supports the argument that the human need for cooperation generated autonomous communication even in a repressive dictatorship (Fitzpatrick and Lüdtke 2009).

These grassroots public spaces provided a vent for independent expression and revealed the limits of state control and its efforts to totally indoctrinate the population. These islands of separateness and "hidden transcripts" of rumors connected individuals into discursive communities, which under conditions of dictatorship were fragmented and peripheral, lacked political influence, and did not facilitate interconnectedness of the whole society. Instead, they lingered as embryos of a public sphere, finding expression in the national discussion of the constitution as autonomous, and sometimes liberal, voices in the staged public sphere. The development of the public sphere picked up momentum after de-Stalinization in the 1950s and 1960s, and later in the 1970s became more internationalized (Rittersporn et al. 2003, pp. 448–50). Fitzpatrick and Kotkin, however, disbelieved that popular opinion and a drive for freedom played a decisive role in the 1989–1991 revolutions, but rather the political decisions of the leadership (Fitzpatrick 2014, pp. 379–80).

References

Alexopoulos, Golfo. 2006. "Soviet Citizenship, More or Less: Rights, Emotions, and States of Civic Belonging." *Kritika: Explorations in Russian and Eurasian History* 7 (3): 487–528.

Almond, Gabriel A., and Sidney Verba. 1989. *The Civic Culture: Political Attitudes and Democracy in Five Nations*. Newbury Park, CA: Sage.

Azadovsky, M. K., ed. 1934. *Lenin v Folklore. Pamiati V. I. Lenina.* 1924–1934. Moscow: Gosudarstvennoe izdatel'stvo.

Barber, John. 1990. "Working-Class Culture and Political Culture in the 1930s." In *The Culture of the Stalin Period*, edited by Hans Guenther, 3–14. Basingstoke: Palgrave Macmillan.

Berelowitch, Alexei, and Victor Danilov, eds. 2012. *Sovetskaia derevnia glazami VChK-OGPU-NKVD, Dokumenty i materialy*. Vol. 4. Moscow: ROSSPEN.

Berkhin, I. B. 1972. "K istorii razrabotki Konstitutsii SSSR, 1936 g." In *Stroitel'stvo Sovetskogo dosudarstva*, edited by E. N. Gorodetskii et al., 63–80. Moscow: Gosudarstvennoe izdatel'stvo.

Bullard, Reader W. 2000. *Inside Stalin's Russia: The Diaries of Reader Bullard, 1930–1934*. Charlbury, UK: Day Books.

Danilov, Viktor Petrovich, Roberta Thompson Manning, and Lynne Viola, eds. 2002. *Tragediia sovestskoi derevni: Kollektivizatsiia I raskulachivanie: dokumenty i materialy*. Vol. 4. Moscow: ROSSPEN.

Davies, Sarah. 1997. *Popular Opinion in Stalin's Russia: Terror, Propaganda and Dissent, 1934–1941*. Cambridge: Cambridge University Press.

Difranceisco, Wayne, and Zvi Gitelman. 1984. "Soviet Political Culture and 'Covert Participation' in Policy Implementation." *The American Political Science Review* 78 (3): 603–21.

Fitzpatrick, Sheila. 1994. *Stalin's Peasants: Resistance and Survival in the Russian Village After Collectivization*. Oxford: Oxford University Press.

———. 1996. "Supplicants and Citizens: Public Letter-Writing in Soviet Russia in the 1930s." *Slavic Review* 55 (1): 78–105.
———. 2008. "Popular Opinion in Russia Under Pre-war Stalinism." In *Popular Opinion in Totalitarian Regimes: Fascism, Nazism, Communism*, edited by Paul Corner, 17–32. Oxford: Oxford University Press.
———. 2014. "Popular Opinion Under Communist Regimes." In *The Oxford Handbook of the History of Communism*, edited by Stephen A. Smith, 371–86. New York: Oxford University Press.
Fitzpatrick, Sheila and Alf Lüdtke. 2009. "Energizing the Everyday. On the Breaking and Making of Social Bonds in Nazism and Stalinism." In *Beyond Totalitarianism. Stalinism and Nazism Compared*, edited by Michael Geyer and Sheila Fitzpatrick, 266–301. New York: Cambridge University Press.
Garros, Véronique, Natalia Korenevskaya, and Thomas Lahusen, eds. 1997. *Intimacy and Terror: Soviet Diaries of the 1930s*. New York: New Press.
Getty, J. Arch. 2013. *Practicing Stalinism: Bolsheviks, Boyars, and the Persistence of Tradition*. New Haven, CT: Yale University Press.
Getty, J. Arch, and Oleg V. Naumov. 1999. *The Road to Terror: Stalin and the Self-destruction of the Bolsheviks, 1932–1939*. New Haven, CT: Yale University Press.
Goldman, Wendy Z. 2007. *Terror and Democracy in the Age of Stalin*. Cambridge: Cambridge University Press.
Gosudarstvenny Arkhiv Rossiiskoi Federatsii (GARF) [State Archives of Russian Federation].
Harvard Project on the Soviet Social System (HPSSS). http://hcl.harvard.edu/collections/hpsss/index.html.
Hellbeck, Jochen. 1996. "Speaking Out: Languages of Affirmation and Dissent in Stalinist Russia." *Kritika: Explorations in Russian and Eurasian History* 1 (1): 71–96.
———. 2009. "Liberation from Autonomy: Mapping Self-understandings in Stalin's Time." In *Popular Opinion in Totalitarian Regimes: Fascism, Nazism, Communism*, edited by Paul Corner, 49–63. Oxford: Oxford University Press.
Inkeles, Alex, and Raymond Bauer. 1959. *The Soviet Citizen: Daily Life in a Totalitarian Society*. Cambridge, MA: Harvard University Press.
Khaustov, V. N., V. P. Naumov, and N. S. Plotnikova, eds. 2003. *Lubianka. Stalin I VChK-GPU-OGPU-NKVD. 1922–1936*. Moscow: Materik.
Kotkin, Stephen. 1997. *Magnetic Mountain: Stalinism as a Civilization*. Oakland: University of California Press.
Kozlov, V. A., ed. 1992. *Neizvestnaia Rossia. 20 vek*. Vyp. 2. Moscow: Istoricheskoe nasledie.
Kukushkin, Yury S., and Nikolai S. Timofeev. 2004. *Samoupravlenie krestian Rossii (19– nachalo 20 v)*. Moscow: MGU.

Kulakov, A. A., V. V. Smirnov, and L. P. Kolodnikova, eds. 2005. *Obshchestvo I vlast': Rossiiskaia provintsiia*. Vol. 2. Moscow: Institut Rossiiskoi Istorii RAN.
Markov, O. 1978. "Ekaterina Pavlovna Peshkova i ee pomoshch politzakluchennym." In *Pamiat': Istoricheskii sbornik*. Vol. 1, 313–25. New York: Chalidze.
Miller, Frank J. 1991. *Folklore for Stalin: Russian Folklore and Pseudofolklore of the Stalin Era*. New York: M. E. Sharpe.
Osterhammel, Jürgen. 2014. *The Transformation of the World: A Global History of the Nineteenth Century*. Princeton, NJ: Princeton University Press.
Petrone, Karen. 2000. *Life Has Become More Joyous, Comrades: Celebrations in the Time of Stalin*. Bloomington: Indiana University Press.
Piaskovsky, A. V. 1930. *Lenin v russkoi narodnoi skazke i vostochnoi legende*. Leningrad: Molodaia gvardiia.
Pirani, Simon. 2008. "Mass Mobilization Versus Participatory Democracy: Moscow Workers and the Bolshevik Expropriation of Political Power." In *A Dream Deferred: New Studies in Russian and Soviet Labor History*, edited by Donald A. Filtzer et al., 95–128. Bern: Peter Lang.
Popov, I. Y. 1998. "Dnevnik: Protsess 'Prompartii' v dnevnike inzhenera I. Y. Popova." *Otechestvennye Archivy* (2): 42–73; (3): 62–90.
Rittersporn, Gábor T., Malte Rolf, and Jan C. Behrends. 2003. "Open Spaces and Public Realm: Thoughts on the Public Sphere in Soviet-Type Systems." In *Public Spheres in Soviet-Type Societies*, edited by Gábor T. Rittersporn, Malte Rolf, and Jan C. Behrends, 423–52. Frankfurt am Main: Peter Lang.
Rossiisky Gosudarstvenny Arkhiv Sotsial'noi Politicheskoi Istorii (RGASPI) [Russian State Archives of Social and Political History].
Scott, John. 1989. *Behind the Urals: An American Worker in Russia's City of Steel*. Bloomington: Indiana University Press.
Shaporina, L. V. 2012. *Dnevniki*. Vol. 1. Moscow: NLO.
Shkarovsky, M. V. 2003. *Alexandro-Nevskoe bratstvo, 1918–1932 gody*. Saint-Petersburg. http://www.anbratstvo.ru/content/m-v-shkarovskiy-fenomen-aleksandro-nevskogo-bratstva. Accessed August 14, 2017.
Siegelbaum, Lewis, and Andrei Sokolov. 2004. *Stalinism as a Way of Life*. New Haven, CT: Yale University Press.
Tsentral'ny Gosudarstvenny Arkhiv Istoriko-Politicheskikh Dokumentov Sankt-Peterburga (TsGAIPD SPb) [Central State Archives of Historical–Political Documents in Saint-Petersburg].
Yekelchyk, Serhy. 2014. *Stalin's Citizens: Everyday Politics in the Wake of Total War*. Oxford: Oxford University Press.
Yurchak, Alexei. 2005. *Everything Was Forever, Until It Was No More: The Last Soviet Generation*. Princeton, NJ: Princeton University Press.

CHAPTER 7

State's Goals for the Nationwide Discussion

In a September 1935 letter, Stalin suggested to Molotov the adoption of referenda: "The constitution should consist of (about) 7 chapters ... 6. Rights and duties of the citizens (civic freedoms, freedom of associations, church, and so on). 7. Election system ... I think we should introduce [a practice of] referendum [underlined by Stalin—OV]" (RGASPI f. 558, op. 1, d. 5388, ll. 209–10; Kosheleva et al. 1996, pp. 253–4). The Russian wording of the last point (*vvesti referendum*) implies the introduction of referenda as a general practice, not a specific referendum on the constitution. This suggestion was implemented in Article 49: "The Presidium TsIK [Central Executive Committee] ... conducts a population survey (referendum) [as in original—OV] on its own initiative or at the demand of one of the Union Republics." The article uses the Russian term *vsenarodny opros* (survey), which does not necessarily involve voting, in contrast to the definition of *referendum* in the *Oxford English Dictionary*: "a general vote by the electorate on a single political question." The constitutional discussion in 1936 did not involve voting and the first all-Union referendum took place in the USSR only in March 1991. Nevertheless, such campaigns of popular discussion without voting were held in 1927 when *Krestianskaia Gazeta* invited its readers to evaluate in its "All-Union forum" the results of the construction of socialism (Velikanova 2013a, pp. 172–5), and then in 1936 to discuss the law on abortion.

Why were so many efforts directed at mobilizing popular opinion around the constitution?

© The Author(s) 2018
O. Velikanova, *Mass Political Culture Under Stalinism*,
https://doi.org/10.1007/978-3-319-78443-4_7

Official discourse and Soviet historiography announced the goals of the discussion as "development of Soviet democracy, communist education of the masses, and political participation for fighting all shortcomings and ineffective bureaucracy." Universal participation in state administration was seen as a feature of communism, according to N. Bukharin's and E. Preobrazhensky's *ABC of Communism* (1920). Historiography translates this into the modern language of social science and conceptualizes the goals further: from sampling popular opinion, socialization, and enlightenment to a mobilization strategy in order to inculcate Stalinist values into society (Sokolov 2009; Getty 1991, p. 23).

1. Monitoring popular moods was among the goals of the campaign (Getty 1991, p. 23; Fitzpatrick 1999, p. 178). Authorities were always interested in popular opinions: since 1918, they had received regular secret police, party, Komsomol, and military reports on the political mood and memorandums on the secret scanning of private correspondence. Numerous recommendations and comments in the campaign were carefully collected and filed, but not for incorporation into the law or bringing them into practice: only 20 recommendations and some editorial corrections found their way into the constitution and thousands of others were neglected (see Chapter 12). The goal of this monitoring was a test for Sovietness (see #3 below).

2. A more obvious function of the discussion of the constitution was to educate and infuse the millions herded into conference halls and "red corners" with the Soviet ideology. Education, especially political education, was a cornerstone of the Enlightenment project and its descendants—the Bolsheviks. They firmly believed in the power of education and propaganda to change the human psyche. A younger generation, who had no personal experience of capitalism, was educated in Soviet schools and the army in the new spirit. But the older generation, with their prerevolutionary values, would be reeducated in the system of political education—in the classes and seminars where the constitution was "studied" in several rounds and via newspapers with their normative message. It was in this top-down instruction that a sense of political community, as an attribute of the New Man and harmonious society, would be ideally fostered. These public events guided by the party, cultural workers, and propagandists structured the perception of the new law and correspondingly the comments (Photo 7.1).

3. Implicitly, the discussion represented a new way of power legitimation through sham appeals for the direct expression of the people's

7 STATE'S GOALS FOR THE NATIONWIDE DISCUSSION 101

Photo 7.1 Political seminar (*kruzhok*). Note the portrait of Stalin, bust of Lenin, and a slogan "Under the banner of Lenin, under the guidance of Stalin, forward to Communism." Leningrad. 1930s. Photographer unknown. Author's family archive

will, and, ultimately, to the principle of popular sovereignty. Legitimacy is a consensus achieved in the relations between society and political power, under which the right of the latter to govern is recognized (Medushevsky 2016, p. 113). As a fundamental feature of a political regime, legitimacy has at least two main components: on the one hand, the perception of the government order as acceptable by the major part of society, and on the other, the ruling elite's confidence in its right to exercise power.

After the social disruptions of the first Five-Year Plan, the restoration of balance in society–power relations was vital. When Stalin halted mass repressions in 1933, he showed his concern about the prestige of power: "The method of mass disorderly arrests under the new conditions produces only [a] negative [impression], decreasing the authority [*avtoritet*] of Soviet power" (Kulakov et al. 2005, pp. 153–4; Shearer and Khaustov 2015, pp. 143–7). The dictator played softball when useful and hardball when needed, such as during the Great Terror, when priorities other than prestige became important to him. In 1937–1938, a flood of arrests resulted in a loss of the legitimacy of power in significant cross sections of the population.

Any political system tries to project strength and stability to win popular support. The Harvard Project interviews of the 1950s confirmed that the image of a strong regime, a strong military, and a well-articulated international mission played an important role in ensuring the loyalty of the younger generation and inhibiting any disloyalty in the old one (Inkeles and Bauer 1959, p. 285). In 1936, the constitution enhanced the legitimacy of the Soviet system in the eyes of both foreign and domestic observers, though it was a short-term and not universal phenomenon (Solomon 1996, pp. 191–4). We will see in Chapters 9 and 11 that many citizens frequently did not believe in the niceties of the new law from the very beginning. The rest understood a short while later that the constitution did not work in practice—its legal terms actually cloaked the antilegal, dictatorial nature of the regime.

As for the Soviet government, it was its permanent concern to reestablish and reconfirm its legitimacy. For a government created in a coup, which then disbanded the Constituent Assembly and triggered a civil war, these were not easy tasks, especially when the major promise of the Bolsheviks to bring "improvement of life" to the population was not achieved. According to Max Weber, of three types of legitimacy—traditional, charismatic, and legal—the charismatic or revolutionary mode, being unstable, compels the government to constantly confirm its right to rule by incessant victories and frequent appeals to the cult of the charismatic leader. The weak self-confidence of the government produced sporadic panics among the party elite, as in the days of Lenin's illness and death in 1923–1924 and during the War Scare of 1927 (Velikanova 2001, pp. 51–2, 67–89). Though the legitimacy of the regime tends to increase with its longevity,[1] especially in the eyes of the

---

[1] According to Rose, in durable systems, support becomes a matter of habit, because it is the only one people know (Rose et al. 2011, p. 16).

younger generation, the insecurity of the Soviet rulers about their popular support produced recurring mobilization campaigns and ultimately repressions to intimidate and excise the doubters. Fear of a "fifth column" and conspiracies speaks clearly about the permanent anxiety at the top. The party's self-perception of isolation from society pushed it to incessantly solicit evidence of popular support and to stage political performances in organizing mass demonstrations, festivals, and campaigns. Suspecting a lack of genuine loyalty on the part of the majority of the population and seeking legitimation, the party did not know any means of governing other than mobilization and intimidation. Scholars interpreted the connection between a heightened feeling of external threat and waves of domestic repressions as a reflection of the deep insecurity of the Soviet government (Hoffmann 2011, p. 207; Velikanova 2013b, pp. 73, 88; Getty 1991, p. 34). Seeking to enhance its legitimacy, the state aimed to complement the revolutionary mode of legitimacy with the legal, or bureaucratic, type in Weber's categorization and presented a nationwide discussion as a direct exercise of the people's sovereignty. By the very fact of participating in the discussion, the population would give the government a legal mandate to rule. The writer Mikhail Prishvin expressed it this way: "The government will now have to draw on the people ['s will]. That is why they start speaking so often of the 'people' and I had [finally] believed in the constitution." In his diary entry from 4 December, the day of adoption of the constitution, he perspicaciously explained the goal of the discussion in religious terms: "[The government] is quite sincere [about the constitution] and expects real hosannas [expressing gratitude for salvation], that is, expressions of the authentic feelings of the people, and then, after they are confident of the genuineness of the hosannas, [they will] say, 'Now lettest Thou Thy servant depart in peace'[2] [*nyne otpuskaesh s mirom raba tvoego*]: speak, write whatever you want freely [*vasha volia*]." This exclamation is appropriate when a big enterprise is completed or a great goal achieved. Prishvin meant that the discussion was a kind of test for Sovietness, after which freedom would be allowed (Prishvin 2010, pp. 298, 382). The turn to mass repressions in 1937 implied that society did not pass the test.

4. In other terms, the nationwide discussion was an orchestrated exercise in political conformity. It was a case of sociopolitical

---

[2] Song of Simeon (Luke 2:29).

mobilization—an important feature of Stalinism intended to control the public and involve it in activities that shaped attitudes and perceptions. It was one of the modern state instruments of social management—"to empower and enthuse the masses so that they might be willing to contribute fully to the state's goals" (Priestland 2007, p. 35). It showed its effectiveness in the extraordinary situation of World War I in all combatant countries. The war showed that modern states had now acquired the technological ability to control their populations at a new level and to direct them toward state goals through new forms of mass mobilization, surveillance, registration techniques, policing, and excisionary state violence. Total mass mobilization and political violence were elements of the emergency mode of Stalin's power in his endeavor to quickly modernize the country and fashion a perfect society. That is why we so often see his erratic policies—consolidating and repressive, inclusion for loyalists and excision for alleged enemies, a carrot and a stick.

As social mobilization, the 1936 discussion ran simultaneously with many other campaigns, both consolidating and confrontational, according to the typology of Sergei Krassil'nikov: the state loan campaign, the nationwide discussion of an abortion ban,[3] Stakhanovism, the report campaign in the soviets, the show trial of the United Trotskyist–Zinovievist Center in August 1936, and the "verification" of party documents, as discussed earlier (Krassil'nikov 2013, p. 20; Tolts 2016). Everything in the Soviet Union was actually a mobilization, as one historian noted. The goal of all campaigns was to artificially invigorate elements of the state and society—the soviets, the party, and the population—objectively demotivated by the lack of material incentives inherent in socialism.

An important condition of mobilization was totality, requiring an all-embracing participation. In its drive for totality, the state aimed to monopolize all the public communication space, politicizing even the private sphere—for example, presenting housing as a gift from Stalin (Brooks 2000, p. 74)—and appropriating critical discourse when the

---

[3] The law was adopted on 27 June 1936 and was in effect until 1955. According to Mark Tolts, it led to a temporary two-year 2 million increase in births, an increase in female mortality (about 2000 every year, only measured in cities), and an increase in infant murders, which comprised up to 14% of all registered murders (25% in 1940 in Leningrad). State support of mothers was insufficient. The pension for the second child was 25% of average salary and gradually declined.

party solicited critical comments about the constitution and the soviets, invited denunciations, and prompted self-criticism. The *staged* public sphere, as Gabor Rittersporn called it, imposed discursive conventions and newspeak, simultaneously silenced all deviants, and aimed to mold homogeneous public opinion, uniform values, and ultimately a new person with a new consciousness.

5. Other implicit functions of mobilization were the solicitation of support, increasing industrial output, and most important—consolidation through mass education and socialization. Attempting to homogenize society, the constitution campaign conditioned citizens to the ideal type of socialism, and in turn they learned how to come to terms with the requirements of the system. By inviting people to discuss the constitution in meetings and to propose amendments, the campaign promoted the sense of unity so eagerly envisaged by utopians in the Kremlin.

It was one more exercise in consolidation on the way to the harmonious society of socialism, which for a moment resonated with the hopes of different population groups. Nikolai Ustrialov praised this unifying message of the constitution in his diary in December 1936: "A demonstration of solidarity and fraternity throughout the land." The former émigré and outcast, now a repatriate and journalist, followed the whole of Stalin's radio speech on the constitution with delight, recorded his impression in detail, and remarked that for a country with a weak national consciousness, it was time to become aware of its identity as a whole (Schloegel 2012, p. 226). A professor's wife and activist, Liubov' Shtange, expressed the same emotion in her diary: "Last night new Constitution was adopted. I won't say anything about it: I feel the same way as the rest of the country, that is, absolute, infinite delight." A skeptic, Andrei Arzhilovsky, a former prisoner, joined the public rally for the first time: "Yesterday the city celebrated the ratification of Stalin's constitution. It approved unanimous, direct, secret voting. Everyone, no matter what his past, has the right to vote and to run for office … Of course, there's more idiocy and herd behavior than enthusiasm … In any case, at least the finger-pointing has ended" (Garros et al. 1997, pp. 131, 181).[4]

---

[4] Diaries of L. Shtange and A. Arzhilovsky (8 December 1936). Shtange's husband had been arrested and incarcerated in 1928, so she may have been very careful about what she wrote in her diary. We find mostly neutral and positive words about everyday life and scarce notes on politics in her diary.

A special event designed to unite the people and connect them with their leader was a live radio broadcast of Stalin's speech at the 8th Congress of Soviets on 25 November 1936, in which he reviewed the results of the discussion. The entire population was assembled around radios: in plants, institutions, schools, and military units, even in Vladivostok in the middle of night. It is said that 25 million people listened. Because of this event, many villages finally received a radio connection. All diarists remembered this emotional moment of "direct" contact with Stalin (see Chapter 12). The forced, ceaseless broadcast on the streets, in dormitories, and hotels united people by a common soundtrack and, according to Ustrialov, "transformed us all into citizens of the world" (Schloegel 2012, p. 224).

Nevertheless, despite the rhetoric of unification and the drive for totality, we will see that the referendum documents exposed the tense, aggressive, and confrontational nature of social relations in the USSR, both in popular discourse and in the official practice of the elimination of critics. This campaign was integrational in its intention but confrontational in its practice. Arzhilovsky acknowledged: "No, comrades, no constitution can plaster over the great fissure in the Russian land" (Garros et al. 1997, p. 141). Only few months after he joined the celebration, Arzhilovsky conveyed distrust of the constitution results—despite formal enfranchisement, "former people" were still under suspicion and he wisely decided to refrain from a solicited critique of the bureaucrats.

> Nothing we, former people like me, do will be acceptable; everywhere they look they'll see intent to discredit the innocent communists. They are not building a classless society in the broad sense of the word; they are simply pulling the wool over people's eyes. And they know how to do it. For no matter what I say, it will all be twisted to mean something bad; everything will be interpreted as an attempt to discredit the party, an assault by a class enemy. They will never allow us to be equal, and they never will believe that we've forgotten and forgiven everything. We are damned, from now until the end of our lives. (Garros et al. 1997, p. 158)

Dictated by the communist ideal, the need for integration was also a condition for survival of the Bolshevik regime in the deeply divided nation. In its effort to fix the balance of social forces and to expand the social base of the regime, the constitution renounced the principle of proletarian supremacy and class struggle, and declared the "power of all toilers." The constitution claimed that class and national disparity had been overcome and replaced by a unified entity—*narod*. Replacing the words "the deputies of the workers and peasants" with "deputies of the toilers (*trudiashchiesia*)," it embodied this new vision of society. Besides, the declaration of the already constructed foundation of socialism presented promises that had by this time been fulfilled in order to convince the population to wait with patience on the way to the bright future of communism. In its integrational message, the constitution belonged to the Soviet system of symbols that included the myths of the October Revolution, the Civil War, the figures of Lenin and Stalin, and later victory in war.

With its mobilizational, integrational, monitoring and educational functions, the campaign in the summer and fall of 1936 belonged to the practices of social engineering—the "taming" of society by the inculcation of patterns of thinking and behavior.

REFERENCES

Brooks, Jeffrey. 2000. *Thank You, Comrade Stalin! Soviet Public Culture from Revolution to Cold War*. Princeton: Princeton University Press.
Fitzpatrick, Sheila. 1999. *Everyday Stalinism*. New York: Oxford University Press.
Garros, Véronique, Natalia Korenevskaya, and Thomas Lahusen, eds. 1997. *Intimacy and Terror: Soviet Diaries of the 1930s*. New York: New Press.
Getty, A. 1991. "State and Society Under Stalin: Constitutions and Elections in the 1930s." *Slavic Review* 50 (1): 18–35.
Hoffmann, David L. 2011. *Cultivating the Masses: Modern State Practices and Soviet Socialism, 1914–1939*. Ithaca, NY: Cornell University Press.
Inkeles, Alex, and Raymond Bauer. 1959. *The Soviet Citizen: Daily Life in a Totalitarian Society*. Cambridge, MA: Harvard University Press.
Kosheleva, L., V. Lel'chuk, et al., eds. 1996. *Pis'ma I. V. Stalina V. M. Molotovu, 1925–1936 gg*. Moscow: Molodaia Gvardiia.
Krassil'nikov, S. A., ed. 2013. *Sotsial'naia mobilizatsia v stalinskom obschestve (konets 1920–1930e gody)*. Novosibirsk: NGU.
Kulakov, A. A., V. V. Smirnov, and L. P. Kolodnikova, eds. 2005. *Obshchestvo I vlast': Rossiiskaia provintsiia*. Vol. 2. Moscow: Institut Rossiiskoi Istorii RAN.
Medushevsky, A. N. 2016. "Kak Stalinu udalos' obmanut' Zapad: Priniatie Konstitutsii 1936 goda s pozitii politicheskogo piara." *Otechestvennye nauki I sovremennost'* (3): 122–38.

Priestland, David. 2007. *Stalinism and the Politics of Mobilization: Ideas, Power, and Terror in Inter-War Russia*. Oxford: Oxford University Press.
Prishvin, Mikhail. 2010. *Dnevniki, 1936–1937*. St. Petersburg: Rostock.
Rose, Richard, William Mishler, and Neil Munro. 2011. *Popular Support for an Undemocratic Regime*. Cambridge: Cambridge University Press.
Rossiisky Gosudarstvenny Archiv Sotsial'noi Politicheskoi Istorii (RGASPI) [Russian State Archives of Social and Political History].
Schloegel, Karl. 2012. *Moscow, 1937*. Cambridge: Polity Press.
Shearer, David, and Vladimir Khaustov. 2015. *Stalin and the Lubianka: A Documentary History of the Political Police and Security Organs in the Soviet Union, 1922–1953*. New Haven, CT: Yale University Press.
Sokolov, A. K. 2009. "Konstitutsia 1936 goda i ku'turnoe nasledie stalinskogo sotsialisma." *Sotsiologiia istorii*, 137–63. St. Petersburg: Aliteia.
Solomon, Peter H. 1996. *Soviet Criminal Justice Under Stalin*. Cambridge: Cambridge University Press.
Tolts, Mark. 2016. "Price of Revolution: Family in Soviet Russia." Interview by Mikhail Sokolov. Price of Revolution. *Echo of Moscow*, 25 September 2016. http://echo.msk.ru/programs/cenapobedy/1843808-echo/. Accessed on December 17, 2016.
Velikanova, Olga. 2001. *The Public Perception of the Cult of Lenin Based on Archival Materials*. Lewiston, NY: Edwin Mellen.
———. 2013a. *Popular Perceptions of Soviet Politics in the 1920s*. Basingstoke: Palgrave Macmillan.
———. 2013b. "The First Stalin Mass Operation (1927)." *The Soviet and Post-Soviet Review* 40 (1): 64–89.

PART II

Popular Perceptions of the Constitution

CHAPTER 8

The Economic Condition at the Grassroots

To understand popular reactions to the constitution and how workers and peasants felt during the recurring discussion sessions, let us look at the economic context of everyday life and the peasants' mood.

The few descriptions of the 1936 economy existing in historiography focus mostly on the macro process, which presents positive growth after the strains of the first Five-Year Plan. At the grassroots, however, the economic circumstances did not look so optimistic. After a good harvest in 1933 when the famine receded, relative economic improvements made it possible to end the rationing of meat, fish, sugar, potatoes, and fats on 1 October 1935 and of manufactured goods on 1 January 1936. Naum Jasny called the period of 1934–1936 "three good years." Khlevniuk wrote that in 1934, Stalin initiated the shift from "leftist" extremes of rationing as the norm to an emphasis on trade and a monetary economy (Khlevniuk 2010, pp. 248–9).

The economic (and political) landscape in 1936 is characterized by scholars as ambivalent and inconsistent. For villagers, it looked quite different than for workers and urbanites; for Muscovites, everyday life was not as hard as for the citizens of the small town in the Urals where Andrei Arzhilovsky lived. These constituencies saw the economy differently, because of diverse state norms of supply. The first half of the year was easier than the second. State statistics were more optimistic than conversations in the food lines. The British Foreign Office, using scarce sources available to diplomats residing in Moscow, reported on the economy in 1936: "Materially the [conditions of the] average workman is 30% worse off than in 1913. ... The housing question is indescribably bad—far worse than in 1913" (British F.O. 371, 1936, vol. 20351, p. 30).

The huge growth in industrial production in 1936 was marked by an increase in the production of consumer goods from 18 in 1935 to 27.2% of all investment in industry, exceeding the annual plan by 5.8%. In the branches providing clothes and footwear to the population, growth measured in physical terms was 23.9% for cotton textiles and 37.3% for leather footwear. In the food industry, the production of meat products expanded particularly rapidly (Davies 2014, p. 321). The shortage of consumer goods, however, was so acute that people did not notice this growth: L. Shtange, the professor's wife and activist living in Moscow, the city with the best supply in the country, still complained about a lack of clothing and shoes in 1937 (Garros et al. 1997, p. 209).

Growth rates slowed in the last quarter of 1936. Besides the global economic crisis, unrealistic planning, and industrial disorganization due to repressions and Stakhanovism, a significant reason for this slowdown was the overburdening of the economy with defense spending. In 1936, the Soviet Union spent 16% of its budget on defense, considerably more than the 11% in the previous year, showing 45% growth in one year. The armed forces increased from about one million people in 1935 to 1,300,000 in 1936 and up to 1,700,000 in 1937 and became the largest in the world (Manning 1993, p. 132; Harrison and Davies 1997). Comparing the military and consumer sectors, R. W. Davies showed that in 1936, armaments production was more than twice that of 1932, while the production of consumer goods increased by only 27.2% (Davies 2014, pp. 321, 326). Between 1936 and 1940, increases in military spending severely strained an already overtaxed economy and resulted in growing supply problems throughout industry and agriculture. Cultural factors also influenced the way people reacted to the economic hardships: while the leadership expected a miraculous socialist growth, both the leaders and the populace tended to blame conspiracies and deliberate wrecking by enemies rather than objective economic constraints (Manning 1993, pp. 135, 141).

The massive crop failure became the major disaster of the year, the worst since 1932. The news about crop failure had already started trickling in when in the summer of 1936, at a meeting with the combine drivers, Stalin, inspired by the good harvest of 1935, set the goal

8 THE ECONOMIC CONDITION AT THE GRASSROOTS   113

for increasing grain output (*urozhainost'*) by 50% in the next three to four years. Due to drought, the grain crop dropped 18–25%, according to various estimates, to approximately 56 million tons (Manning 1993, pp. 118, 120; Davies 2014, p. 353). It was accompanied by livestock slaughtering and a typhus epidemic in the Smolensk, Briansk, and Kalinin *oblasts* (Berelowitch and Danilov 2012, pp. 374–6; TsGAIPD SPb f. 24, op. 2v, d. 1860, l. 41; Khaustov and Samuelson 2010, p. 159). Long lines—a common reflection of the shortages—formed in cities partly because peasants also flooded into buy bread, as people from depleted small towns traveled to major cities and industrial centers with a better supply: "The bread shortage has just added to all the usual hassles. People stand in line for six or eight hours at a time and talk about the possibility of war. … I am starving, after all. … [We are] quite a hungry bunch of people. It's a happy country, but still a lot of people don't have enough to eat," wrote Arzhilovsky in December 1936, referring to the famous Stalin motto "Life became better, comrades" (Garros et al. 1997, pp. 130–1, 144).

In July, the NKVD *svodki* informed the rulers about the crop failure and food shortages in many European provinces: in the Volga, Orenburg, and Chelyabinsk regions, in the Bashkir and Tatar autonomous republics, and in the non-Black Earth zone (Saratov, Ivanovo, Kursk, Gorky, Stalingrad, Voronezh *oblasts*, Stavropol) (Davies 2014, p. 353).[1] In December 1936, the NKVD registered cases of hunger swelling in the Saratov *oblast'*, and in February 1937 informed the rulers about deaths from starvation there and in the Volga German Republic (Berelowitch and Danilov 2012, pp. 367–81). In some locales, cannibalism was reported (Khaustov and Samuelson 2010, p. 158). M. Kalinin received letters from the countryside: "In Kursk and Voronezh *oblasts*, famine and total destitution reign. Very many residents stay without bread for several days. Instead of bread they eat various plants. People prowl like wild beasts, seeking a piece of bread" (RGASPI f. 78, op. 1, d. 592, l. 33).[2] The Soviet press kept the famine secret and tried to manufacture a positive picture, while Soviet officials like Kalinin and the deputy commissar of agriculture of the Russian Federative Republic (RSFSR), N. Lisitsyn, assured the public the harvest was good. Any "philistine" talk about crop failure could result in arrest and charges of

---

[1] The harvest was good in the south and in Western Siberia.
[2] 12 April 1937.

counterrevolutionary propaganda. This happened to citizens Khrolov and Vorozhtsov, who were arrested for conversations at a sanatorium in August 1936. Among the topics they discussed were "food difficulties" in some regions and violent methods of grain procurement: "There is a shortage of bread in their region [in Gorky *oblast'*], so peasants go at night to the cities and stand in breadlines. ... There was an incident. Members of the village soviet came to a peasant's hut [to procure the state quota] and at that very moment, he was drying groats in a pan. They took the grain from the pan straightaway" (Kulakov et al. 2005, pp. 317–9).[3]

R. W. Davies estimates that the 1936 harvest was almost certainly as poor as that of 1932,[4] but the government now conducted a sharply different policy which prevented an increase in deaths from hunger and malnutrition (Danilov et al. 2002, p. 27; Davies 2014, p. 365). A new understanding of social conditions in the countryside influenced the attitude of the government toward the problem of crop failure. In 1932, it viewed peasants as class enemies and saboteurs and left them to starve without aid. Now they viewed villages as successfully collectivized with enemies eradicated, and consequently did not punish the peasantry for "sabotaging" procurement. In 1936, the government decreased the state delivery obligations by 44% and directed food aid and seeds to the afflicted regions, which arrived in winter (Danilov et al. 2002, p. 30; Khlevniuk et al. 2001, pp. 632, 639, 648, 674, 696; Davies 2014, pp. 370–81). As E. Osokina noted, none of the party or NKVD reports included accusations of sabotage against peasants. Most of the starvation deaths occurred among individual peasants, not among collective farmers, who received aid (Osokina 2001, p. 162). "As early as July and August of 1936, mortality was 50–60% greater than in the same months of 1935, with the increase being greater in the countryside than in the towns" (Davies 2014, p. 364). The government managed to cope with crop failure much better than in 1932–1933. It had already curtailed the export of grain and fodder in August and stopped it altogether by February 1937, decreasing grain exports from 1517 thousand tons in 1935 to 321 thousand tons. The grain reserves accumulated in plentiful 1935 allowed famine relief to collective farms and additional supplies

---

[3] Interrogation record, 25 February 1937.

[4] According to *kolkhoz* reports, they harvested 571.3 million centners of grain and beans in 1935 and 464.8 million centners in 1936.

of bread and flour to the cities in the fourth quarter, but the situation "remained severely strained throughout the first half of 1937" until the next very rich harvest (Manning 1993, pp. 122–3, 131; Davies 2014, pp. 352, 422). In addition, households were not as vulnerable as in 1932, because in 1934–1936 private plots supported peasants and *kolkhoz* markets developed. As a result, the famine was not as disastrous as in 1932–1933: starvation was limited to several thousand people. Nevertheless, lines in the cities, shortages in everything, and starving villagers created unfavorable conditions for praising the achievements and celebrating socialism. Discontented people generalized: "What kind of socialism was built? You even have to fight [in lines] to get bread. We stand in lines for hours: when is there time to work?" (Osokina 2001, p. 164).

With trade liberalized the previous year, the government on 20 January 1936 permitted the rural population of the areas that fulfilled the state procurements to trade bread on the markets. That summer, responsibility to maintain the farmers markets was imposed on local soviets—evidence of a trade revival. But this liberalization, obviously a result of a good harvest, continued only briefly. Following the June 1936 Central Committee (CC) Plenum decision, the NKVD circular from 20 June prohibited collective farms and individuals from trading bread, grain, and flour at the farmers markets (Osokina 2001, p. 161; Danilov et al. 2002, p. 794). As skeptical peasants had predicted, the free trade of bread was postponed in August–September 1936 when the government learned about the crop failure.

Shortages in food and industrial consumer goods were endemic, producing lines and speculation. The government struggled with this persistent problem by organizing commissions, raising prices, and conducting repressions: on 19 July, the Politburo issued a decree to allocate more textiles and footwear to four major European cities, with prices increased by 25–30% and accompanied by a round of arrests of speculators. "The decision also instructed the NKVD to exile up to 5000 speculators from the four towns. By the beginning of September, 4003 persons had been sentenced by the NKVD *troiki* [extralegal courts] in four towns, and in 25 regions an additional 1635 persons were sentenced by the courts" (Davies 2014, pp. 347, 349). On 19 September, an engineer from Moscow wrote to Molotov that when searching for children's shoes he visited 40 stores in one day and finally found a pair for 48 rubles—almost one-third of the average monthly wage. "In an interview with Chastene [a French journalist], you announced to the whole USSR and the world that prices will be lowered in the next two years. However, in a few months you raised the prices on textile and shoes. It's too bad. You are accountable for that. Why do you make people angry? ... Discontent grows. ... This has continued for ten years. For how much longer?" (Livshin et al. 2002, pp. 312–3).

The tactics employed by the population in the countryside anticipating famine were quite natural—flight from the collective farms and refusal to work. Documents show how desperate the situation was. In some regions, mass refusal to work the collective farm fields increased dramatically—as much as 40% in August in the Stalingrad *oblast'*; in July, 55% in the *kolkhoz* Dubrava, Voronezh *oblast'*; and in December, 90–95% in that *oblast'*. The problem of motivating people to work in the fields was endemic for the collective farms, but now evasion of field work grew into strike dimensions. In the Krasny Stroitel' collective farm, Voronezh *oblast'* peasant women beat the *kolkhoz* chair who pressed them to work. The reason: no payments for workdays[5]—neither in money nor kind (Berelowitch and Danilov 2012, pp. 280, 332; TsGAIPD SPb f. 24, op. 2v, d. 1850, l. 49; Fitzpatrick 1996, pp. 145–8). People remembered the previous year: "With the good harvest we got only one kilogram per workday; this year we won't get even that." In the *kolkhoz* Stalinets, Saratov *krai*, foreman Arefiev, 70 years old, said: "I would not press members of my team to work without [payment of] bread. It's enough to deceive them. Six years of promises, but no bread. We are starving" (TsGAIPD SPb f. 24, op. 2v, d. 1860, l. 69). With the prospects of a bad harvest, *kolkhozniks* did not expect compensation after the mandatory delivery of state procurement in the fall and looked for alternative means to survive the difficult time ahead. They did not rely on collective farms, but preferred to work their private vegetable plots to guarantee at least subsistence, and they rushed to the woods to gather mushrooms and berries (Berelowitch and Danilov 2012, pp. 279, 292; TsGAIPD SPb f. 24, op. 2v, d. 1850, ll. 63, 258).

This desperate situation on a collective farm is described by a 16-year-old boy:

To VTsIK, Kalinin from citizen Goriachev Fedor Petrovich, village Kletino Nerl' *raion*, Kalinin *oblast'* [about May 1937].

---

[5] The workday (*trudoden'*) was a measurement of work according to which *kolkhozniks* were paid in money and kind.

This is my request to pay attention to my circumstances. On 12 April 1937, my father, a *kolkhoz* chair, hanged himself. In October 1936 he was elected a temporary chair for two weeks, but in the fall all the people went away to work elsewhere, so he had to work as the chair all winter. Because in 1936 there was a crop failure, we did not have seeds for sowing. ... By the beginning of the sowing season there was only one man in the *kolkhoz* [and] me—Goriachev Fedor and my comrade S. F. Guchkov. My father many times appealed to village soviet and the *raion ispolkom*, but got no support from these organizations. He was very much shocked by this situation. On 10 April 1937, comrade M. S. Rozonov refused categorically to be a brigade leader because he appeared to be alone with only two 16-year-old boys, when we had to sow 82 hectares [202.6 acres]. My father wrote a note and hanged himself: "No more force. I can't work anymore." He left us five children: (1) Ponia, 21 years old, but she is a student in Moscow. (2) Me—Fedia, 16 years (3) Klaudia, 12 years (4) Vania, 7 years (5) Niusha, 4 years (6) Serezha, 9 months (7) babushka, 75 years (she has a broken leg), and (8) Mama. After father's death our family had five pounds of bread. However, the same day, we got help—80 kg of flour. ... Now we have eaten this flour and I do not know what we'll eat further. I ask you to consider this situation. Goriachev Fedor.

In the following interview, Fedor answered the questions of a certain representative:

There were 35 households in the *kolkhoz*, but all went away and only 15 households remained. Absolutely all the able-bodied people left the *kolkhoz*, because in 1935 they got no payment for workdays, or very little. Only the elderly stayed in the *kolkhoz*. Nobody could work. In the spring for eight–ten days we plowed alone with my comrade—I, 16 years old, and my comrade, 17 years, and also my father—no more able-bodied. There were a few women, but they did not go out to work because they went every day [to the city] to buy bread—all together seven–eight women. Yes, about eight days we plowed by ourselves with my comrade. My father had no time to work [in the field], because he had to attend meetings or go to the village soviet. [Question: Did you have meetings in the *kolkhoz*?] Yes, every other day. Representatives from the RIK [region executive committee] visited us. ... They pressed father because the *kolkhozniks* fled. He reported to the local soviet that he has no people to work [in the fields], but they pressed him—do your business. But he is not responsible for people fleeing. Who can stop them? [Question: So people left the *kolkhoz* without his permission?] They do not need any permission. ... They did not ask permission. (RGASPI f. 78, op. 1, d. 592, ll. 57–60)

To get such a permit issued by the *kolkhoz* or village soviet chair was difficult but important, as an ID-substitute was necessary to get jobs elsewhere. But the lack of permission ID did not prevent the outpouring from the collective farms to the towns. Fear of hunger made the peasants bypass the law. The process of the depopulation of villages increased during collectivization when the industrial workforce grew by 1,300,000 a year (plus the extraction of peasants to the Gulag) and continued through the 1930s and 1940s. Though not every departing peasant got permission, the number of permissions issued in the Orenburg *oblast'* grew two to three times in comparison with 1935 (TsGAIPD SPb f. 24, op. 2v, d. 1860, ll. 111–3). The total nonagricultural employed labor force increased in 1936 by 1.3 million persons—6% (Davies 2014, p. 353).

In October, many collective farms had no grain for the members to pay in kind and could not fulfill state quotas. A summary of yearly reports compiled by *kolkhozes* between 1934 and 1939 shows that 10,000 *kolkhozes* in the country did not pay grain from the 1936 harvest to members; 100,000 did not pay potatoes; and 26.5% of *kolkhozes* did not pay a monetary share (Danilov et al. 2002, p. 27). The village officials did what they could in these dire conditions. Facing a lack of grain and mass flight, some *kolkhoz* chairs refused to deliver the state procurement quotas (their primary obligation before paying the members), but instead distributed available grain among the *kolkhoz* members, neglecting the law giving priority to state delivery (TsGAIPD SPb f. 24, op. 2v, d. 1860, l. 61). The reason: otherwise the *kolkhozniks* would flee to the cities. "First we should provide the members, and the state will get the leftovers." In Yaroslav *oblast'* in August, the chair of the Voroshilov *kolkhoz*, A. A. Danilov, gathered several chairs and colluded to boycott the state delivery. Danilov spoke at the village soviet plenum, but party representatives from the *raion* prevented a strike (Berelowitch and Danilov 2012, p. 327). The village officials contrived to spoil the grain with weeds, expecting the state would not accept grain of poor quality (unsuitable for storage) and that it would go to members of the farm, who could eat it anyway (Berelowitch and Danilov 2012, pp. 307, 322–7). The NKVD reported that many *kolkhoz* leaders broke the law by neglecting the creation of seed reserves (*zasypka*) and instead distributed grain to members before the state procurement delivery. Many delayed harvesting and threshing, expecting that the state would lower the quotas in view of the crop failure. Collective farmers frequently disrupted the *kolkhoz* meetings with demands to pay grain to peasants for workdays before state delivery—such protesters were arrested in the Makarov, Cherkess, Aktarsk, Bakur, Novorepin, Ershov, Kistendei, and Romanov *raions* in the Saratov *oblast'* (TsGAIPD SPb f. 24, op. 2v, d. 1860, ll. 75, 78). Such resistance at the grassroots, prioritizing local needs at the expense of state duties, was called by NKVD "antistate tendencies among some leaders of *kolkhozes* and *raion* organizations." They took place in the West and East Siberian *krai*, Kazakhstan, North Caucasus, Krasnoyarsk, Kirov, Saratov, Gorky *krais*, Tatar autonomous republic, Kuibyshev, Yaroslav, Stalingrad, Kursk, Sverdlovsk, Cheliabinsk, Orenburg, Voronezh *oblasts*, Bashkiria, Georgia, and Ukraine (TsGAIPD SPb f. 24, op. 2v, d. 1852, l. 132). It was an open challenge to the *kolkhoz* system, designed as a whole to drain resources from the village and to supply industry and the military. This "antistate" economic behavior contributed to the escalation of repressions. After the harvest, many party and soviet locals were arrested—for instance, the chief of the agricultural department on the Voronezh *oblast'* party committee, S. I. Bulatov—for low payments to collective farmers for workdays, as well as the Tatarsky *oblast'* party committee's secretary for a loss of livestock (Khaustov and Samuelson 2010, pp. 157–8). "Antistate tendencies" (or agricultural strikes) against procurement were reported through the fall of 1936 and winter of 1937 (Danilov et al. 2002, pp. 845, 848).

Another form of resistance common in 1936 was the "antimachinery (or anticombine) mood" among the *kolkhoz* chairs and population. Machine-breaking was widely reported during collectivization and opposed the cult of technology (an element of Soviet ethics). Official sources interpreted both intentional and accidental breakage and cases of negligence as intentional wrecking by class enemies, numbering 2250 cases in the USSR, or 14.9% of all cases of "enemy assaults" on collective farms in 1931 (Viola 1996, p. 218). With the introduction of machinery in the *kolkhozes*, the new phenomenon of machine–breaking, which Viola compared with Luddism,[6] was justified in the popular narrative. Unrelated to politics, anticombine incidents were often a part of hidden feuds within the village, for machinists became a privileged group in the

---

[6] The Luddites were a social movement of British textile artisans in the early nineteenth century who often destroyed mechanized looms in protest against the changes produced by the Industrial Revolution, which they felt were leaving them without work.

kolkhoz; they received passports, unlike other members, and more—a wage and a minimum income in cash and kind guaranteed by the state since 1935 (Fitzpatrick 1996, p. 141). There was another reason for dislike of the combines: in the peculiar conditions of 1936, when the harvest was so poor, a compulsory share of it went to machine operators as payment and thus became a loss for other members. "Now the harvest is so bad, but you have to pay grain for the combine"; that is why the chairs of the *kolkhozes* Krasnyi Pakhar', Chapaev in the Saratov *oblast'*, and Podol'sky in the Western *Oblast'* refused to use combines (TsGAIPD SPb, f. 24, op. 2v, d. 1850, ll. 136, 238, 39; Koval' 2009, p. 237). Paradoxically, combiners alleviating the rural labor competed with rank-and-file *kolkhozniks*, leaving the latter without work. If the combine harvested all the grain, the collective farmers would not earn workdays and would not receive payment in the fall. Worse, peasants complained about the low quality of combine work—up to 10 or even 20% of grain was lost, blown away, or otherwise (TsGAIPD SPb f. 24, op. 2v, d. 1850, ll. 161, 204). *Pravda* recognized that even in the advanced *kolkhozes*, a combine could harvest only half the grain in the fields, and advised peasants to use simpler machines for the remainder (*Pravda* 5 August 1936). Anonymous forms of protest such as throwing iron objects into machines and littering fields with iron sticks in order to break the combines were reported in 1936 and interpreted as wrecking (Berelowitch and Danilov 2012, pp. 275, 277, 313; TsGAIPD SPb f. 24, op. 2v, d. 1850, l. 136). Selfish economic motives were blamed in a November 1933 report from the Machine-Tractor Stations' political department describing the collective farmers' grievances over the large sums paid for machinery use and their belief that manual labor was more productive (Viola 1996, p. 218). Antimachinery tempers resulted from the demotivating organization of work in the *kolkhozes*.

The most common way for peasants to escape the coming famine and *kolkhoz* serfdom was flight. To prevent this, freedom of outmigration for collective farmers was restricted. In 1933, the state issued internal passports to city dwellers, regulating access to work and housing. To avert panic migration resulting from famine in the countryside, villagers (excepting machinists) were excluded from passportization and depended on the village soviet, which could reject or issue identification (*spravka*) permitting departure. This resembled conditions of serfdom. Only in the period 1976–1981 did Soviet peasants acquire passports and the right of mobility.

Starting in July 1936, when the drought had ensured a crop failure, whole labor teams fled to industrial centers or *sovkhozy*, including foremen, Young Communist League (Komsomol), and party members. By August, the flight had become massive. The NKVD arrested those agitating for flight, but it was futile. Peasants said: "Drought. You won't get bread in the *kolkhoz* anyway; you need to find a job in other places, or you will die from hunger" (TsGAIPD SPb f. 24, op. 2v, d. 1850, l. 48). The tractor operators fled too: "There is no point in working. The *kolkhoz* does not provide payment and bread; we do not want to go hungry, unclothed, and barefoot." Crowds besieged the village soviets demanding the permits to leave. Many left without papers. Because of the resulting lack of a labor force, the entire harvest was in jeopardy: delays led to additional losses of grain (Berelowitch and Danilov 2012, pp. 303, 309).

Only on 6 November did *Pravda* finally recognize the drought, but not the troubles: "In agriculture, an ominous enemy impedes continuing *kolkhoz* achievements—the extraordinary drought over the entire territory of the USSR. ... In front of all our achievements, such as the *kolkhoz* labor discipline, the socialist enthusiasm in the fields, and the army of tractors created by the Bolsheviks, the threatening ghost of cataclysm has receded. It has no place in the country of victorious socialism."

Under such conditions, peasants were pressed to discuss the charter. The economic situation in the countryside influenced the mood and behavior of the rural population. Unsurprisingly, attendance at the meetings was a problem. A collective farm organizer explained: "A *kolkhoznik* is not up to discussing the constitution because he is almost starving" (Berelowitch and Danilov 2012, p. 345; Garros et al. 1997, p. 297). It was against this background of a poor harvest, the threat of hunger, and the exodus from *kolkhozes* that the exclusion of peasants from constitutional guarantees, such as the passport system and social welfare, exacerbated their desire to abandon the countryside and move to the city or a construction site. There they would be eligible for social benefits and full citizenship.

REFERENCES

Berelowitch, Alexei, and Victor Danilov, eds. 2012. *Sovetskaia derevnia glazami VChK-OGPU-NKVD: Dokumenty i materialy*. Vol. 4. Moscow: ROSSPEN.
British Foreign Office–Russia correspondence, 1781–1945. 1975. Wilmington, DE and London, UK: Scholarly Resources.

Danilov, Viktor Petrovich, Roberta Thompson Manning, and Lynne Viola, eds. 2002. *Tragediia sovestskoi derevni: Kollektivizatsiia I raskulachivanie; Dokumenty i materialy*. Vol. 4. Moscow: ROSSPEN.
Davies, R. W. 2014. *The Industrialisation of Soviet Russia, Volume 6, The Years of Progress: The Soviet Economy, 1934–1936*. Basingstoke, UK: Palgrave Macmillan.
Fitzpatrick, Sheila. 1996. *Stalin's Peasants: Resistance and Survival in the Russian Village After Collectivization*. Oxford: Oxford University Press.
Garros, Véronique, Natalia Korenevskaya, and Thomas Lahusen, eds. 1997. *Intimacy and Terror: Soviet Diaries of the 1930s*. New York: New Press.
Harrison, Mark, and R. W. Davies. 1997. "The Soviet Military-Economic Effort During the Second Five-Year Plan (1933–1937)." *Europe-Asia Studies* 49 (3): 369–406.
Khaustov, V., and L. Samuelson. 2010. *Stalin, NKVD i repressii, 1936–1938 gg*. Moscow: ROSSPEN.
Khlevniuk, Oleg. 2010. *Khoziain: Stalin i utyerzhdenie stalinskoi diktatury*. Moscow: ROSSPEN.
Khlevniuk, O. V., R. W. Davies, L. P. Kosheleva, E. A. Rees, and L. A. Rogovaia, eds. 2001. *Stalin I Kaganovich. Perepiska. 1931–1936 gg*. Moscow: ROSSPEN.
Koval', N. 2009. "Put' k nishchete: Vospominania." In *Rossiiskaia i sovetskaia derevnia pervoi poloviny XX veka glazami krestian*, edited by N. F. Gritsenko, 233–42. Moscow: Russkii Put'.
Kulakov, A. A., V. V. Smirnov, and L. P. Kolodnikova, eds. 2005. *Obshchestvo i vlast': Rossiiskaia provintsia*. Vol. 2. Moscow: Institut Rossiiskoi Istorii RAN.
Livshin, A. Y., I. B. Orlov, and O. V. Khlevniuk, eds. 2002. *Pis'ma vo Vlast', 1928–1939*. Moscow: ROSSPEN.
Manning, Roberta T. 1993. "The Soviet Economic Crisis of 1936–1940 and the Great Purges." In *Stalinist Terror: New Perspectives*, edited by J. Arch Getty and Roberta T. Manning, 116–41. Cambridge: Cambridge University Press.
Osokina, Elena. 2001. *Our Daily Bread: Socialist Distribution and the Art of Survival in Stalin's Russia, 1927–1941*. Armonk, NY: E. Sharpe.
Rossiisky Gosudarstvenny Archiv Sotsial'noi Politicheskoi Istorii (RGASPI) [Russian State Archives of Social and Political History].
Tsentral'ny Gosudarstvenny Arkhiv Istoriko–politicheskikh Dokumentov Sankt-Peterburga (TsGAIPD SPb) [Central State Archives of Historical–Political Documents in Saint-Petersburg].
Viola, Lynne. 1996. *Peasant Rebels Under Stalin: Collectivization and the Culture of Peasant Resistance*. Oxford: Oxford University Press.

CHAPTER 9

Liberal Discourse

The wide range of opinions voiced in 1936 was another reflection of meaningful political participation demonstrated by the populace rather than the simple parroting of propaganda. Categorizing the polyphony of popular reactions, one can distinguish several themes of popular concern—direct secret elections, civil rights, citizenship, rule of law, welfare, democratic procedures, and local administration. Citizens' comments characterizing Soviet popular political culture can be thematically grouped into two major categories. The first is comments supporting democratic, civic, moderate, conciliatory, tolerant (for example, of religion) values and appreciating individual rights, all of which are close to our understanding of liberal values.

The second group of opinions supported regulation, excision, and discrimination and can be categorized as antiliberal discourse. Intolerance toward anyone different, aggression toward sanctioned minorities, hatred of enemies, generalized hostility, but respect for authority, and adherence to values perceived as endorsed by the leadership are usually associated with the authoritarian (H. Arendt, T. Adorno) or totalitarian (A. Etkind and L. Gozman, A. Krylova and others) type of personality and political culture. Some opinions revealing a commitment to collectivism over individualism, statism, patron–client relationships, and the personification of power are often associated with traditional peasant societies.[1]

---

[1] Orlov and Dolgova (2008) suggest the following categories in the Soviet political culture: traditional, Western-modernist, and Soviet elements. In the latter, they include

This categorization, dictated by the nature of my sources, will form the strategy for the following analysis. It will be taken in the context of official culture that promoted the virtues of a New Man: loyalty to socialism, collectivism, antireligiosity, modesty, humanity, altruism, self-perfection, and an illiberal subjectivity (Hoffmann 2003, pp. 45–7). In this chapter, I argue that the concern of many citizens about individual and civil rights, the workings of the soviets, election reform, and legality, as well as political engagement, speaks in favor of the existence of liberal elements in the Soviet mass political culture.

Democracy was the primary issue under discussion and the common people had their own ideas about it. Don Cossack, who worked as a bookkeeper, said after the war in an interview: "My opinion is that the Russian people are not prepared for democratic rule. You need a period of preparation for them. But the Russian people (*narod*) are so wise that they can develop self-rule. With the free vote as in 1913 [author meant 1613], they met in the Zemski Sobor. If they could meet again this way, if they could collect their own representatives, if the system of parties had not been suppressed, they could do it" (HPSSS Schedule A, Vol. 1, Case 5, p. 53). Another correspondent believed that only with the help of foreigners could self-governing be successful in Belorussia: "(Question: Do you think it would be good for Belorussians to have their own independent state?) Yes, it would be good, but Americans should stay there for a long while. (Question: What do you mean, Americans should stay there?) American soldiers; something like in Germany, because people in our regions don't know how to behave. They should be taught that to steal, to lie, and to kill is not good" (HPSSS Schedule A, Vol. 34, Case 109, p. 34). Another minor *kolkhoz* official and teacher from Ukraine "emphasized very heavily the democratic inclinations of the Russian peasantry, saying they were not fooled by the pseudodemocracy of choosing their own collective farm chairman and alike" (HPSSS Schedule A, Vol. 25, Case 494, p. 49).

9.1 The Judicial Innovations of the Constitution

The judicial innovations of the constitution provoked vivid interest among the citizens. A part of the "moderation" trend in politics during 1934–1936 was the turn to more legality and the partial rehabilitation

Communist eschatology, the cult of the leader (*vozhdism*), conflict consciousness, and egalitarianism.

of the rule of law. After decades of upholding "revolutionary" extralegal practices and mass arrests of peasants during collectivization, the new turn realized a tendency for more stability and order that had been sporadically initiated by the government over time to keep control.

The innovations of the constitution included new rules for elections of the judges, the rise of the role of defense, and procurator approval of arrests. They corresponded to the reorganization of the judicial system, conducted between 1934 and 1936 and directed toward reviving legal procedures and improving the administration of justice. But the main purpose of the reorganization was centralization and control over the judges, procurators, and investigators (Solomon 1996, pp. 274, 297). This reorganization corresponded to the dual model persistent in Soviet politics—with one hand the government strengthened the legal system, with the other hand it continued extralegal operations. According to the draft, all levels of courts were to be elected by the appropriate soviets, but people's courts, the lowest level, were to be elected by direct, equal, and secret voting of the whole electorate of each region. In Leningrad and Smolensk, between 5 and 7% of comments suggested that all judges and procurators should be elected in a democratic procedure (Getty 1991, p. 25). In Gorky *krai*, 15 comments out of 400 supported the election of educated judges, who would report regularly and could be recalled, while ten comments were for the appointment of judges, with one voice against the attorneys in courts and one for introduction of the death sentence (Kulakov et al. 2005, pp. 389–435). The anxious population endorsed the legal innovations of the constitution, which ignited the expectations and demands for repressions to stop. Many believed that people who were arrested would now be pardoned and released from the prisons (HPSSS Schedule A, Vol. 34, Case 109, p. 34; Vol. 29, Case 633, p. 25; RGASPI f. 5, op. 1, d. 232, ll. 57, 86).

Both the leaders and the common people were dissatisfied with the low qualifications of the legal officials. In 1934–1935, the government tried to expand legal education for judges (Solomon 1996, pp. 185–91). Standardized education potentially enhanced uniformity and state control over the judiciary. As Soviet official statistics showed, by 1 June 1936, over 50% of procurators and the people's judges in the Russian Federative Republic (RSFSR) had no legal training, with only 5% having completed a course of law studies at university level (British F.O. 371, 1936, vol. 20351, pp. 122–3; Solomon 1996, p. 186). To address the problem of low competency, a review of all judges was ordered by the Central Committee (CC) on 10 July 1934, leading to the removal of 12% identified as incompetent. But their replacements proved no better (Solomon 1996, p. 185). People within the discussion endorsed the idea of the election and the revocation of judges and procurators, insisting that judges have appropriate education and qualifications (GARF f. 3316, op. 41, d. 207, l. 146).[2] The constitution, however, did not require any legal knowledge or formal training for judges. Educated cadres were in short supply in all fields.

A part of judicial reorganization was empowerment of the institution of defense in the Soviet courts. Previously, the old class of advocates had been destroyed and Soviet courts showed a lack of confidence toward defense counsel. Only the growth of the new Soviet cadres, "assimilated to our Soviet viewpoint," made a turn in favor of advocacy both "timely and appropriate," as Nikolai Krylenko, head of the Commissariat of Justice, stated in September 1936. The idea of the independence of all parties in court, however, was framed in a peculiar way by Krylenko, an officer with an affinity to extralegality and simplification of procedure. Krylenko made it clear that though the defense should be independent, "definite" political control and a "definite" direction of the defense on the part of the government organs are necessary because "our defense should be a Soviet defense" (*Sovietskaia Yustitsia* 26 September 1936). Independence of judges—not subject to dismissal or to outside control by other institutions within the system of government—is a crucial characteristic of the effective modern state. But starting in 1936, local party committees regularly reviewed the work of the courts and procuracy. A few attempts to ignore the directives of the party and soviet authorities were undertaken by some judges, who cited the constitution in support. Independence remained unrealized after 1936 as long as the recruitment, budgeting, and supervising of legal officials were still under party and soviet control (Solomon 1996, pp. 286–97).

In the course of preparing for the elections of the people's judges by secret ballot, *Sovetstkaia Yustitsia* published the list of qualities necessary in a Soviet judge under the new constitution. The order was as follows: (a) fidelity to socialism and to the party of Lenin and Stalin; (b) a political, Bolshevik steadfastness and uncompromising attitude in the struggle with enemy; (c) political experience; (d) education and culture; (e) thoughtfulness and seriousness in relation to people; and (f) calmness and sagacity. These qualities should ensure that judicial

---

[2] Seven suggestions in Gorky *krai*.

personnel would be "independent and answerable only to the law" (*Sovietskaia Yustitsia* 5 November 1936). Loyalty was in first place and qualifications—in fourth place. Such a priority was a typical requirement for all Soviet functionaries.

The emphasis of the draft on an open judicial process and the right of the accused to a defense (Article 111) found resonance in society and produced a cluster of suggestions from below. Article 109 about people's judges attracted vivid interest and elicited 1551 comments—ranking it sixth. A population who hardly had the historical opportunity to develop strong traditions of legal culture now, after the outrage of collectivization, showed an appreciation for lawfulness—not overwhelming but repetitive demands (32 in my archival records) for an independent, open court and the accountability of judges (26 recommendations in one report). Some correspondents thoughtfully suggested paying judges from the central budget to secure independence from local authorities. Concerned citizens in their comments wanted more rule of law, less arbitrariness: "Disfranchisement should be imposed only by the court, not the village soviet," as was the old practice according to the 1918 constitution (GARF f. 3316, op. 8, d. 225, l. 93). Approval of legal innovations could reflect a craving for normalcy in an unsettled society and some continuity with the prerevolutionary culture, when legal proceedings were an accepted means of resolving conflicts, even in rural settings (Burbank 2004, p. 72).

This group of comments suggests the existence of a certain degree of legal consciousness in the public mind, although the majority generally showed a weak understanding of how the law operated. Article 127[3] constitutionalized the requirement of the procurator's approval for an arrest, as promoted by procurator Andrei Vyshinsky, in order to restrict the NKVD's power, and had been introduced earlier in June 1935 following a secret Politburo instruction from 8 May 1933, "On the Procedure of Arrests." The procurator's approval requirement produced numerous protests among the rural population—1098 out of 3218 comments on this article (GARF f. 3316, op. 8, d. 226, l. 131). The confusion of the people was understandable; in rural areas, villagers had never seen procurators and even police (called militia in the USSR) were in short supply: "We have no procurator in our village. So a hooligan will roughhouse and nobody can stop him without a procurator's

---

[3] "Citizens of the USSR are guaranteed inviolability of the person. No person may be placed under arrest except by the decision of a court or with the sanction of a procurator."

permission?" (GARF f. 3316, op. 8, d. 225, l. 75). People saw the requirement of the procurator sanction as an impediment to justice, especially in distant villages. According to customary law, minor crimes like the theft of a horse were usually resolved on the spot by direct, immediate action—often by fists (Chudakov 2012, p. 106). Eight percent of Leningrad respondents and 13.3% of Smolensk residents rejected the need for a procurator sanction (Getty 1991, p. 25). People often demanded the right of every citizen to detain an offender caught in the act (GARF, f. 3316, op. 41, d. 207, l. 191; d. 147, l. 67; op. 40, d. 40, l. 20; f. 1235, op. 76, d. 153, ll. 118, 431).

In conditions of judicial ignorance, habitual arbitrariness, and frequent retreats to extralegality, combined with the fresh memory of the mass deportations of dekulakization, the officials and population had only a vague understanding of who had the right to arrest. Because of the absence of police in many villages and the possession of legal weapons by party officials, this civil war practice of arbitrariness was repeatedly overused by local authorities. Though the law limited the right to arrest to only police, the procuracy, and the NKVD, all authorities—chairmen of *kolkhoz* or soviet or party secretaries—exercised it as a matter of course—for example, to force peasants onto the collective farm. Justifications of the protests against the procurator's approval for the arrest (calling for no police or procurators in villages) made one thing clear: discontent originated more from the customary legal traditions and a misunderstanding of the judicial procedure rather than from popular approval of unlimited and arbitrary local power.

Despite misunderstandings, discussion of the constitution played an educational role, making people aware of their rights. We know that in later decades the constitution became a weapon of the entire Soviet dissident movement, which constantly pointed to the discrepancy between the law and practice. This pattern originated in 1936. In the extralegal chaos of the Great Terror, victims constantly demanded implementation of the constitution's provisions. As the wife of an arrested man wrote to Molotov in December 1936: "The right to work is written in our Stalin's constitution," but she was fired and could find no other job (Livshin et al. 2002, p. 321). A respondent to the postwar interview recalled such an episode:

> In the spring of 1938 in our school in the Donbas, a Ukrainian teacher, 35 years old, married, with two children, was arrested. In the constitution it says that the arrest of a person by the police can occur only on permission by the procurator. When two militiamen came at 11 o'clock

at night to arrest him, he did not open the door and asked them through the door whether they had a permit from the procurator to arrest him. They answered, "No." The teacher told them that, according to Stalin's Constitution, they had no right to arrest him without any permit from the procurator. The militiamen said they had only an order from the *nachal'nik* [boss] of the militia office. But the teacher demanded the procurator's permit. Then one militiaman remained and the other went to the *nachal'nik* of the militia and told him the story. The *nachal'nik* of the militia ... instructed the militiaman not to pay any attention to the teacher's demand and, if the teacher should make further resistance and not open the door, to break the door down and arrest him forcibly. When they began to break down the door, the teacher opened the door and was arrested. ... His wife told me later that he was accused of counterrevolutionary activities, of telling some political jokes. (HPSSS Schedule A, Vol. 9, Case 118, pp. 23–4)

The constitutional principal regarding procuratorial approval was neglected in practice in 1937–1938. Another interviewee, a Ukrainian mechanic, said: "In the Stalin Constitution, which we all had to learn, it was said that one could only be arrested upon the presentation of evidence by the state prosecutor and with judicial guarantees. But when in 1937 the NKVD led me directly from my place of work to prison, I saw no trace of these guarantees, and if I had tried to draw on my constitutional rights, that would only have worsened my situation" (HPSSS Schedule A, Vol. 36, Case 492, p. 54). Modern surveys show that legal awareness in Russian society continues to be in its embryonic state (Dubin 2010, p. 83).

9.2 THE WORKINGS OF THE SOVIETS AND ELECTORAL REFORM

The workings of the soviets and electoral reform formed the core of the new constitution both for its authors and its readers. Equal elections with secret ballots are the key element in democracies and exactly this innovation was suggested by Stalin personally in 1935, becoming a motivation for reform of the entire constitution. The new electoral system canceled class restrictions, the inequality of city and village voters, and indirect many-step elections. This "social reconciliation" policy, however, co-occurred with continuing repressions on the basis of social origin.

M. Kalinin's and the Central Executive Committee's (TsIK) instructions (see Chapter 6) on the mechanism of the discussion and elections directed popular discontent against members of local soviets and their mismanagement. It was easy to set the population against the "boyars"; blaming those in the middle of the power hierarchy had a long historical tradition. After the Revolution, the peasant masses initially supported the soviets as potential instruments of autonomous self-governance. But gradually they grew disillusioned with the village and provincial soviets, which became more and more controlled by the party-state. During the 1920s, the party's central bureaucracy subdued the soviets, taking over their governing functions. Finally, the soviets transformed from organs of self-government to subservient agencies for collecting taxes and promoting state interests. One peasant wrote: "There is concern among the peasants that the people who are sitting in the VIKs [provincial soviets] are not our people, they don't know the peasants' needs" (TsGAIPD SPb f. 16, op. 6, d. 6916, l. 80). The independence of the elected deputies was questionable. The idea of representing the people's interests against the pressure of the higher administration and state bureaucracy was not realistic. The ineffectiveness of the soviets, the appointment system, the barring of the wealthier peasants from soviet elections, and the nomination of outsiders caused popular distrust of these bodies and discouraged villagers from voting in annual elections, resulting in low participation. In 1922, turnout was only 22.3% and in 1924 it was so low that many places saw their results canceled. Officials (and later Soviet historiography) attributed such absenteeism to backwardness, a general indifference to politics, poor communication, and huge distances. The main cause was, however, the powerlessness of the soviets and disillusionment in this institution. In a group of 2073 private letters from 1924 to 1925, 96% were dissatisfied with local soviet authorities (Izmozik 1996, p. 289).

> People absolutely lost trust in power and stopped attending gatherings … Now when the reelection of the soviet is announced, … citizens speak directly: "We won't go anyway; we have nothing to do there; our voice is not heard there. Let the chair of soviet Cherdakov elect himself like in the March elections."
>
> The power is appointed from the top to the bottom. The chair and the secretary of the soviet are not elected, but are sent here from elsewhere. If he is good or bad—it's not your business. Even in the Tsarist times, we elected our elder and a head, but now Soviet authorities do not trust us [to choose]. (RGASPI f. 17, op. 85, d. 529, l. 280; GARF f. 396, op. 1, d. 1, l. 29)

Demands for the equal representation of all strata of the peasantry and of political parity between peasants and the proletariat promoted the principle of universality of rights throughout the postrevolutionary decade. This basic tenet of democracy was used as a standard when peasants referred to the violation of their rights stated in the Russian Federation (RSFSR) constitution of 1925: "Examining the constitution, one inevitably comes upon Article 9, in which any person from the city is given more privileges than a peasant; it reads that [factory] workers have one representative to the Congress of Soviets for every 25,000 people, whereas peasants have the same one representative for every 125,000 people. For me, a peasant, this seems very odd. I am thinking that there are sons there and stepsons here" (RGASPI f. 17, op. 84, d. 916, ll. 2–7).

In the 1920s, peasants often demanded changes to the constitution in their favor: free multicandidate elections and equality of the poor and wealthy peasants in the soviets (RGASPI f. 17, op. 21, d. 3075, l. 20; f. 17, op. 85, d. 354, l. 14; Krukova 2001, pp. 208–9; Danilov et al. 1999, p. 577; Klimin 2007, p. 180). The disproportionate representation of the poor villagers promoted by the party within the local soviets, as well as their pursuit of state interests rather than those of peasants, dissatisfied the majority of the countryside with this institute (Male 1971, p. 99).

In the middle of the 1930s, under the new social conditions after dekulakization, when the remaining villagers were equalized in *kolkhoz*, the problem of wealthy peasants' representation receded, but not the problem of the effectiveness of soviets. Soviets received a plethora of criticism from above and below, especially in distant rural areas. It was a soviet's authority to collect taxes and duties, to issue passports and ID documents for those who wanted to depart the village. The arbitrariness and abuse of power (such as arrests and arbitrary levying of fines), theft, and drunkenness of the soviet chairs were the major sources of peasant's grievances (Fitzpatrick 1994, pp. 175–84). Neglect of legal procedure was a norm and dekulakization only made things worse. The Central Executive Committee (TsIK) *svodka* about the 1934 soviet elections and decree from 15 May 1936 revealed a failure of the majority of soviets to implement voters' requests and of deputies to report on their work to the voters (TsGAIPD SPb f. 24, op. 2v, d. 1755, ll. 118, 136–7, 140–1). In this general setting, the improvement of soviets' work was imperative.

The constitution and the targeted efforts of the campaign organizers stirred up a new wave of hope and criticism among the population. In numerous demands from below (45 in my records, 4% in Getty's data, and 2% in Gorky *krai*), we can hear the frustration with the workings of the soviet system and the desire for more accountability, transparency of the local administration, and prompt answers to inquiries. Articles 142 and 95, concerning regular reporting by the deputies to the voters and revoking inefficient deputies, got respectively 1048 and 395 comments out of 43,427 registered, with 305 recommendations on the frequency of reports (GARF f. 3316, op. 8, d. 226, l. 162). These comments expressed one of the foundations of democracy—the deputies should be responsible to the electorate. But with the phony elections, deputies depended more on their superiors than on their constituencies.

Voronezh leaders informed TsIK, "The anticipation and demands to the soviets grew; the majority of all suggestions (about the constitution) is related to the local powers" (GARF f. 1235, op. 76, d. 161, l. 230). *Pravda* wrote, "The Soviet citizen ... criticizes without mercy unworthy leaders, bureaucrats who do not help him to make his work more efficient, his life more cultured" (*Pravda* 27 September 1936). Here, criticism solicited from above during the soviet report campaign in the summer and fall of 1936 found resonance in the popular discontent. Some participants rejected the right of immunity for local deputies. When criticizing local bureaucrats, the people sometimes questioned the top authorities: "Does the Supreme Soviet report regularly to the voters?" "Who had elected Stalin? We or somebody else?" (GARF f. 3316, op. 41, d. 207, l. 172; Berelowitch and Danilov 2012, p. 346). But criticism aimed at high targets was not the intention of the masterminds in the Kremlin. Rather, they planned to discipline the intermediate bureaucrats by using the hands of the people. British diplomat MacKillop observed in September 1936 that a Soviet citizen, invited to criticize "must ... surrender his critical faculty and use it for the still immovable establishment of those in high office—he must not use it against them—by helping them to detect and to eliminate the inefficient among those minor office-holders with whom he comes into daily contact and by generally reducing that sense of security among elected persons" (British F.O. 371, 1936, vol. 20351, p. 48).

People greeted the new election law as an opportunity to bring to power their genuine representatives, who would defend their interests against the party-state. "In future elections we should organize ourselves in order to elect our own people to the soviets, not aliens. ... In new elections using the Constitution, people will elect a people's government, which will grant freedom. [As a result,] those who want to will stay in the *kolkhoz*; others will get a piece of land and work as in the old ways. Communists and Jews will leave Ukraine for Great Russia. Ukraine will be independent. New power will restore the churches." The speaker, Vatazhenko (Ukraine), was arrested for this talk (TsGAIPD SPb f. 24, op. 2v, d. 1858, l. 230; GARF f. 3316, op. 8, d. 222, l. 73; Berelowitch and Danilov 2012, pp. 340–1, 346, 350, 364). People insisted on multiple-candidate elections at all levels: "Before elections to the village, *raion*, up to the Supreme Soviet, public and party organizations should nominate more than one candidate from among the best people, so that people could make a choice freely" (GARF f. 3316, op. 8, d. 226, l. 162). They asserted the right to nominate candidates by nonaffiliated units—local organizations and working collectives, agricultural and sports units, tractor stations, housewives' groups (44 proposals)—and by individuals (25 proposals, TsIK estimates) (RGASPI f. 17, op. 120, d. 232, ll. 83–5; GARF f. 3316, op. 8, d. 226, l. 160; Berelowitch and Danilov 2012, p. 286). Ordinary people saw nomination by individuals and self-nominations as direct democracy. But not Stalin. He rejected self-nomination at the June 1937 CC Plenum (Kurliandsky 2011, p. 488). The collective farm, however, finally became the nominating institution according to the subsequent 1937 clarification to the election law. Nomination of candidates was a crucial moment that allowed the party-state to control the elections. A Leningrad worker, Lebedev, saw this clearly: "Anyway, we'll elect only low-level officials. We won't be able to nominate the candidates to high offices. They will be nominated from the top. Our business is only to give our votes" (TsGAIPD SPb f. 24, op. 2v, d. 2664, l. 270) (Photo 9.1).

Chapter XI, "Electoral System," got a huge number of comments—totaling 6369—14.2% of all proposals sorted by the TsIK (GARF f. 3316, op. 8, d. 222, l. 158). Of this number, Article 135, which introduced universal voting rights and canceled the institution of disenfranchisement, received 4716 comments and was second after Article 120 on pension benefits (GARF f. 3316, op. 8, d. 222, ll. 156–60).[4]

There is no surprise that the question of citizens' rights was at the center of discussion. It presented a radical shift in policy and involved

---

[4] Statistical review, Organizational Department of the Presidium of TsIK SSSR ("Kolichestvo predlozhenii k Proektu Konstitutsii SSSR"), received by 15 November 1936. See Tables 12.1 and 12.2 in Chapter 12.

Photo 9.1 Collective farmers of cooperative Zaklinie, Luga *raion*, Leningrad *oblast'*, near the polling station on the day of elections of the Supreme Soviet of the USSR. December 1937. Courtesy of the Central State Archives of Documentary Films, Photographs, and Sound Recordings, Saint-Petersburg (TsGAKFFD SPb)

the personal interests of millions previously excluded from full citizenship. After the Revolution, the Constitution of 1918 legalized the class struggle principle, which deprived a variety of people called "former"—such as priests, kulaks, former tsarist police, traders, and nobility—of the rights of citizenship, categorizing them as *lishentsy* (RSFSR Constitution 1918, Article 4, Chapter 13, no. 65). Initially, this group numbered 2–3% of the population—if we believe Stalin (1947, p. 31). The Constitution of 1924 expanded the category. The government itemized the list of prerevolutionary positions and titles that precluded their owners and families from voting, and added to a category of former people—those not loyal to the Soviet government. In the second half of the 1920s, the Bolsheviks toughened restrictions on the franchise again, to exclude White Army officers, members of "counterrevolutionary parties," victims of political repression, and their family members, making the group three times bigger. According to estimates, these unfortunates comprised 7.7% of adults in the towns and 3.5% in the countryside—more than 5 million people (Smith 2002, p. 131). Fitzpatrick estimates their number as 8.6% of all adults in 1929, and Sergei Krassil'nikov as 3,716,855 people, or 4.89% of all voters. Collectivization enlarged this constituency because of deported peasants, but according to Molotov,[5] in 1934, after some softening of policy, the disenfranchised comprised 2.5%, or more than two million out of 91 million voters (Fitzpatrick 1999, p. 249; Krassil'nikov 1998, Table 1, and passim; RGASPI f. 82, op. 2, d. 247, l. 29). The decision about who to disfranchise was made by local election committees following nomination by soviets, OGPU, or financial organs. According to A. Dobkin, an older and non-Russian population dominated in this group. The share of clergy with families was 20% among lishentsy in the countryside and 5–8% in the cites; merchants—up to 40% in RSFSR cities; artisans and "exploiters" using hired labor up to 27% in cities and villages (Dobkin 1992, p. 606).[6] For the *lishentsy*, disfranchisement was actually a matter of life or death because the state stripped access not only to voting but also to housing, food rations, education, and jobs; it penalized them with higher taxes, and, most perilously, it made them the first targets in periodic mass operations. Documents record the waves of suicides among the disfranchised (Alexopoulos 1997, p. 127). Both Krassil'nikov and Dobkin concluded that those ostracized were not so much political opponents of the regime, as they were independent, energetic, and entrepreneurial elements of society who were able to self-organize and build the foundation of a civil society.

The elimination of disfranchisement was the primary innovation of the constitution that roiled the society. Arzhilovsky recorded in his diary the TsIK decree from 14 March 1937, which ordered an end to judicial cases that restricted voting rights because of social origin, wealth, or past activities. "But," he continued, "there are no signs of improvement in our life. They always be saying 'class enemies' are everywhere." He was right. The inclusive message of the constitution and the granting of voting rights to the "class alien elements" did not directly affect the practice of the NKVD, which continued to persecute specific groups because of

---

[5] Molotov's report at the 7th Soviet Congress, 6 February 1935.
[6] No date specified, but probably at the end of the 1920s.

their social origin or past affiliation with now-banned parties. Ultimately, the number of "alien elements" did not decrease among those arrested in 1936—and comprised 26.9% (Khaustov and Samuelson 2010, p. 66). Preventive mass operations targeted alien elements: kulaks and mullahs from Azerbaijan (16 December 1936 Politburo order), church people (27 March 1937 NKVD circular), and former Mensheviks (29 April 1937 NKVD circular) (Khaustov and Samuelson 2010, pp. 52, 66, 68). The narrative of reconciliation obviously belonged to the sphere of ideology—what ought to be—rather than to political reality.

The article about universal voting rights divided society. Comments against the inclusive conciliation policy will be discussed in Chapter 10. Here, I focus on approval comments. The voting rights provisions of the constitution encouraged numerous general assertions in favor of grand democratic principles that went to the newspapers and the TsIK. Citizens often preferred "moving with the flow". More pragmatic support came from those who felt discriminated against, with their rights violated: believers, kulaks, *kolkhozniks*, and even workers. Welcoming universal voting rights, believers wanted more; they wanted a reversal of the previous brutal policies: liberation of imprisoned priests and parishioners, the reopening of churches, compliance with religious freedom, and an end to abuses and arbitrary taxes on churches (GARF f. 5263, op. 1, d. 32, l. 9). The *kolkhozniks* were another group dissatisfied with their second-class status: the inaccessibility of social benefits, heavy taxes on collective farms, exclusion from decision-making, and inability to leave the *kolkhoz*. "There is no improvement for the *kolkhoznik* in the constitution. It opened the way for the kulak and the priest, but nothing has changed for us." "The constitution is good only for workers" (RGASPI f. 17, op. 120, d. 232, l. 86; Sokolov 1998, p. 137). Peasants used exactly the terms of citizenship and discrimination when they demanded their share of welfare provisions and to take part in decision-making (see Chapter 12).

The workers, formally a "privileged" class, also used this occasion and voiced loud grievances about exploitation. They requested that the constitutional norm of a seven-hour working day, granted by Article 119 for "the great majority of the workers," be implemented in reality and reported the practice in the provinces of twelve, seventeen, and even nineteen hour workdays without any compensation for overtime or days off (GARF f. 3316, op. 41, d. 81, ll. 53, 67). They humbly asked for the right to have a land lot, a small house, and livestock, in order to grow supplemental foodstuff. With only their meager wages, "the workers can't support their families as the *kolkhozes* still produce too little food for the market."

> Let me write my opinion following the new constitution and freedom of opinion and press. I lost my health at the construction of socialism and I am unable to work in production now. I am exhausted, weak, and drained, but have nothing and do not know how to live. I have two children and no home. I would like to have a chance to get without pay some allotment to build a small hut or dugout and a vegetable garden in order not to burden the state [requesting a pension]. A proletarian living on land should have a right to toil the small piece of land. I have never had a hut and vegetable garden, and now I have a desire to live peacefully and independently. Could you also permit artisanship without hiring labor and high taxes—just to subsist? Please permit the trade of building materials like bricks and timber for individuals. (GARF f. 1235, op. 76, d. 153, l. 328; f. 3316, op. 8, d. 225, l. 3; f. 3316, op. 41, d. 81, l. 53; TsGAIPD SPb f. 24, op. 2v, d. 1772, l. 51)

Formerly, a huge majority of industrial workers owned their share of land in the village commune, along with the houses to which they usually returned after retirement. There was no longer such a practice after collectivization, as the plea of this worker conveys. This request listed the everyday hardships that the proletariat endured in a country of a dictatorship of the proletariat: malnutrition, scarcity, homelessness, and a miserable retirement. But the fate of the deported kulaks was far worse.

9.3 THE RIGHTS OF SPECIAL SETTLERS IN LIGHT OF THE CONSTITUTION

The most vocal group in support of universal voting was the exiled kulaks in special settlements comprising 1,056,633 persons in September 1936. During collectivization in 1930–1931, 1.8 million were deported, including their families, into internal exile to the North, Far East, and Siberia, to work as forced laborers with the goals of colonizing the hinterlands and exploiting natural resources while, to use the official parlance, reeducating themselves to become socialist citizens. By 1 January 1932, only 1.3 million remained in special settlements: 500,000 had either fled or died (Pokrovsky et al. 2006, pp. 47, 310, 532, 797). These exiled peasants enthusiastically greeted enfranchisement but they also expected liberation and freedom of movement. Enfranchisement led to legal and administrative confusion around the freedom to move, rooted in significant part in the extralegal practice of the peasants' deportation with no formal verdict or exact terms defined. As Lynne Viola and Sergei Krassil'nikov wrote, the mass banishment during collectivization was conducted not by the judiciary but by soviet administrative organs. According to law, such administrative exile inflicted individual, not family, deportation, and free, not forced, labor, and was limited to five years. The extraordinary practice of family deportation, with forced labor and no terms of exile, violated the law and created a legal vacuum around the question of liberation that allowed authorities to manipulate the issue with bylaws and instructions according to their immediate needs (Pokrovsky et al. 2006, p. 22; Viola 2007, pp. 155–9).

After the publication and adoption of the constitution, those exiled during collectivization requested permission to return home, and many of them left the special settlements without authorization. The NKVD reported the mass return of deportees as early as July 1936 (Berelowitch and Danilov 2012, p. 283; Fitzpatrick 1994, pp. 240–1). The writer Mikhail Prishvin in his diary entry from 10 June 1937 depicted wanderers who appeared on Russian roads—peasant-deportees who were walking home. The picture is tragic: "Now when summer warm days came, people with yellowish-green faces appeared on the northern highway. They drag slowly, like turtles, swinging. I asked one where he was coming from—'from Arkhangelsk.' He worked in exile for seven years in timber rafting, lost all family, and now is returning to his *izba* (hut) in his native village. Others are children of the kulaks, whose fathers died doing forestry work. ... They wander for about two months, overnighting in the villages." These "ghosts" moved Prishvin to write a letter to Molotov asking if in seven years these poor people had not yet earned a ticket back home, at least in cattle cars. "Beside natural sympathy, these human shadows are politically undesirable as they conflict with the picture of a happy life in the country, which we are trying to design. Even if they learned there in the North to keep absolutely total silence, their appearance is a crying shame" (Prishvin 2010, pp. 622–3).

Article 135 of the constitution, which introduced universal voting rights and reinstated the citizenship of millions, had been a part of the discourse in the villages and special settlements, in the Lubianka and the Kremlin for years. The period between 1930 and 1936 was a marked by fluctuations in policy—from concessions to restrictions—regarding the rights of the special settlers. The TsIK decree of 3 July 1931 established a term of five years for the special settlers, which in principle ended the term for those exiled during collectivization in 1934–1935, but partial and selective rehabilitation of their rights started earlier. To motivate labor, concessions were made to the youth and good workers who demonstrated their loyalty. For example, in May 1932, the TsIK restored rights to a group of 931 deportees—the shock workers. An important concession for the youth was the TsIK instruction of 17 March 1933, which enfranchised the children of the deportees who came of age. The OGPU sought to profit from this concession, instructing local offices to use this chance to motivate young people to raise productivity, to recruit them as informers, and also "for the purpose of splitting the constituency of the exiled"—an old ChK-OGPU practice. The TsIK decree of 27 May 1934 specified that hard-working, loyal deportees nominated by OGPU officers could acquire civil rights after the five years of exile and the shock workers among young people even before this time (Pokrovsky et al. 2006, pp. 83, 89, 99). But in a few days, on 9 June, internal OGPU instruction no. 43 went to local departments imposing a restriction of enfranchisement. First, this instruction—"About the mechanism of restoration of civil rights for *spetsposelentsy*," signed by OGPU deputy chief G. Yagoda, Gulag chief M. Berman, and G. A. Molchanov (Secret Political Department, OGPU)—warned local officers against "mass rehabilitation" but instead to select individuals. Second, the instruction imposed a cumbersome bureaucratic rehabilitation procedure. Third, it urged using the enfranchisement "to detach the youth from the counterrevolutionary older generation and to recruit new informants [among youth]." Last, the document permitted the rehabilitated to leave the special settlements but instructed the OGPU to press them to stay, and for this purpose to introduce a few privileges (Pokrovsky et al. 2006, pp. 506, 508, 569–72).

It seems that the rulers were firm in their belief that youth would be on the side of the government. In a report about the political moods of Ural deportees, the *chekists* emphasized that the mood of the youth is very distinct from the rebellious moods and actions of the older exiles. "Young people consider themselves to be not guilty and grumble about their parents. Conflict with adults reflects the splitting [of the constituency]. The groups of young people visit the *comendature*, offices of forestry departments, and declare their break with their relatives and demand improvement of living conditions. On the eve of the October holidays, the youth expressed their wish to participate in a celebration and even to volunteer to build a club."[7] Youth was the target group in recruiting informers. According to the OGPU, in Ural exile, every 20 families had on average one informer, and about 30% of the informers were youth.

The question about the right to return became central. By 1 November 1934, 31,364 exiles were rehabilitated, and despite pressure to stay, 75% of them left the special settlements; in the Northern *krai*—90%. To stop their departure, on 25 January 1935, the TsIK approved the prohibition, suggested by the OGPU, for the rehabilitated to leave their place of exile (Pokrovsky et al. 2006, p. 661). This was a break with the earlier OGPU "Temporary statute (*polozhenie*) about rights and duties of special settlers" from 25 October 1931, which regulated all peasant exile life in the 1930s and established the "full restoration of all civil rights five years after deportation" (Pokrovsky et al. 2006, p. 36). This point of the statute had maintained the spirit of thousands of deportees, but was now canceled.

Inconsistency about the right to return to one's native place, join a *kolkhoz*, and restore one's possessions found expression in a debate at the Second Congress of Outstanding Kolkhozniks in February 1935. The adopted Kolkhoz Statute contained a clause allowing the admission to collective farms of expropriated kulaks who had reformed themselves and were no longer enemies of the Soviet government (Fitzpatrick 1994, p. 123). However, at the Congress and later during the constitution discussion, *kolkhoz* activists expressed anxiety about revenge from the kulaks. "I believe that, as a result, those who were activists during dekulakization and the elimination of kulaks will suffer now. If the kulaks come to power, they will persecute those activists because kulaks still continue to feel a big hatred" (GARF f. 3316, op. 40, d. 14, l. 33).[8] Siegelbaum and Geldern agree with Fitzpatrick's observation elsewhere that "the party leadership proved to be more conciliatory towards the bulk of the peasantry than did the activists" (Geldern and Siegelbaum 1935). While the Kolkhoz Statute inspired deportees, a reverse movement came

---

[7] 19 December 1930, Report of Ural *oblast'* plenipotentiary G. P. Matson to the head of the Secret Operative Department (SOU), OGPU, E. G. Evdokimov "About the conditions of kulak exile."

[8] The author, K. E. Porkhomenko, Western *oblast'*, Gordeevsky *raion*, probably belonged to the activists.

in August 1935 arising from a Gulag clarification sent to all chiefs of special settlements to allow admission to collective farms only in places of exile, not in the returnees' native localities (Pokrovsky et al. 2006, p. 581).[9] Such manipulation, when secret instructions denigrated the operation of publicly announced policies, was a common practice.

At that moment, in the midst of this ambiguity, the constitution draft was published and aroused a new wave of hope and many cases of spontaneous unauthorized departures of settlers. In the general confusion on the legal status of the deportees, the returnees were often accepted in *kolkhozes*, which at that time experienced a depletion of the workforce (Fitzpatrick 1994, p. 365).

The next problem of the returnees was the question of homes and possessions. They demanded not only voting rights and membership in the *kolkhoz* but also their homes and property (RGASPI f. 17, op. 120, d. 232, ll. 49, 51; f. 5, op. 1, d. 232, l. 51; Sokolov 1998, p. 139). This understandably met opposition among the beneficiaries of collectivization. A certain V. N. Chimorodov from Voronehz *oblast'* protested: "[The constitution] implies that the popes and kulaks are full citizens and have the right to receive their confiscated homes, which are now in the *kolkhoz* ['s possession]. For that reason, we ask to ban them from voting [meaning from restoration of rights—OV]" (GARF f. 3316, op. 40, d. 14, l. 57). The arbitrary nature of collectivization caused a backlash resulting in new conflicts. In some places, peoples' courts sanctioned the restoration of possession rights to former kulaks (in Northern Caucasus); in other places, returnees occupied their confiscated homes without any authorization (Berelowitch and Danilov 2012, pp. 283, 285).

With such uncertainty about their status, special settlers expected the adoption of the constitution would help them. The newspapers and authorities received an incessant flow of questions and complaints about the rights of deported kulaks. Many had been deported without trial and did not know their terms: "We do not consider ourselves to be deprived of the rights according to the court decision, but only by NKVD [power], because we did not hear any sentence, any trial, but they simply exiled us to another area and that's it" (GARF f. 3316, op. 41, d. 86, ll. 2a, 2a (verso), 2b, 2b (verso); f. 3316, op. 40, d. 14, ll. 33, 57).

[9] The Gulag clarification to local organs about the application of the Statute article to special settlers with reinstated voting rights, August 1935.

These peasants asked about their status. To numerous questions and inquiries, the secretariat of the TsIK Presidium answered in January 1937: "There is to be no return of dekulakized (confiscated) property because it was confiscated according to law. The constitution does not imply such a return" (GARF f. 3316, op. 29, d. 793, ll. 11, 17, 32, 45, 59, 73).[10] The August 1937 letter of the chief of the Gulag, I. I. Pliner, to Yezhov reflected the understanding of the necessity to clarify the legal status of the special settlers according to the new constitution: "In the last three–four months, he wrote, the flow of complaints by the settlers [*trudposelentsy*] grew significantly. They write to central and local government institutions and complain that after the adoption of the new Constitution there is no change in their legal status. ... At the time I do not deem it necessary to allow former kulaks to leave their place of exile but rather to uphold the TsIK decree from 25 January 1935 forbidding them to leave exile until ... 1943" (Pokrovsky et al. 2006, p. 591). The NKVD did not consider the constitution applied to them. For too many deportees, rehabilitation according to Article 135 was nominal since they were not allowed to leave their place of exile (Khlevniuk 2010, p. 244). In contrast to the published and discussed constitution, the inaccessibility of the laws' publications and secret instructions issued by the Gulag caused additional pain for citizens.

Another flow of letters with inquiries followed during the preparation for elections in 1937 (GARF f. 3316, op. 29, d. 793, ll. 71–3). The Gulag instruction from 15 October 1937 confirmed the voting rights of the settlers, though again restricting their mobility. The central election committee and NKVD agreed that voting identification documents (*spravka*) should be issued for special settlers by the commandants of the settlements to then be taken away at the polls in exchange for a ballot (Pokrovsky et al. 2006, p. 593). Restoration of civil rights was incomplete and sabotaged at any level of administration. We see a common practice when the constitution, law, or decree granting rights to citizens was curtailed by normative instructions and bylaws that restricted those rights. "Normative acts quenched the power of law," wrote Lynne Viola and Sergei Krassil'nikov, the compilers of the document collection on the special settlers. The authors abstain there from using the term "the *legal* status of *spetspereselentsy*," as the notion of legality does not reflect the

---

[10] December 1936–January 1937. Requests for clarifications of the constitution.

reality of their condition. "It was a quasilegal procedure, with norms and rules not restricted by any legal or justice institutions, but established and changed by political authority. ... The law was an instrument in the hands of regime organs [NKVD] supervising the groups of special settlers" (Pokrovsky et al. 2006, pp. 21–2, 38). Finally, by April 1937 as many as 136,350 former deportees, though rehabilitated, still resided in or near special settlements (Ivnitsky 2004, pp. 143, 147; Pokrovsky et al. 2006, p. 603).[11] This twist-and-turn policy of rehabilitation lasted for a short period, until July 1937, when, according to the infamous Order No. 00447, thousands of former kulaks who had fled or returned from exile became victims of a new mass operation directed first of all against returnees (Viola 2007, pp. 163–4).

Article 121 announced the right to education. Free education was a great achievement of socialism. Children of the *lishentsy* formally gained access to high education according to a government decree from 29 December 1935. A Belorussian correspondent told an interviewer that his father was dekulakized, arrested, and disfranchised. In 1933, he tried to enter Leningrad University but was not accepted. In 1936, due to the new constitution, he successfully enrolled at the teachers' institute in Vitebsk (HPSSS Schedule A, Vol. 36, Case 142, p. 45).

At the beginning of 1936, Vyshinsky offered to expand this decree to children of deportees but did not receive approval. Only selected applications, for example groups of young men from Leningrad and Igarka, were approved in 1936 (Khlevniuk 2010, pp. 245–7; Pokrovsky et al. 2006, p. 111). Children of special settlers got the right to move to nearby cities with educational institutions only in the spring of 1939, according to a new NKVD statute. But as always, there was a great distance between law and practice: the letters of young people relate their inability to realize their right to an education. The seventh-grade student Vasily Melusov wrote to the commandant of the special settlement in the village of Berezovka, Pikhtov *raion*, in Siberia on 23 July 1939. "[In May I wrote to you and] on 25 June I have sent an application to Tomsk Forestry College via [you] the commandant receiving no answer. ... Obviously you held my documents with the purpose of keeping me from education. However, Article 121 of the Constitution (the Fundamental law) of the USSR declares the right of USSR citizens for education,

---

[11] The total number of special settlers was 859,366 by 1 October 1938.

but—alas!—not in our settlement" (Pokrovsky et al. 2006, pp. 1010, 1013). Not only was the right to education impossible to realize for many young citizens but the right to freedom itself was equally unattainable. The TsIK decree from 1938 to liberate sixteen-year-old children of the special settlers was only one-third successful: out of 165,050, only 50,569 were liberated by 1941. Liberal measures were hardly implemented (Ivnitsky 2004, p. 149). Ultimately, the exile and all restrictions on the kulaks and special settlers officially ended only after Stalin's death—in 1954.

The approvals of the enfranchisement of special settlers in the discussion materials cannot be interpreted as a reflection of liberal attitudes per se, but they were a part of the discourse endorsing a new conciliation policy and individual and political rights of citizens.

9.4 Skepticism About Fair Elections

The constitution inspired hope in citizens, who welcomed the state's new direction toward civil rights. Too many, however, were skeptical: "Universal and secret voting—it's just on paper; still only the nominees of the Communists will be elected [*proidut*]" (TsGAIPD SPb f. 24, op. 2v, d. 1860, ll. 7–8, 18–20, 63; d. 2664, ll. 232, 270). Repetitive expressions of disbelief in the new freedoms reflected the accumulated experience of the two decades when much was promised but little realized. Citizens actually remembered only one major effective retreat from the harsh Bolshevik policies—the New Economic Policy. But even this single concession was reversed in 1928. The adult generation who remembered the prerevolutionary past and witnessed a myriad of unrealized promises and declarations had abundant grounds for disbelief. A recent disappointment was the first Five-Year Plan. American military intelligence reported: "Another cause of serious discontent was 'the bluff about Five-Year Plan.' They [the people] were promised after the completion of the plan a period of rest and prosperity" (Reynolds 1984, Reel X, pp. 0366, 0439; HPSSS Schedule A, Vol. 36, Case 1705, p. 68). The archival sources reflect popular anticipation (HPSSS Schedule A, Vol. 13, Case 167, p. 30). The results of the first Five-Year Plan were indeed inadequate: real wages fell by about 50% in industry and continued to fall until 1934. In the cities, the standard of living fell and the countryside was decimated by famine. A worker stated: "A good state would be one without Communists because they only promise to better the position of the workers. When will we finally see this improvement?

The first Five-Year Plan has already ended and where are their promises?" (Goldman 2007, pp. 20, 31).

While the constitution democratized the election procedure, people suspected that falsification and fraud would be used in future elections to guarantee the results necessary for the party. "Is it a new democracy if the party will compile the list [of candidates] and introduce it to the masses for approval and they vote without thinking?" (Danilov et al. 2002, p. 426). A diary recorded such a conversation: "Yesterday Stroshkov, the chairman of a local artel, blurted out, 'The Constitution is one thing, but local authorities are something else. Everything will be at their discretion: who can be allowed [to run for office] and who cannot.' And he may be right, the red-faced thug. They can find subversive meaning in the most well-intentioned criticism. Myself, I do not expect any real change," noted the worker Arzhilovsky (Garros et al. 1997, p. 127). But disbelief was a crime. Arzhilovsky was arrested, his diary confiscated, the statements of skepticism about the victory of socialism were underlined by an NKVD officer and brought him a death sentence. Pig farm worker Gontarev, Mostov *raion*, Odessa *oblast'*, was sent to a labor camp for five years for discrediting the constitution in November 1936 by talking to other workers about the government's lies in the constitution, saying that the liberties would not be realized (Berelowitch and Danilov 2012, p. 364). The same fate befell another worker in February 1937, who said: "We have no freedom of speech. In what newspaper can I criticize the CC secretary Andreev? We have no democracy; our democracy is fake; any bourgeois country has more democracy than the USSR" (TsGAIPD SPb f. 24, op. 2v, d. 2685, l. 1–2).

A certain Gaponov in Leningrad expected arrests of the people's candidates together with their supporters. "If the people's candidates win, the dictatorship will dismiss them. Do not be fooled by the widening of liberties!" (TsGAIPD SPb f. 24, op. 2v, d. 1860, l. 20). "The election was arranged in a way that the results were predetermined. It's interesting what will be a mechanism of elections now and how it will be arranged to secure the results necessary for the party." "Even if the people elect their representatives, the Bolsheviks, under the conditions of their dictatorship, will do everything to dismiss them. Give us freedom of parties and the press, and then we'll see who wins." "The counting of votes will be arranged in favor of the Bolsheviks" (TsGAIPD SPb f. 24, op. 2v, d. 1860, ll. 19–20).

Every day brought confirmation of the truth behind these skeptical comments. Delegates' elections to the local and all-nation soviet congresses in the summer and fall of 1936 were conducted according the old norms (including unequal representation of urban and rural soviets), as specified by the TsIK instruction from 2 August 1936 following Stalin's remark at the CC June Plenum. But voters hurried to realize their new rights in practice. *Pravda* wrote approvingly that electors felt compelled by the constitution draft to exercise their right to dismiss ineffective cadres immediately—in the fall elections and report campaign in the local soviets—even before formal approval of the constitution.

While the population attempted to realize new freedoms, they had already been violated here and there. The officials continued to behave in the old suppressive ways. In October, the NKVD reported with alarm of voters nominating and electing to the local soviet congresses "anti-Soviet elements", *lishentsy*, or former counterrevolutionaries. The NKVD quickly dismissed such delegates from the congress list: in Malaia Vishera, Podporozhie, Novoselsky *raion* in Leningrad *oblast'*, Zeldsky *raion*, Odesskaia *oblast'*, and others (Berelowitch and Danilov 2012, pp. 354–5, 363–4). The kulak *lishenets* Afanasy Popov in the Caucasus was deprived of the deputy mandate in the middle of the congress, while delegates "Khoptiar, suspected in spying, and Zaidman, Trotskyist," in Vinnitsa *oblast'*, were arrested (TsGAIPD SPb f. 24, op. 2v, d. 1860, ll. 3, 14–5; d. 2664, l. 231; Berelowitch and Danilov 2012, pp. 354–5, 365). Security bodies and the party directly intervened in the elections, blocking undesirable candidates and imposing the nominees. In Tikhvin *raion*, Leningrad *oblast'*, the voters declined the candidacy of village soviet chair Sokolov, but the *raion* representative said, "You can vote him out, but my word is final: Sokolov will stay as chair" (Berelowitch and Danilov 2012, p. 354). As skeptics predicted, the old practice of party and NKVD control over elections and manipulation continued: the unwanted candidates were excluded from the voting lists or arrested. Another method of manipulation was "an informal quota system," or *raznariadka* (TsGAIPD SPb f. 24, op. 2v, d. 2664; Kulakov et al. 2005, p. 447). For example, the Gorky *krai* soviet leader instructed the staff: "Elections to the *krai* [soviet] congress should guarantee [winners include] 34 per cent women, 40–45 per cent nonparty people, 22 per cent workers, and 30 per cent *kolkhozniks*" (Kulakov et al. 2005, pp. 385–447; Yekelchyk 2014, pp. 199–202). This sorting took place at the moment of nomination. The plenum of the Gorky *krai* party committee in September 1936 directly instructed party officials to scrutinize the cadres of the candidates and manage the elections of the deputies

(Kulakov et al. 2005, pp. 384–5).[12] Thus, already in the fall of 1936, the local elections of the delegates to the soviet congresses saw the test of the new freedoms implementation. The NKVD reported that socially alien elements used the report campaign and elections for anti-Soviet agitation (Berelowitch and Danilov 2012, pp. 346–58). Elected former kulaks and members of now banned parties were blocked via something akin to "criminal checks".

In the fall of 1936, when the NKVD en masse warned high party authorities of the people's intent to use a secret procedure to vote out Communists from local positions, they already had precedents (Berelowitch and Danilov 2012, pp. 340–1, 346, 350). In 1937, such warnings multiplied as soviet and party officials realized the threat to their positions of power. Their misgivings were voiced in the debates on the new election procedure at the February–March 1937 CC Plenum. Arch Getty analyzed this debate from the perspective of officials' resistance to the initiatives of the center (Getty 1991, p. 29; 2013a, Chapter 7), but the subject of the debate—energizing of anti-Soviet forces in the population—was also internalized by the decision-makers. As a result, repressions targeted not only officials and elite, but the masses—NKVD decrees from 27 March, 25 April and 8 June 1937 directed operations against churchmen and believers[13]; operations against former kulaks and other anti-Soviet elements started in July 1937. Experiments with freely contested elections, announced by A. A. Zhdanov at the plenum to purge officials, continued as well. May 1937 elections in the local Communist Party committees led to 50% rotation and to over 70% rotation in the trade unions (Goldman 2007, pp. 147–8). On 2 July, the press published the procedures governing elections to the Supreme Soviet—the ballots were printed to accommodate several candidates. According to Getty, the frightened local officials "tried to convince Moscow of the dangers of contested elections" and thus precipitated the mass operations of the Great Terror (Getty 2013b, p. 229)

---

[12] The information of the Gorky *krai* soviet chair Yu. M. Kaganovich about the preparation of the extraordinary soviet congresses at the 10th Plenum of the VKPb *Krai* Committee, 28 September 1936.

[13] The decrees stressed preparations of the church people to elections according to the new liberties of the constitution. Sixty-four percent of the arrested 31,359 in church operations between August and November 1937 were believers, others—churchmen.

Photo 9.2 Polling station no. 19 in Leningrad, December 1937. The slogan reads "On 12 December 1937 here will take place a secret voting to elect the Supreme Soviet of the USSR." M. P. Yanov. Courtesy of the Central State Archives of Documentary Films, Photographs, and Sound Recordings, Saint-Petersburg (TsGAKFFD SPb)

unleashed in July 1937.[14] Contested elections were secretly cancelled in October 1937 just before the election to the Supreme Soviet. In December, the people were disappointed to find only one name on each ballot (Photo 9.2). The intelligent and critically minded Leningradian Liubov' Shaporina put in her diary:

> During the studies of the election law in all enterprises and institutions, the public asked if they could take the ballot and go home to ponder what candidate to vote for. Answer: yes. I entered the booth where I was supposed to read the ballot and choose my candidate to the Supreme Soviet … [but] we have on the ballot one name, selected in advance. I had

---

[14]The history of the elections to the Supreme Soviet in 1937 deserves to be studied further, with meticulous analysis of the October CC Plenum (see Getty 2013b; Brandenberger 2011; Pavlova 2003).

a laugh attack in the booth. For a time, I could not make the appropriate calm face. At the exit I met Yuri with a stony expression on his face. I raised my collar [to hide my face—OV]—it was incredibly laughable. In the yard I met Petrov-Vodkin and Dmitriev. V. V. [Dmitriev] talked about something and wildly laughed. ...We all laughed. (Shaporina 2012, p. 219)

Finally, popular skepticism about the election reform was well justified.

This disbelief demonstrates a faculty for rational and critical thinking in the popular mind—the ability to analyze the political process, to connect cause and consequence. These skeptical comments evidence the distance that some individuals managed to keep from the state—and the fortitude underlying their opposition to the state's falsehoods embodied in its constitution. The liberal undercurrent was pronounced in support of judicial innovations, accountability of the soviets' administration, universal voting rights, and especially in reactions to proclaimed individual freedoms.

9.5 New Freedoms in the Popular Discourse

Individual rights, guaranteed safe from government interference, and the protection of minority rights are generally considered the essential elements of a liberal democracy. The 1936 discussion characterizes popular views on the principles announced in the constitution draft—freedom of assembly, press, religion, mobility, and the inviolability of person, home, and private correspondence.

The freedom to unite in public organizations declared by Article 126[15] stood in sharp contrast to reality: by the 1930s, the party-state had suppressed all independent voluntary associations of any kind. After crushing the party of Socialists-Revolutionaries and the Mensheviks at the beginning of the 1920s, the All-Union Communist Party (of Bolsheviks) (VKPb) remained the single party in the country, though this one-party system had never been institutionalized in previous constitutions. By describing it as a party of the most active and politically conscious citizens, the 1936 Constitution's Article 126 enhanced the

---

[15] "In conformity with the interests of the working people, ... citizens of the U.S.S.R. are ensured the right to unite in public organizations—trade unions, cooperative associations, youth, sport and defense organizations, cultural, technical, and scientific societies; and the most active and politically conscious citizens ... unite in the Communist Party of the Soviet Union, which is the vanguard of the working people in their struggle to strengthen and develop the socialist system and is the leading core of all organizations of the working people, both public and state."

party's role, especially in its formula "the All-Union Communist Party (of Bolsheviks) ... is the leading core of all organizations of the working people, both public and state." This formula confirmed the status of the party organization at plants, schools, *kolkhozes*, and local soviets as supervisor of their executives, and thus institutionalized the party-state. The next constitution in 1977 established the party as "the leading and directing force of the Soviet society."

Common people reading Articles 125 and 126 often missed the point that political freedoms were guaranteed to citizens "in conformity with the interests of the working people, and in order to strengthen the socialist system." It was an important limitation meant to bar critique of the regime. Although the article did not mention political parties, it raised expectations in public about the revival of a multiparty system. A certain Grigory Gorunov, called a former Socialist-Revolutionary in the NKVD report, interpreted Article 126 as follows: "The constitution permits parties and liberties, so now we'll organize our own party and press and will conduct our own policy" (RGASPI f. 17, op. 120, d. 232, l. 52; TsGAIPD SPb f. 24, op. 2v, d. 1860, l. 7). The engineer Glebov from Leningrad recommended that the government permit political parties; otherwise, he warned, they will go underground. (RGASPI f. 17, op. 120, d. 232, l. 52). People still did not forget their experience of a multiparty system, as many nostalgic references to the prerevolutionary past or to Western political systems showed. The comments were mostly abstract in nature, approving liberties in principle; peasants, however, were quite explicit in their demand for Peasant Unions to protect their interests. "We ask you [the government] to allow a Peasant Union because without it we are like a flock without a shepherd; we have no place to ask any advice." "I suggest complementing Article 126 about enhancing self-organization [with an addition] to grant the *kolkhoz* and individual peasantry the right to organize a Peasant Union at every village soviet to convey directly all [the peasants'] needs and requests to central agricultural agencies. The village soviets and *kolkhoz* offices, because of their bureaucratic attitude, in most cases lead *kolkhozes* not to an affluent and cultured life, but to destruction and deterioration." (GARF f. 3316, op. 41, d. 207, l. 195; RGASPI f. 17, op. 120, d. 232, l. 52; f. 5, op. 1, d. 232, l. 79). The voices from the countryside demanded equal rights with workers, effective representation in power, and protection of their specific political and economic interests. These requests for a peasant political party or trade union, widespread in the 1920s, lessened after the eradication of the most active and entrepreneurial farmers from the village during collectivization, but demands were still voiced during the constitution discussion (Velikanova 2013, pp. 118–58; RGASPI f. 17, op. 120, d. 232, ll. 79, 83; f. 5, op. 1, d. 232, ll. 74, 79; TsGAIPD SPb f. 24, op. 2v, d. 1860, l. 8; GARF f. 3316, op. 40, d. 14, ll. 69–70; Sokolov 1998, p. 149). The political movement in the countryside for the Peasant Union indicates strongly the efficiency of the forces of modernity in transforming even a conservative constituency like the peasantry. It undermines the maxim of Max Weber about the pattern in peasants' behavior in European revolutions: "to switch from the most thoroughgoing radicalism [during the Revolution] to a state of apathy or political reaction, once their immediate economic demands had been satisfied" (Beetham 1985, p. 188).

Here too, skeptics contributed to the conversation: "Anyway, those who dare to organize a party will be razed to the ground." Those dreaming about democratic pluralism overlooked the discouraging note in Molotov's interview with the French journalist Chastene, published in *Izvestia* on 24 March 1936: the question about the multiparty system in the USSR "is not relevant as we approach the disappearance of conflicting classes, and respectively the parties representing them." *Pravda*, in editorials and articles written by officials, often underscored the incompatibility of the multiparty system with the harmonious world of socialism. "There are no conditions in our country for any party opposed to the Bolshevik one" (*Pravda* 1, 4, 6 November 1936). Finally, Stalin dismissed the need for other parties in a speech at the 8th Soviet Congress "because all classes are friendly now, without antagonistic interests," thus conveying his ideal of a homogeneous communist society (Stalin 1947, p. 21).

While state supremacy was recognized by the masses as a given (to be discussed in Chapter 10), support for individual rights also found its place in the popular discourse. One of the correspondents advised: "The violation of the main rights of man and citizen not only undermines citizenship but also ignites hatred in a person against the state and the desire to destroy such a state" (RGASPI f. 17, op. 120, d. 232, l. 52). The articles about individual rights were in sharp antagonism with the very recent experience of collectivization. After dispossession of the kulaks, when pillows, mirrors, and coats had been confiscated, typically without taking any inventory, or simply robbed, personal property was now declared protected by the law. The new constitution claimed the households of collective, individual farmers, and artisans inviolable, including livestock and hens. "Earned by labor, possessions, income, savings, house, household, instruments, and personal belongings are protected by the socialist state" (*Pravda* 14 June 1936). The new Family Legislation confirmed property rights.

Article 9 permitted the small private subsidiary economy of individual out-*kolkhoz* peasants and handicraftsmen. This inspired the expectations that pressure on independent peasants to join *kolkhoz* would end. Most collectivized peasants interpreted this concession to individual farmers as the beginning of a return to the pre-*kolkhoz* system—this was a popular subject of rumors in the countryside. Their logic: if there was no more pressure on the out-*kolkhoz* farmers to join collective farms, then *kolhozniks* would also be free to exit. For peasants, no pressure meant freedom to stay out of the collective farms, and in this case, they implied, nobody would stay in the *kolkhoz*. The dreamers fantasized even further: that after cancellation of the *kolkhoz*, peasants would be given land (RGASPI f. 5, op. 1, d. 232, l. 49; f. 17, op. 120, d. 232, l. 49).

The numerous expectations of the end of collective farms were accompanied by a small number of requests for the right to travel abroad and for such "luxuries" as receiving foreign newspapers (GARF f. 1235, op. 76, d. 153, l. 73 verso; f. 3316, op. 8, d. 225, l. 73, 114; d. 226, l. 152). Such requests sounded quite extravagant in a country where permissions to go abroad were approved by the Politburo. The constitution inspired freedom-lovers like a certain Savin from West Siberian *krai*, Diaschinsky *raion*. In his letter to *Krestianskaia Gazeta*, he demanded freedom of trade, days off for all, low taxes, ending repressions, and control of crime. But his main emphasis was on religious freedom: "Give all citizens full freedom, no suppression of beliefs in any nation, open all temples—Orthodox and other denominations. Liberate all exiled priests and other persons. Village soviets and other state institutions should not harass the churches and other denominations; all citizens should practice the faith that they want" (Danilov et al. 2002, p. 822; *Kresianskaia Gazeta* 17 August 1936). Savin's letter demonstrated inclusive views and tolerance when he defended the rights of minorities. The letter does not show if he was a believer or not, but he raised his voice for all faiths, not only the Orthodox. Such tolerance, however, was rare: disregard of the rights of minorities (individual farmers and believers) was a particular trend in the discussants' understanding of democracy. Even as late as the 1990s, Russian citizens showed concern first and foremost for their own rights, neglecting the rights of others, including minorities. In 2006, from a third to half of young people in Russia showed a willingness to suppress the rights of "others," of minorities and deviants (Gibson and Duch 1993, p. 88; Zorkaia 2010, p. 24). Such an understanding was noticeable even among the Russian "democrats" who guided reforms in the 1990s (Lukin 2000, p. 265).

Article 127, which guaranteed the inviolability of the person, found strong resonance and got 3218 comments (ranking it fifth). "Farmers are very happy with the inviolability of the person in the Constitution—now soviet officials won't come to arrest us for debts as in the past" (GARF f. 3316, op. 41, d. 207, l. 191; d. 81, l. 84; RGASPI f. 17, op. 120, d. 232, ll. 83–5). A certain Tkachenko, maligned and excluded from the party, addressed Kalinin: "According to Soviet laws, do I have a right to wash away the black spot of slander from me? I want to know how the constitutional law provides inviolability of person to me, an honest man, and to a slanderer in our Soviet conditions" (RGASPI f. 78, op. 1, d. 592, l. 25). The article resonated with the growing sense of dignity and self-worth among citizens.

Self-esteem and individualism revealed itself in ten (TsIK data) requests to protect citizens from humiliation by cursing and insults. These comments responded to Article 123: "any advocacy of racial or national exclusiveness or hatred and contempt is punishable by law." The voices in the discussion against verbal aggressiveness, emboldened by a feeling of personal autonomy, belonged to a liberal discourse. Obscene language (*mat*) after the revolution flooded public spaces and new population groups—women and children. A contemporary philologist, Selischev, observed the attempts to condemn the proliferation of vulgarisms in party and youth publications in the 1920s. He discussed a source of obscenity and vulgarisms within criminal groups and believed that the phenomenon migrated from the city factory milieu toward villages and youth (Selischev 1928, pp. 74, 80). At 4 a.m. on 27 February 1937, while walking to take his place in a food line, Arzhilovsky "heard a young woman, a worker, swearing. She used the same filthy language that men are prone to use. The other women were laughing at her outbursts. And in fact, all the women are constantly exposed to coarse language; they know the hidden meaning to all the words, so why not use them themselves? Equality in all things" (Garros et al. 1997, p. 149). The observer sarcastically interpreted everyday brutalization as a result of the drive to equality.

As a reaction to the vulgarization of language and in line with the enlightenment trend in Bolshevism, an attempt at "linguistic engineering" (Katarina Clark's expression) produced in the 1920s an official campaign of a "struggle for cultured speech": the Komsomol campaigned against foul language; the pedagogue Makarenko and writer Maxim Gorky advised adults to censor their speech; and politeness was invoked as a requirement for the new Soviet elite and bureaucrats (Hoffmann 2003, pp. 42–3, 67; Clark 1998, p. 208; Smith 1998; *Komsomol'skaia Pravda*, no. 162, 1925; Laursen 2007). Some local soviets—in the Sverdlovsk, Omsk, and Kuban' *oblasts*—introduced fines for cursing and thus hoped to replenish their scarce budgets (Rittersporn 2014, p. 228). Despite these efforts, swearing and rudeness persisted in society. Campaigns in the press against verbal aggressiveness juxtaposed a powerful but crude vernacular, associated with proletarian origins, against cultured speech, which the masses instinctively associated with "bourgeois" manners and upbringing. Shaporina, who was of noble origin, wrote in 1946: "[She was] very cultured, well-mannered, and I often rebuked her for being too 'ladylike' (*barynia*). I know from my experience that this gentleness hindered and hinders me in contemporary life, preventing me from when in Rome, doing as the Romans do (*s volkami zhit'– po volch'i vyt'*)" (Shaporina 2017, p. 33). Besides the antibourgeois tenor in the vernacular and the general coarsening of mores as a result of wars and the exodus of the cultural elite after the Revolution, some historians see the persistence of cursing as a vent for long-suppressed frustrations of the Soviet citizens, as a means of symbolic self-assertion for a population reduced to silence (Rittersporn 2014, p. 205). More convincing is the positing of *mat* as an antireligious declaration or an often unconscious resistance to lifeless and dull Bolshevik speech, a kind of "secret" language of a subaltern group, in James Scott's terms. Facing a flood of verbal violence, members of the old intelligentsia—but also those unrooted, humiliated, and marginalized elements, who desperately sought a new Soviet identity, security, and integration—believed that the "blessed" new constitution could stop swearing (GARF f. 1235, op. 76, d. 153, l. 126; f. 3316, op. 8, d. 225, l. 75; op. 41, d. 207, l. 16; op. 40, d. 40, l. 13). It is yet more evidence of the common belief in the power of words and texts (a constitution) to change reality. Correspondents in 1936 suggested toughening punishment as the way to stop cursing (GARF f. 3316, op. 8, d. 225, ll. 75, 135; op. 41, d. 85, ll. 42–3, 45–6; d. 86, l. 19; f. 3316, op. 40, d. 15, l. 117; RGASPI f. 17, op. 120, d. 232, ll. 56, 87). Already existing decrees against insults, however, did not work. A gap between the law and practice in the USSR was common: in the discussion, people often demanded the introduction of a law that had already been in force but rarely implemented. The swearing epidemic remained incurable for decades: in 1999, half of surveyed Russians had reported having been a victim of verbal abuse (Dubin 2010, p. 86).

These calls for human dignity were a part of modern subjectivity[16] and a new feature for the workers and peasants in their transformation to a modern personality. Inspired by the liberating promises of the Revolution, it was endorsed by the official inculcation of civility (Taylor 1989, p. 211). The growth of self-worth accompanied the process of the formation of the Russian working class. Stephen Smith showed that already during the 1905 Revolution, "Russian workers had developed a heightened sensitivity to the innate value of the human person." In labor strikes, demands for polite treatment in the workplace went hand in hand with economic and political issues. The traditional form of familiar address, *ty*, used by foremen and supervisors when communicating with the workers, became perceived as intolerable by the first generation of the proletarians. In the period 1901–1913, the Factory Inspectorate registered a tenfold increase in annual complaints about "bad treatment" and a demand for respectful treatment was in one-fifth of all strike resolutions between 1907 and 1914 (Smith 1998, pp. 105–6; Figes and Kolonitsky 1999, pp. 115–6). One of the innovations of the February Revolution in 1917 was Order No. 1, introducing the more formal address, *vy*, to soldiers in the army.

Mechanisms of modernization—migration to cities, industrial discipline, education—launched the process of individuation in former peasants and proletarians. A sign of this was the perception of a loss of citizenship (*lishenie prav*) in the USSR as a source of shame for individuals, while the acquisition of full citizenship was perceived by many former outcasts as a restoration of honor (Alexopoulos 2006, p. 514). In our sources, we hear the voices of the disenfranchised who defended their dignity. An artisan, I. Anokhin protested against the practice of displaying the lists of *lishentsy* in public places in villages and small towns on the eve of elections: "I have a family and children. Placing my name on the fence [*zabor*], like a citizen without rights, defames my good name … [It] puts the stamp of outcast on me."

---

[16]The idea of natural autonomy and dignity are central in the modern Western self.

Another voice: "I am a loyal member of the Churikov [religious] sect and like a free citizen living in free Soviet republic, I have the right to think freely, go and spend time where I want and need" (Dobkin 1992, pp. 620, 622). These expressions of self-validation and individuation were noteworthy in the context of many centuries of a peasant collectivist commune mentality and anti-individualist Soviet mores. In official discourse, dignity and respectability had a quite ambiguous place and were often overshadowed by subordination of the individual to the collective good and by self-denial in favor of the collective. The word "individualist" had a negative connotation in the Soviet vernacular. Not self-esteem, but modesty was one of the ideal features of the new Soviet Man, inculcated by propaganda, inter alia, through the ascetic images of Lenin and Stalin, who served as role models. This mindset was propped up by those in power at any level to make sure that their subordinates did not appropriate their superiors' places, and exemplified in a Soviet colloquialism *ne vesovyvaisia!*, which can be translated as "Do not stand out!" or "Keep a low profile!" Reflecting the feeling of "unworthiness" hidden in the subconscious, many letters and appeals began with excuses for bothering the addressee.

Freedom of mobility was in demand in the country, with 1.3 million exiled peasants, *kolkhoz* bondage, and the administrative system of "regime" cities with limited residency. Nine comments collected by TsIK requested introducing the right to settle anywhere inside the country without restrictions; and seven (my records), the right to change workplaces. This freedom was not introduced in the charter, but the demand came organically from below. These citizens disapproved of the reduction of freedom of movement resulting from the establishment of *kolkhozes*, exclusion of collective farmers from the internal passport system, and the introduction of residency registration in the cities. In the summer of 1936, under conditions of massive flight from collective farms in the face of famine, the basic freedom of movement became vital for common folk, who often compared their status with that of fugitive serfs.

Article 128 about the inviolability of the home produced various readings—the majority of discussants stood for the restriction of this right (to be discussed in Chapter 10); others were in favor. This principle in Western constitutions was based on private property. After the nationalization of real estate in 1918, bringing with it the absence of private property in the USSR, the inviolability of the home was a falsehood. State property on real estate made the state a distributor of housing according to its interests in favor of privileged social groups. An economy of shortages made any resource an instrument of wealth redistribution and thus of control. In this condition, tenants' rights were inevitably vulnerable. Soviet urbanites obtained their living space free, according to the written order of the local soviet, which was omnipotent in the distribution of housing. The order gave "the right of occupation" or "using the living space." The urban housing crisis, arbitrariness and corruption of allocating agencies, and the uncertain status of various housing facilities made the "housing problem" central in cities and towns. Tenants had no right to sell, buy, exchange, or lease at will the accommodations where they lived. They totally depended on the authorities in this key sphere. Distribution of housing and the institution of registration in a certain place became instruments of control over the population, regulating the people's mobility and way of life (Meerovich 2008, pp. 196–7, 294–5).

Many citizens understood very well the weakness of the principle of real estate inviolability under socialism without private property rights. This constitution article provoked endless inquiries about the issues of inheritance, exchange, bequest, and the lease of housing, which were not clearly established by law (GARF f. 3316, op. 29, d. 793, ll. 12–4). Reflecting the routine of arrests, many comments endorsed the principle that only a police warrant gives the right to intrude into a home and make searches.

More complicated was the legal status of dormitories and housing facilities affiliated with a particular plant or factory, where eviction of the retired, sick, or fired was common practice. The workers at the shoe factory in Leningrad enthusiastically supported Article 128 and insisted that nobody except the court could evict a resident or make him or her share a living space (GARF f. 3316, op. 8, d. 225, ll. 75, 149; op. 41, d. 207, l. 17; d. 85, ll. 4, 11, 13–4, 18). Such interpretation of the article, however, was wrong: factory barracks remained exterritorial for law. In July 1937, the TsIK secretary answered Podolsk worker M. A. Zhukov, explaining that the article does not imply that eviction from plant housing is illegal. It rather means "Nobody can enter a citizen's dwelling without his consent (except the power organs with the appropriate warrant). ... As for the question of eviction of a tenant who no longer works in the plant, this is regulated by the rules of dwelling *usage*. The new constitution's Article 128 has nothing to do with this question." One TsIK clarification—"The eviction is acceptable by court decision"—contradicted another clarification: "Instruct the courts that they should not accept such lawsuits about eviction" (GARF f. 3316, op. 29, d. 793, ll.

11, 22, 30, 90, 119, 133).[17] Numerous inquiries and evasive answers from officials, who instructed supplicants to "seek a lawyer's consultation," demonstrate how unfree and vulnerable Soviet citizens were when it came to their basic human rights.

The discussion of the constitution for the first time educated a new generation of Soviet citizens in the language of civil rights. For example, the woman's discontent about the ban on abortion in 1936 expressed her concern in civil rights terms—as a restriction of the personal human rights of all women (GARF f. 3316, op. 41, d. 82, ll. 1–2). An underground leaflet from 1939 signed by the National Labor Union of the New Generation urged: "Fight for the rights that Stalin has taken from you! Restoration of religion, political views, legality, and equality before the law is our aim. ... In respecting the rights and freedoms of others, one is strengthening his own rights and freedoms. ... Restoration of the right to work, freedom of occupation, and equality is our aim. ... All citizens of Russia must have the right to choose their work" (Reynolds 1984, Enclosure to report 10516 from 26 October 1939).

The concern of many citizens about individual and civil rights, the effective workings of the soviets, election reform, and the rule of law, as well as their political engagement, support the existence in Stalinist society of a liberal political subculture with democratic elements. An illiberal system still admitted a liberal subject with limited autonomy (Fitzpatrick 2005; Tikhomirov 2013, pp. 117–8).[18] The evidence of liberal discourse challenges the monolithic argument about "the death of liberal man in Stalinist Russia," articulated in debates on Stalinist subjectivity in historiography (Krylova 2000). Discussed here, pockets of liberal political culture, though marginal, add an alternative perspective to the view of indiscriminate consumption by society of the state's ideological production (Dobrenko et al. 2004, p. 700). The comments reflected creative, independent political engagement and rational attitudes to be distinguished from those praising Stalin's constitution, who originated in servile and emotional conformity, uncritically accepting everything emanating from the authorities. It is the democratic character of the constitution and a shift in official discourse that inspired these "liberal"

---

[17] "Clarifications about the Constitution."

[18] The letters to the regime, according to A. Tikhomirov, showed that the Soviet people conceptualized themselves not only as supplicants but also as individuals and citizens.

voices and allowed them to be heard in the summer and fall of 1936. The transient moment of discussion allowed "unsettled identities to consolidate" around one or another set of values. But the previous and later practices of the regime precluded this stratum of the population from becoming "a competent, self-confident, experienced body of citizens." They tended to remain "democratic aspirants" (Almond and Verba 1965, p. 25). Lacking proper experience in Stalin's USSR, they had few chances to develop their confidence and competence. The fake, demagogic democratism of the political system, as well as persecutions, led to the isolation of liberal elements in society. They still existed, however, in "the islands of separateness" such as professional and private life, as well as in religious and intellectual groups. As one of the correspondents warned in the discussion of 1936, these "aspirants" turned to the semi-underground. Only much later did dissidents generate peaceful activities to protect human rights, but this will come only in the 1960s and 1970s. These dissidents will make the constitution their banner.

REFERENCES

Alexopoulos, Golfo. 1997. "The Ritual Lament: A Narrative of Appeal in the 1920s and 1930s." *Russian History* 24 (1–2): 117–29.
———. 2006. "Soviet Citizenship, More or Less: Rights, Emotions, and States of Civic Belonging." *Kritika: Explorations in Russian and Eurasian History* 7 (3): 487–528.
Almond, Gabriel A., and Sidney Verba. 1965. *The Civic Culture: Political Attitudes and Democracy in Five Nations*. Newbury Park, CA: Sage.
Beetham, David. 1985. *Max Weber and the Theory of Modern Politics*. Cambridge, UK: Polity.
Berelowitch, Alexei, and Victor Danilov, eds. 2012. *Sovetskaia derevnia glazami VChK-OGPU-NKVD: Dokumenty i materialy*. Vol. 4. Moscow: ROSSPEN.
Brandenberger, David. 2011. *Propaganda State in Crisis. Soviet Ideology, Indoctrination and Terror Under Stalin, 1928–1941*. New Heaven: Yale University Press.
British Foreign Office—Russia Correspondence, 1781–1945. 1975. Wilmington, DE: Scholarly Resources.
Burbank, Jane. 2004. *Russian Peasants Go to Court: Legal Culture in the Countryside, 1905–1917*. Bloomington: Indiana University Press.
Chudakov, Alexander. 2012. *Lozhitsia mgla na starye stupeni*. Moscow: Vremia.
Clark, Katerina. 1998. *Petersburg: Crucible of Cultural Revolution*. Cambridge, MA: Harvard University Press.

Danilov, Viktor, Roberta Manning, and Lynne Viola. 1999. Vol. 2; 2002. Vol. 4. *Tragediia sovestskoi derevni: kollektivizatsiia I raskulachivanie: Dokumenty i materialy.* Moscow: ROSSPEN.
Dobkin, A. I. 1992. "Lishentsy, 1918–1936." In *Zvenia: Istoricheskii al'manakh.* Vol. 2, 600–10. Moscow: Feniks-Atheneum.
Dobrenko, E. A., Jesse Savage, and Gust Olson. 2004. "Socialism as Will and Representation, or What Legacy Are We Rejecting?" *Kritika: Explorations in Russian and Eurasian History* 5 (4): 675–708.
Dubin, Boris. 2010. "The Worth of Life and the Limits of Law: Russian Opinions on the Death Penalty, Russian Laws, and the System of Justice." *Russian Social Sciences Review* 51 (3): 69–88.
Figes, Orlando, and Boris Kolonitsky. 1999. *Interpreting the Russian Revolution: The Language and Symbols of 1917.* New Haven, CT: Yale University Press.
Fitzpatrick, Sheila. 1994. *Stalin's Peasants: Resistance and Survival in the Russian Village After Collectivization.* Oxford: Oxford University Press.
———. 1999. *Everyday Stalinism.* Oxford: Oxford University Press.
———. 2005. *Tear Off the Masks! Identity and Imposture in Twentieth-Century Russia.* Princeton, NJ: Princeton University Press.
Garros, Véronique, Natalia Korenevskaya, and Thomas Lahusen. 1997. *Intimacy and Terror: Soviet Diaries of the 1930s.* New York: New Press.
Geldern, James von, and Lewis Siegelbaum. 1935. "The Second Kolkhoz Charter." *Seventeen Moments in Soviet History.* http://soviethistory.msu.edu/1936-2/second-kolkhoz-charter/. Accessed September 22, 2017.
Getty, A. 1991. "State and Society Under Stalin: Constitutions and Elections in the 1930s." *Slavic Review* 50 (1): 18–35.
———. 2013a. *Practicing Stalinism: Bolsheviks, Boyars, and the Persistence of Tradition.* New Haven, CT: Yale University Press.
———. 2013b. "Pre-election Fever: The Origins of the 1937 Mass Operations." In *The Anatomy of Terror. Political Violence Under Stalin,* edited by J. Harris, 216–35. Oxford: Oxford University Press.
Gibson, James I., and Raymond M. Duch. 1993. "Emerging Democratic Values in Soviet Political Culture." In *Public Opinion and Regime Change: The New Politics of Post-Soviet Societies,* edited by Arthur H. Miller, William M. Reisinger, and Vicki L. Hesli. Boulder, CO: Westview.
Goldman, Wendy Z. 2007. *Terror and Democracy in the Age of Stalin.* Cambridge: Cambridge University Press.
Gosudarstvenny Arkhiv Rossiiskoi Federatsii (GARF) [State Archives of Russian Federation].
Harvard Project on the Soviet Social System. *Harvard College Library Digital Collection.* http://hcl.harvard.edu/collections/hpsss/index.html.
Hoffmann, David L. 2003. *Stalinist Values: The Cultural Norms of Soviet Modernity, 1917–1941.* Ithaca, NY: Cornell University Press.

Ivnitsky, N. A. 2004. *Sud'ba raskulachennukh v SSSR*. Moscow: Sobranie.
Izmozik, Vladlen S. 1996. "Voices from the Twenties: Private Correspondence Intercepted by the OGPU." *Russian Review* 55 (2): 287–308.
Khaustov, V., and L. Samuelson. 2010. *Stalin, NKVD i repressii, 1936–1938 gg*. Moscow: ROSSPEN.
Khlevniuk, Oleg. 2010. *Khoziain: Stalin i utyerzhdenie stalinskoi diktatury*. Moscow: ROSSPEN.
Klimin, I. I. 2007. *Rossiiskoe krest'ianstvo v gody novoi ekonomicheskoi politiki (1921–1927)*. Vol. 1. Saint-Petersburg: Izdatel'stvo Politekhnicheskogo universiteta.
Krassil'nikov, Sergei. 1998. *Na izlomah sotsial'noi struktury: Marginaly v poslerevolutsionnom rossiiskom obschestve (1917– konets 1930-h godov)*. Novosibirsk: NGU.
Krukova, Svetlana, ed. 2001. *Krestianskie istorii*. Moscow: ROSSPEN.
Krylova, Anna. 2000. "The Tenacious Liberal Subject in Soviet Studies." *Kritika: Explorations in Russian and Eurasian History* 1 (1): 119–46.
Kulakov, A. A., V. V. Smirnov, and L. P. Kolodnikova, eds. 2005. *Obshchestvo I vlast': Rossiiskaia provintsiai*. Vol. 2. Moscow: Institute Rossiiskoi Istorii RAN.
Kurliandsky, Igor. 2011. *Stalin, Vlast', Religia*. Moscow: Kuchkovo Pole.
Laursen, Eric. 2007. "Bad Words Are Not Allowed! Language and Transformation in Mikhail Bulgakov's *Heart of a Dog*." *Slavic and East European Journal* 51 (3): 491–513.
Livshin, A. Y., I. B. Orlov, and O. V. Khlevniuk, eds. 2002. *Pis'ma vo Vlast', 1928–1939*. Moscow: ROSSPEN.
Lukin, Alexander. 2000. *The Political Culture of the Russian "Democrats"*. Oxford: Oxford University Press.
Male, Donald J. 1971. *Russian Peasant Organization Before Collectivization: A Study of Commune and Gathering, 1925–1930*. Cambridge: Cambridge University Press.
Meerovich, M. 2008. *Nakazanie Zhilischem: Zhilischnaia politika v SSSR kak sredstvo upravleniia liud'mi (1917–1937 gody)*. Moscow: ROSSPEN.
Orlov, I. B., and E. O. Dolgova. 2008. *Politicheskaia kul'tura rossiian v XX veke: Preemstvennost' I razryvy*. Sergiev Posad: SPGI.
Pavlova, I. V. 2003. "1937. Vybory kak mistifikatsia, terror kak real'nost'." *Voprosy Istorii* 10: 19–37.
Pokrovsky, N. N., V. P. Danilov, S. A. Krassil'nikov, and L. Viola, eds. 2006. *Politburo and Krestianstvo: Vysylka, Spetsposelenie, 1930–1940*. Vol. 2. Moscow: ROSSPEN.
Prishvin, M. M. 2010. *Diaries, 1936–1937*. Saint-Petersburg: Rostok.
Reynolds, Dale. 1984. *U. S. Military Intelligence Reports: Soviet Union, 1919–1941*. Frederick, MD: University Publications of America.

Rittersporn, Gábor. 2014. *Anguish, Anger, and Folkways in Soviet Russia.* Pittsburgh: University of Pittsburgh Press.
Rossiisky Gosudarstvenny Archiv Sotsial'noi Politicheskoi Istorii (RGASPI) [Russian State Archives of Social and Political History].
RSFSR Constitution. 1918. *Marxists Internet Archive.* https://www.marxists.org/history/ussr/government/constitution/1918/article4.htm. Accessed November 23, 2015.
Selischev, A. M. 1928. *Yazyk revolutsionnoi epokhi: Iz nabliudenii nad russkim yazykom (1917–1926).* Moscow: Rabotnik Prosvescheniia.
Shaporina, Liubov'. 2012. *Dnevnik.* Vol. 1. Moscow: NLO.
———. 2017. *Dnevnik.* Vol. 2. Moscow: NLO.
Smith, S. A. 1998. "The Social Meaning of Swearing: Workers and Bad Language in Late Imperial and Early Soviet Russia." *Past and Present* 160 (1): 167–202.
———. 2002. *The Russian Revolution: A Very Short Introduction.* Oxford: Oxford University Press.
Sokolov, Andrei, ed. 1998. *Obschestvo i vlast'. 1930e gody.* Moscow: ROSSPEN.
Solomon, Peter H. 1996. *Soviet Criminal Justice Under Stalin.* Cambridge: Cambridge University Press.
Stalin, I. V. 1947. *Doklad o proekte konstitutsii SSSR.* Moscow: OGIZ.
Taylor, Charles. 1989. *Sources of the Self: The Making of Modern Identity.* Cambridge: Cambridge University Press.
Tikhomirov, Alexey. 2013. "The Regime of Forced Trust: Making and Breaking Emotional Bonds Between People and State in Soviet Russia, 1917–1941." *Slavonic and East European Review* 91 (1): 117–8.
Tsentral'ny Gosudarstvenny Arkhiv Istoriko–politicheskikh Dokumentov Sankt-Peterburga (TsGAIPD SPb) [Central State Archives of Historical–Political Documents in Saint-Petersburg].
Tsentral'ny Gosudarstvenny Arkhiv Kinofotofonodokumentov Sankt-Peterburga (TsGAKFFD SPb) [Central State Archives of Documentary Films, Photographs, and Sound Recordings of Saint-Petersburg].
Velikanova, Olga. 2013. *Popular Perceptions of Soviet Politics in the 1920s: Disenchantment of the Dreamers.* Basingstoke, UK: Palgrave Macmillan.
Viola, Lynne. 2007. *The Unknown Gulag: The Lost World of Stalin's Special Settlements.* Oxford: Oxford University Press.
Yekelchyk, Serhy. 2014. *Stalin's Citizens: Everyday Politics in the Wake of Total War.* Oxford: Oxford University Press.
Zorkaia, Natalia. 2010. "'Nostalgia for the Past', or What Lessons Young People Could Have Learned and Did Learn." *Russian Social Science Review* 51 (2): 4–31.

CHAPTER 10

Voices Against Liberties

Among the polyphony of opinions, two major pattern-driven currents existed—liberal versus antiliberal. The clamor for civil rights and support for the innovations of the constitution contrasted with mass disapproval of the new liberties, demands for continuing segregation of the "former people," and strengthening of punishments—a major finding of this research that deserves analysis and will get full attention in this chapter.

But first a few reservations about the opinions should be discussed here. As soon as the constitution was granted from above to the population, its support among the masses swung toward maximization as many swam with the tide, uncritically accepting everything emanating from the top, sometimes even without understanding—for example, the concept of the secret vote. This phenomenon is well known to sociologists. But opposition to the liberal principles of the constitution should logically have had a reverse tendency, toward minimization, as nonconformists swam against the tide and had to overcome the frustration and danger of defying the powers above. Protests against liberties conflicted with the official truth manifested in the constitution, and with Stalin himself. In our attempt to analyze these two trends, we should keep in mind these pressures—of loyalty and fear, conformity and individual reasoning. It is noteworthy that the widespread mood of rejection of the "holy" constitution was not reported by the People's Commissariat for Internal Affairs (NKVD) or party observers as anti-Soviet or disloyal. In contrast, unauthorized meetings of believers to discuss the constitution, though absolutely legal, were reported as suspicious. Apparently, blatant constitutional freedoms did not live alongside the cultural code that ruled the perceptions and behavior of activists and reporting officials.

The expansion of the franchise met extremely articulate opposition. Rejection of this innovation reflected a high intolerance and hostility in society against the people defined as "enemies" or as "others"—for example, "former people," clergy, and individual homestead farmers. Starting from the Civil War, the new Soviet identity was promoted through an official incitement of class hatred and the planting of images of internal and external enemies. When the constitution annulled a pillar of Soviet identity—internal foes—it met numerous protests. In my records, 108 comments, and 7.7% in Smolensk, 17% in Leningrad, and 30.6% in Gorky *krai*, were against expansion of the franchise to former "enemies." Article 135 stated, "Elections of deputies are universal: all citizens of the USSR irrespective of race or nationality, religion, educational and residential qualifications, social origin, property status, or past activities, have the right to vote in the election of deputies and to be elected." Arch Getty generalized that "in rural areas, and indeed across the USSR, around 17 per cent of all suggestions represented a protest against allowing formerly disenfranchised persons ... to vote," but the origin of this number is not clear. In the information *svodka* no. 3/13 from 1 November 1936, Article 135 got 4716 suggestions (10.8%) and Part XI, "Elections System," got 6369 comments (14.6%) out of 43,427 calculated comments, but in any event these numbers included both *protests and approvals* (Getty 2013, p. 210; GARF f. 3316, op. 8, d. 222, ll. 123, 158). Half—48%—of the 4716 comments argued with Stalin's thesis that the class structure of Soviet society had changed, that classes were emancipated and entirely transformed, with no political contradictions between them. And he heard this message. This opposition, counter to the "sacred" constitution, provides us with one more important argument about popular opinions. If, generally, comments in the discussion are a priori assumed to have been manipulated by the official framework, through intimidation, propaganda, and selection, and as such tended to be more supportive and celebratory, the *counter*-constitutional utterances, sometimes arguing with Stalin himself, undermine the universality of such an assumption. The large group of comments criticizing Stalin's thesis of social conciliation seems more independent than those voices glorifying the constitution as a "gift" of the Great Stalin to Soviet citizens.

Arguing with the constitution, these citizens insisted on the preservation of hostile anti-Soviet attitudes in the population: "Former merchants, kulaks, and other exploiters have not yet transformed themselves and forgotten their former wealth. During elections they can propagate their views and attract unstable, hesitant citizens. Former people should be restricted in their rights" (Kulakov et al. 2005, p. 428; GARF f. 3316, op. 41, d. 126, l. 147). Such aggressive intolerance predominated over the voices of inclusion and reconciliation: "I agree with the article. ... Many former people became new people and participate in the construction of socialism" (Fitzpatrick 1999, p. 179; Getty 1991, pp. 26–7; GARF f. 3316, op. 41, d. 184, l. 63). The major popular argument against enfranchisement and reconciliation with former enemies was fear of vengeance from the kulaks if elected to soviets: "I believe that now things will be very bad for those who were activists during dekulakization and kulaks' elimination. If a kulak comes to power, he will harass the activists, as he still has a big hatred" (GARF f. 3316, op. 40, d. 14, l. 33).[1] Another important argument was the collective farmers' unwillingness to return kulaks' property. The peasant Chimorodov wrote to a newspaper: "I can't understand one question. Our village soviet started mass returns of possessions—homes, gardens—to former kulaks, speculators, and other people harmful for Soviet power. ... Soviet administration seized all this from kulaks and speculators in favor of *kolkhoz*. Now the soviet returns these things to them. They told me it's according to the text of Stalin's constitution" (GARF f. 3316, op. 40, d. 14, l. 57; RGASPI f. 78, op. 1, d. 593, l. 138).[2] In Cherkessia, returned deportees seized their property back by force. In Shabal'insk *raion*, Kirov *krai*, *kolkhozes* accepted peasants who returned without permission from a special settlement: the Balyberdin family, Seleznev family, the Kozlovs, and the Valegzhanins got back their houses, estates, property, and cows. The NKVD reported eight such episodes and deported those families back to special settlements (Berelowitch and Danilov 2012, pp. 285, 287). In Borisovka, Kursk *oblast'*, 75 houses were returned to the dekulakized according to the constitution, and 134 kulaks had their voting rights restored. In the fall next year, however, during the show trial against local officials, the party secretary in Borisovka, Fedosov, was charged

---

[1] K. E. Porkhomenko, Western *oblast'*, Gordeevsky *raion*.
[2] V. N. Chimorodov, Voronezh *oblast'*, Troitsky soviet.

with exactly these concessions (Fitzpatrick 1994, p. 307), which—now that the earlier optimistic view of society had changed—were considered reconciliation with the class enemies. Several times during these trials peasants witnessed that kulaks, accepted to *kolkhoz*, had taken revenge on the activists. The deportee V. F. Kulygin, from Kirov *krai*, wrote that it was too early to restore the civil rights of all exiled kulaks: "Many, especially the elders, resist personal transformation and remain hostile to Soviet rule" (GARF f. 3316, op. 41, d. 86, ll. 2a, verso, 2b, verso).[3] Such warnings undoubtedly attracted the attention of the chronically suspicious Stalin. The arguments of the protesters reflected deep layers of the popular mentality, the influence of propaganda, and often personal interests. Beneficiaries of the previous policies opposed the new shift. The practices of the Civil War—ruptures of legality, violence—were sustained during collectivization and now echoed again in the social disagreement surrounding the constitution.

Objections to conferring electoral rights on former class enemies were so numerous that high government spokespersons had to respond. The Central Executive Committee (TsIK) officer I. A. Akulov, in his article in *Izvestia*, dismissed these objections because "they took no account of the fact that the task of building a classless socialist society had been already fulfilled, and so respectively no more class struggle occurred in the USSR" (*Izvestia* 23 November 1936). In his speech published in July, M. Kalinin, was more circumlocutional in answering the critics:

> By giving electoral rights to our antagonists ... we are allowing them to take part in public life. ... There is no doubt that the restoration of electoral rights will not increase the number of our enemies. Naturally, the declared enemies of the Soviet rule will endeavor to increase their counter-revolutionary work. But on the other hand ... those who, as *lishentsy*, were denied the possibility of demonstrating clearly that they were for the Soviet government will join the ranks of the workers as fully enfranchised builders of the socialist society. Not only so, but the universality of the elections will make it possible to distinguish and expose the direct enemies of the Soviet rule. (*Izvestia* 6 July 1936)

---

[3] Such a denunciation from a special settler should be taken critically as the deportees' letters were read by the commandants. The letters were often a means to demonstrate loyalty and earn some privileges in the brutal, unfree conditions of exile. The warnings, however, about hidden enemies were copious.

Such a message opened the door for opportunists and intimidated those who dared to canvass for nonparty candidates.

Finally, the supreme leader answered these concerns at the 8th Congress of Soviets and rejected the idea that former White Guards, kulaks, and priests, if allowed to vote, would present a threat to the Soviet rule. He added ominously that even if these enemies were elected, party officials would be responsible because they had conducted their propaganda poorly (Stalin 1947, p. 30).[4] "If our agitation work will be conducted in the strong Bolshevik way, then people won't let inimical persons enter supreme power organs. It means we should work, not complain, but work hard." This statement of rejection demonstrated, first, that Stalin had heard the people's forewarnings about the threat of the remaining enemies; second, that he believed in the might of propaganda and ideology; and third, his desire to intimidate officials and urge them to work hard.

Stalin's statement conflicted with the letter of the new law and put party officials in a predicament: what should they do if people elect a religious person to a soviet? This is lawful according to the constitution but unwanted according to Stalin's statement. They could easily pay with their lives for the wrong reading of the official message. A peasant, Anna Manuilova, a member of the soviet in the village of Zolotovo, Moscow *oblast'*, wrote to the TsIK in April 1937 that the village administrators blamed her for attending church. "Stalin's Constitution announces freedom of religion and the right of religious persons to vote and be elected. Is it harmful if I, a member of the soviet, attend church or pray at home? I do my work in the soviet well. The chair of the *kolkhoz* answered me at the meeting that I am wrong in connecting religion with the constitution. I asked him directly: Should we elect to the soviet only nonbelievers? Are believers our enemies and should not be elected to the soviets? He answered that I am wrong. Who is right? Who is wrong here?" (RGASPI f. 78, op. 1, d. 592, l. 29). We do not know the TsIK answer. But a logical conclusion for the local officials would be to prevent the nomination and election of newly enfranchised people to the soviets *by any means*—including their elimination.

The persistence of the protests against extending the franchise suggests that the divisive Bolshevik class ideology had a strong reverberation

---

[4] Citation translated by David Priestland (2007, p. 346).

in society. The language and arguments of popular comments parroted official rhetoric from the past and demonstrated so deep an entrenchment of revolutionary values in the public mind that these irreconcilables dared to oppose the new course of politics and criticize Stalin's constitution. These aggressive voices denied freedom of the press, assembly, and speech for "enemies" and former people (2% in Getty's data). Responding to numerous fears that the enemies could use the liberties to obstruct the construction of socialism, the article "Freedom of Assembly" by M. Katanian in *Izvestia* explained that the new constitution granted not freedom in general, but freedom corresponding only to the interests of the working people and designed to strengthen the socialist order.

> There cannot be meetings of criminals—monarchists, Mensheviks, social revolutionaries, and so on. ... [Anyway], the ranks of such people grow thinner every day; they are an insignificant minority. ... The people who are not allowed to make use of these liberties are dying out, for they have no basis for existence. The Soviet state will continue to wage untiring warfare with the relics of capitalism, crushing [them] on the one hand, ... and on the other hand, [it will] reeducate, remold such people, by absorbing them into the general constructive work of our country. For the convening of meetings, no special permission will be required ... though the representatives will apply to those who are in charge of the premises and must make a declaration regarding the placing of these premises at their disposal. (*Izvestia* 6 August 1936)

Thus outlining the limitations, Katanian assured the doubters that everything was under control. It was, however, nearly impossible for officials to interpret and convey the meaning of the constitution to the "laypeople," to explain the new political turn without calling danger on their heads.

Those irreconcilables who objected to the new freedoms could pursue their personal interests—the activists, for example, could protect their benefits and positions, or they could be true believers, defending socialist principles as they understood them. Regardless, inertia could frame popular actions: people possibly found difficulty adjusting to rapid shifts in ideology. The Marxian dictum about the perfectibility of man and society, inherited from the Enlightenment, was epitomized in the constitution's optimistic view on the transformation of "enemies." But many participants in the discussion were inflexible and stubborn, adhering to the well-internalized connection between class origin and political views and disbelieving in the conversion of former people. The narrative of omnipresent enemies held sway among local and central authorities. Debating the inclusive message of the new constitution, popular comments tellingly omit the Christian virtue of forgiveness of former "enemies." Modern surveys confirm that the refusal to believe in the repentance of a criminal, and to forgive him if he has indeed repented, is "notably and unequivocally prevalent" in all strata of the Russian population today (Dubin 2010, p. 80).

Among the possible motives of this irreconcilable position could be a lack of understanding in the minds of the common people. A young female student, for example, told an interviewer after the war that a government should grant freedom of the press. But when asked specifically about the role of government in relation to the press, she answered: "It is the government's responsibility to close down papers that are against the system. Everything must be done on democratic principles, but within the framework of a definite control. Government must see to it that the press tells the truth and does not publish lies or fantasies. Everything that appears in the press must correspond to reality" (HPSSS Schedule A, Vol. 12, Case 145, p. 59). This was a quite common view of liberal freedoms—accessible to the majority, but restricted for the enemies. Such liberties as permission to trade and have a small garden plot were sometimes considered a retreat to capitalism and betrayal of the Revolution. One feature of these protests was a lack of reverence typical of many encomiums to the constitution, which indicates the genuineness of opinion. People vacillated between the new official norms and what they observed in everyday practice.

Protests were numerous against the legalization of the individual out-*kolkhoz* households confirmed in Article 9, which was incompatible with the true believers' understanding of socialism. The individual farmers, recognized in the constitution as equal to *kolkhozniks*, were often targets of hostility in the discussion. *Edinolichniki*—an entrepreneurial market-oriented group numbering between 7 and 10% of the peasantry[5]—resisted collectivization and remained out of the *kolkhoz*

---

[5] The Election Information Bulletin in September 1937 evaluated this group as 10%. Fitzpatrick characterized this social group and evaluated it as 7% (Fitzpatrick 1994, pp. 153–8).

system (GARF f. 1235, op. 76, d. 158, l. 11). They were discriminated against by heavy taxes. The constitution's step toward independents was in opposition to the previous official course—to strangle this group by taxes and administrative pressure. In a July 1934 Kremlin meeting, Stalin called for an offensive on individual peasants "in order to relieve *kolkhozniks* from hesitation [about staying in the *kolkhoz*]." At the Second Congress of Outstanding Kolkhozniks in February 1935, Ya. A. Yakovlev, head of the Central Committee's (CC) agriculture department and an editor of *Krestianskaia Gazeta*, claimed in his report that "it was the government's aim to enroll all the peasantry in collective farms, not to retain the present division of the village into *kolkhozniks* and independents" (Danilov et al. 2002, pp. 12–3; Fitzpatrick 1994, p. 125). In 1935, *edinolichniki* complained in great numbers about taxes and state obligations, which increased by a factor of 9 to 22, ruining their households (Danilov et al. 2002, pp. 476, 560–4). In 1936, this official line underlied a large number of comments that demanded eliminating the stratum of individual households: "Individual farmers provoke the gullible *kolkhozniks* [to believe] that individual life is better. We should eliminate those who hinder us from building a classless socialist society" (GARF f. 3316, op. 41, d. 207, ll. 180, 197; d. 147, l. 52; op. 40, d. 40, ll. 31, 94; RGASPI f. 17, op. 120, d. 232, l. 50; f. 5, op. 1, d. 232, ll. 50, 65–7; TsGAIPD SPb f. 24, op. 2v, d. 1772, ll. 17, 54). Peasants who succumbed to forced collectivization, joined *kolkhozes*, and suffered from their ineffectiveness were antagonized by the out-*kolkhoz* farmers' relative independence and efficiency. Tense relations and internal scores often divided these two parties in the village. In their intolerance and envy, collectivized peasants demonstrated the old communal conformism, collectivism, and egalitarianism. Boris Mironov sees these features of popular culture cultivated in patriarchal families and rural communes as a source of Soviet authoritarianism (Mironov 1994, p. 54). Peasants, though unhappy with the *kolkhoz* system, did not accept peace with the disturbers of the community and uniformity. The *kolkhozniks*' discontent with liberalism in relation to independent farmers—a minority group in the rural world—was echoed in the pronouncements of local officials: "Remnants of class enemies praise the constitution and its article about out-*kolkhoz* farmers. They propagandize that after the constitution's adoption the land will be returned to the independent farmers and their taxes will be waived. By doing that, the class enemy pushes peasants to leave the *kolkhoz*. Such departures were already reported" (Kulakov et al. 2005, p. 386).[6]

At the very top level, Stalin addressed this mass demand in his report at the 8th Congress of Soviets in November 1936 when he reviewed popular comments: "Besides collective farmers among the peasants there are more than one million individual households. What to do with them? Do the authors of this demand suggest that we discard them? It would be unreasonable" (Stalin 1947, p. 24). In spite of Stalin's intervention in defense of *edinolichniki*, the constitution's adoption did not bring an end to excommunicative policies toward them. Official pressure continued and encouraged local administrators and envious neighbors to squeeze *edinolichniki* out of the village. By the end of the decade, the tax burden and ostracism had eliminated this social group.

10.1 Religious Liberties: Popular and Government Views

Aggression toward sanctioned minorities can be read as an indication of authoritarian-type political culture. After individual farmers, another target of antifranchise fever in the constitution discussion was the clergy (GARF f. 3316, op. 8, d. 222, l. 26 verso, 58). The Gorky *krai* soviet by 16 October claimed to have received "around 1,000" anticlerical comments and no approvals out of 4000 systematized suggestions (Kulakov et al. 2005, p. 425); such round numbers, however, may raise concern about their precision. The TsIK received 1061 objections from individuals to the voting rights for clerics plus 730 that were announced at the meetings (80% of antifranchise objections). Another 20% of protests—448 (including 384 individual recommendations)—denied voting rights to "exes," kulaks, "exploiters," White Army and tsarist police officers, prison inmates, and individual farmers (GARF f. 3316, op. 8, d. 226, ll. 154, 120–76).[7] The TsIK reported a similar proportion

---

[6] Speech by the chair of the Gorky *krai* soviet executive committee about preparation for the soviets' congresses, 28 September 1936.

[7] The Information *svodka* 3/13 of Presidium TsIK from 15 October 1936 summarized the materials from the republics, provincial soviets, and 505 central and local newspapers, speeches at the meetings, and individual and collective letters addressed to various institutions and the Presidium itself.

in the *svodka* from 22 July 1936: 52 suggestions against the clergy and 28 against all "former people" (GARF f. 3316, op. 41, d. 207, l. 152). Practical considerations could rationalize the segregation of this second group. Exiled kulaks returning home, for example, threatened the economic interests of the villagers who benefited from dekulakization because kulaks demanded and often seized back their homes and property. It seemed reasonable to perceive former military and police officers as a threat. But the question of why peaceful priests became a target of mass ostracism needs deliberation. This subchapter examines the attitudes to religion and priests in light of the new freedoms.

Previous constitutions of 1918 and 1925 declared freedom of conscience, antireligious and religious propaganda. The last freedom was restricted in 1929 and was not restored in 1936. Despite the old constitutions' provisions, antireligious propaganda and persecutions prevailed in state politics in the 1920s and 1930s, with periods of relative moderation between five subsequent waves of persecutions: the Civil War, 1922, 1929, 1937, and 1958. In the official narrative, the fight with religion was couched in terms of modernization, as a drive for enlightenment and rationalism. A religious worldview was seen as incompatible with communist ideology. A political element in the justification was that the Orthodox Church was a pillar of the monarchy and ally of the Whites in the Civil War. Nineteen years after the Revolution, the real goal of the antireligious campaign and repressions was more social discipline and engineering rather than modernization. The dictatorship saw religion as "dangerous" because of "its informal and uncontrolled nature, which could not be tolerated in authoritarian society" (Panchenko 2012, p. 336).

After splitting the institutional hierarchy of the Patriarchate into Tikhon's branch and Renovationists at the beginning of the 1920s, and a "concordat" with the Soviet state—agreed to by the Metropolitan Sergy in 1927—the most disastrous year for ground-level religion was 1929. The Politburo resolution from 24 January 1929 on intensification of antireligious work was grounded in Stalin's determination to end religion as a part of his "socialist offensive" policy. The secret party CC instruction "Enhancing Antireligious Work," from February 1929, launched the new wave of repressions and arbitrary closures of churches. The fateful government decree "On Religious Organizations," from 8 April 1929, regulated the life of parishes. It requested registration of all members, permission for all activities, and forbade charity and pilgrimages. The decree tried to legally structure the arbitrariness at the grassroots level and centralize control. Gregory Freeze defines the government strategy since 1929 as "to unfetter grass-roots radicalism to combat counterrevolutionary religious circles", but hold "local zealots in check, insisting upon both popular assent and official endorsement" from the TsIK commission (Freeze 1998, pp. 215, 219). Despite the decree's article no. 36, however, that churches' "liquidation can be authorized only by a motivated decree of the Central Executive Committees," the churches were often closed in haste, breaking existing laws, with the decision taken by only the village soviet, and accompanied by confiscation of valuables and arrests of the priests. This was not new. In the previous period of church closures, the zeal of local powers and the Young Communist League (Komsomol) to quickly put an end to religion often conflicted with the letter of the law. The party congresses in 1923 and 1924 repeatedly warned against excessive use of administrative measures by local militants in closing the houses of worship.

The TsIK Cults Commission under P. A. Krasikov operated between 1930 and 1938 and pursued similar attempts to somehow regulate arbitrariness at the village level. Designed to supervise the law in relation to the church and to regulate religious life, the commission repeatedly communicated the grievances of the believers and cases of breaking the law to the CC VKPb and to the procurator general, and reprimanded local organs for many severe law violations in relation to priests and believers—but without success.

In May 1936, the TsIK and Cults Commission directed a circular to local powers with a demand to stop "fighting religious beliefs by administrative measures" (meaning violence and unlawfulness). They warned that those breaking the law by closing churches without TsIK approval would be severely punished. The commission disapproved of the liquidation of 15% of churches in 1934 and 1935, and 36 and 32% in 1936 and 1937 respectively, but it was not very effective—both high authorities and locals in most cases ignored it, or sometimes resisted (Odintsov 2014, pp. 211–3; Fitzpatrick 1999, p. 119). The Soviet government first ignited "revolutionary" ardor on the local level, and then tried to bridle it by commissions and law.

Pondering these attempts at control from above, Sheila Fitzpatrick suggested that "these repeated calls for tolerance ... are evidence not just of the party leaders' moderation and rationality on the question of religion but also—and perhaps more importantly—of the *lack* of tolerance and militant antireligious zest of the party's rank and file" (Fitzpatrick 1994, p. 34). The popular rage against priests articulated in the discussion of the constitution matched the local authorities' practice of "sabotaging" any periodic attempts to regulate religion ordered from the center. Freeze assumes that there was internal discord in the center about methods of antireligious work between the militant League of the Godless (a sponsored public organization) and the moderate CC Antireligious Commission, abolished in December 1929 when all-out secularization began (Freeze 1998, p. 214). Activists and local soviets often relied on their revolutionary instincts, rather than the letter of the law, when they closed churches without legal procedure, capriciously overtaxed the priests, and generally tended to overdo the laws in favor of restriction and prohibition.

Numerous official reports about the revival of religious activities following the constitution's publication may reflect the "regime's obsession with purported subversion by churchmen and believers after the introduction of the new constitution" as "the only organized alternative group able to collective action with highly developed infrastructure and communication network" (Rittersporn 2014, p. 156; Rittersporn et al. 2003, p. 442). Official reports of the Cults Commission, People's Commissariat for Internal Affairs (NKVD) documents, and individual letters confirm the objective increase of religious activities in connection with the constitution (Freeze 1998, pp. 210, 212, 227, 232).[8] After years of hard persecutions, priests and believers happily greeted Article 124, which confirmed freedom of conscience and was read as a promise to reverse the official repressive policy. Only a few skeptics pointed out acidly that religious freedom granted by the previous Constitution of 1925 was not implemented and so churchgoers should not believe in the new constitution (GARF f. 5263, op. 1, d. 32, l. 9; Prishvin 2010, pp. 384, 388). The former Archimandrite of the Kiev-Pechory monastery, P. Ivanov, wrote to the Cults Commission: "Citizens of the USSR had already had these rights according to the previous constitution … but in reality it was open harassment and persecution. … That's why believers do not trust both Article 124 and the whole constitution." Among

---

[8] The security organs and trade unions continuously reported the rise of religious activities, a surge in sectarianism and religiosity in the 1920s, religious opposition and resistance in 1930–1931 and in 1935, driven primarily by the systematic closing of churches, and occasionally with the approach of Easter.

most parishioners, however, the constitution produced new hope, as statistics of the Cults Commission show. In July 1936, the number of petitions (some had 700 signatures) increased by 8.5% compared to the same period in 1935; the number of visitors to the commission increased by 53%. The next month, the number of petitions increased by 36% compared to the previous year, and there was a 95% increase in visitors. In these petitions and complaints, demands to reopen the churches dominated—at 37.7% (1965 petitions). Complaints about overtaxation comprised 18.1% (945). Believers demanding freedoms were more active than the intolerants opposing freedoms: in July and August, the commission received 2318 complaints from the believers, while the TsIK received 52 suggestions against the clergy and religion in July and 1791 in five months (GARF f. 5263, op. 1, d. 32, ll. 84, 89, 91). The NKVD reported:

> Recently in connection with the publication of the draft of the new constitution, one sees an intensification of the activity of the clergy and religious people (to open previously closed churches, create new religious communes, and prevent closing of churches). In this case, the clergy exploit the draft of the new constitution in an anti–Soviet direction; they assemble signatures in villages and prepare declarations to organs of authority, requesting the opening of churches. (Freeze 1998, p. 228)

Having read the draft, parishes started religious processions praying for rain during drought, and some reopened churches without permission (Berelowitch and Danilov 2012, pp. 285, 341–2). The tone of their demands became more persistent: "Bring Article 124 to life and restrict the arbitrariness of the local authorities. Stop harassment of believers and the arbitrary taxation of the church!" Chernov from Virsk in Bashkir republic demanded: "1. Article 124 should be implemented better, rein in local authorities' arbitrariness [*postavit' v ramki*]. 2. Do not overtax the churches and clergy, but establish a percentage taxation. 3. Forbid harassment of church, clergy, and believers. 4. Allow free meetings of believers, church councils, and services at homes without the need of formal permits. 5. Do not allow pressure on workers and employees for their beliefs. 6. Do not close churches by administrative pressure without the consent of a parish." Priest M. Sorokoumovsky sent the list of 22 demands to the Cults Commission (GARF f. 3316, op. 8, d. 222, l. 139; f. 5263, op. 1, d. 32, ll. 11, 9, 83–6). Parishioners requested the freeing of arrested priests and believers, and former clerics asked for access to jobs previously barred to them. Religious people pressed authorities to reopen the churches by mass petitions, by mass demonstrations at the soviets sessions, or by strikes. In the village of Naryshkino, Gorky *krai*, collective farmers demanding the reopening of the church did not go to the fields to harvest (Kulakov et al. 2005, p. 960). Believers wanted nothing more than what the new constitution declared, but local authorities and the NKVD interpreted and reported these requests as undermining activities and arrested church people, as in Voronezh *oblast'*, who demanded opening the churches. When the believers and their priests in Valdai and in Saratov *krai* organized 33 religious processions in July to pray for rain, they faced repression and fines. The priest was surprised: "The Constitution announces the processions' freedom, but they fined me. Why?" (Berelowitch and Danilov 2012, pp. 274, 280–1, 322, 342, 351; GARF f. 5263, op. 1, d. 32, l. 8).

Opposing those voices supporting the liberalization of religious policy, intolerant comments comprised a large part of the discussion. What were their arguments? The militant activists raised their voices and rejected religious liberties. They argued that the church was an old enemy that fought against the Revolution and that the priests did not contribute their labor to the construction of socialism. They were scared that priests elected to soviets could seek revenge on their persecutors. The Red Army soldier Kalganov objected to the franchise because the priests were traitors of working people, and in the future war they may betray the socialist fatherland (GARF f. 3316, op. 8, d. 225, ll. 92–3; f. 3316, op. 40, d. 40, l. 103; d. 15, l. 121; RGASPI f. 89, op. 4, d. 55, l. 19; f. 17, op. 120, d. 232, l. 71; TsGAIPD SPb f. 4000, op. 7, d. 1176, ll. 13, 24). Antifranchisement demands were complemented by numerous suggestions that all houses of worship should be closed and remodeled into cultural institutions (16 demands, TsIK). Freedom of religious rituals, especially baptism and circumcision, should be limited (280, TsIK), religious propaganda should be persecuted (seven, TsIK), religious education of children and priests forbidden, and priests and their children (together with former kulaks and criminals) should be excluded from military service[9] (GARF f. 1235, op. 76, d. 153, l. 124; f. 3316, op. 8, d. 225, l. 72). Indeed, almost all of these limitations were in force

---

[9] As unreliable groups to access the weaponry.

previously and numerous discussants quite belligerently demanded their continuation.

The evidence of exasperation against the priests, church, and religion is interesting when seen against the high degree of religiosity of the population. Two months later, in the January 1937 census, 57% of the USSR's population claimed to be believers. Historiography debates the level of popular religiosity in the 1930s—was it still high or had it decreased? Most scholars think the real number of believers was even higher, as heated covert conversations took place among believers on the eve of the census about whether they should conceal or announce their faith to the census taker. The tendency to hide religiosity prevailed as a means to avoid expected repression, deprivation of rations, and so forth (TsGAIPD SPb f. 24, op. 2v, d. 2486, ll. 36–7, 62, 83). Karpov, the counter in the census, reported to his superiors: "When you ask about religion, the masses answer with great caution and distrust. They consider that it is a trap: if they register as believers—then they can be persecuted. It's better to register as a disbeliever. The populace is in confusion" (GARF f. 3316, op. 29, d. 793, l. 27, verso).

The question about religious affiliation was included in the census at Stalin's insistence. He personally approved the final version of questionnaire. The instruction for counters directed the question toward "current convictions" rather than the religion given to a person by his parents (Schloegel 2012, p. 113). The organizers obviously wanted to know about the progress of secularization and the effectiveness of their antireligious policies. This particular question caused nervousness and even protests in society. On the eve of the census, eight Leningrad workers wrote to the TsIK:

> We ask you to cancel the question about religion in the census. The Constitution granted us freedom of conscience, and rituals, but this question will push many believers to tell untruths, because before the Constitution it was persecuted. Accordingly, many distrust not only mere mortals, but even high officials and party people. You know that in ancient Rome, even the great persecutors of Religion did not use such means to search out believers. We ask you to convey our request to comrade Stalin and to cancel this question in the census. This is a great injustice and God will punish the guilty. (RGASPI f. 78, op. 1, d. 592, n.p.)

Such testimonies reveal the logic behind hiding religiosity, and display the high level of anxiety and mistrust of the state and constitution at the grassroots level.

Evidencing the persistence of religiosity in the 1930s, peasants did not work in the fields on religious holidays. Services still remained in great demand in society, as Arzhilovsky witnessed as a census counter: "The phantom of religion is still alive; even the clergy can make a living. ... In spite of 20 years of reeducation, some people are still religious, and when they come to the census question about religion they give a straightforward answer: believer. Old allegiances, old habits" (Garros et al. 1997, pp. 23, 132, 135).[10] The NKVD *svodki* reported great respect for exiled priests among deported peasants. Exiled to the Far East, deportees refused to work on religious holidays, though deprived of all liberties and under threat of repression and hunger. A crowd of 200 persons requested permission to attend church and asked for a priest to be sent to them (Pokrovsky et al. 2006, pp. 54, 924).

Every time the threat of oppression receded, folk religiosity immediately revived: we see it in the summer of 1936, and during emigration when some former Soviet young people converted (HPSSS Schedule A, Vol. 1, Case 6, pp. 38–40; Vol. 23, Case 470, pp. 41–2; Vol. 14, Case 240, p. 40). Churches were reopened by the population in the territories that had been occupied by the Nazis. In 1955, many adults were baptized (Shaporina 2017, p. 323) and many turned to religion during perestroika. All this shows the resilience of faith in peasant culture despite repressions and modernization. Stephen Smith posits that the onslaught of modernization itself and the specifics of the Russian crisis activated the "magic resources of popular culture" (Smith 2005, pp. 300–2).

An alternative view in historiography opposes this interpretation of the higher rates of religiosity in the USSR and the resulting conclusion about the failure of state propaganda. I. Kurliandsky argues that the antireligious campaign was generally successful, especially among the youth, city dwellers, and the Komsomol (Kurliandsky 2011, p. 486). He suggests that in the census, many people registered as believers only because they were baptized, but were actually not active churchgoers. It is logical that as the local church was closed, people could not attend it and open religious observance inevitably declined because of the lack of priests and

---

[10] See diary of Frolov; diary of Arzhilovsky.

churches (exactly as Bolshevik visionaries anticipated). Soviet statistics confirmed the decline of religion, as expected at the top. In 1934, a survey in the Black Earth *oblast' kolkhozy* found that in the adult group, only 38% of women and 10% of men were still carrying out religious rituals, but in the youth group only 12% of women and 1% of men were doing so (Fitzpatrick 1994, p. 205). Statistics, however, measured outward ritual observance, not inner beliefs. In the census, 45% of youth claimed to be believers. Furthermore, we should take the accuracy of all Soviet surveys and statistics with a grain of salt, as results could be adjusted to match the expectations of the ideological authorities. We can also question how sincere people were in answering direct questions about faith while knowing the official repressive position on religion.

Indirect evidence, however, about the decline of religiosity in the USSR provided another sample of information the government received. The 26 October 1936 note of the chief of the NKVD State Registrar, M. M. Alievsky, analyzed the correlation of weddings and births with periods of fasting and abstinence in the Orthodox tradition—the Great Lent fast in March and the Nativity fast in December. He noted the rise in the number of weddings (out of 100 weddings/year in the countryside) in 1910, 1926, and 1935 in the European part of Russia: 1.2, 7.6, and 9.5 during the period of the fast in March and 1.2, 3.3, and 8.1 in December. In the same way, the seasonal peaks of fertility typical for Imperial Russia became, in 1935, almost level with the same rate in other months (Danilov et al. 2002, pp. 859–61). While seasonal fluctuations in weddings and births in Imperial Russia presented the adherence of the countryside to religious rituals (though generally tending to decrease, as Boris Mironov showed in his *Social History of Russia*), their 1935 even distribution was interpreted in favor of mounting secularization.

Due to excessively optimistic reports from the local officials and imprecise data on church closures, the central authorities by 1936 presumed that only 28% of all religious communities were still in operation and 23.5% of religious buildings (Freeze 1998, pp. 223, 225). The report of the Cults Commission about the situation of religious organizations in the USSR and their attitude to the draft of the new constitution from October 1936 reported 29% of religious buildings functioning in April 1936 out of a prerevolutionary 72,963 (GARF f. 5263, op. 1, d.

32, l. 77) and 21.4% of priests in 1936 out of 112,629 in 1914 (GARF f. 1235, op. 76, d. 58, l. 23).[11]

Such surveys and statistics produced in the high authorities an impression of success for the state's antireligious efforts. In its precensus propaganda, the political leadership projected its high expectations for social advancements. On the very day of the census, *Pravda* predicted the growth of the population, literacy, and education, and insisted that religious beliefs had almost been eradicated (*Pravda* 6 January 1937). In preparation for the census, "the categories of social status were significantly simplified and formulated in such a way as to emphasize the homogeneity of society and progressive meaning of the elimination of all social differences" (Medushevsky 2010, p. 10). But even with such manipulation, the results of the census were incompatible with ideological schemes and shocked the Stalinists, who had scheduled an end to class divisions in the second Five-Year Plan (1933–1937) and the reeducation of citizens into secular New Men. Gregory Freeze explains: "The party probably shared the traditional intelligentsia view that Orthodoxy was largely ritualistic (*obriadoverie*), rooted in quotidian custom rather than conscious belief." So they assumed "an automatic withering away of superstition" as soon as the church superstructure and parish infrastructure were broken and religious services ceased. Correspondingly, local officials concluded that after closing the churches, "everything is finished with religion" and they halted their antireligious propaganda (GARF f. 5263, op. 1, d. 32, ll. 2, 5, 18). The census results, as well as the popular discussion warnings about enemies, did not correspond to the Stalinists' wishful ideological constructions: the population growth (seen as evidence of the achievements of socialism) was lower than extrapolated numbers from the previous census, literacy was not universal, society was split, and religiosity had not withered. Stalin's government disregarded the unexpected census results as false, classified them, and arrested the organizers. The new census of 1939 omitted the questions about religion.

Bolsheviks invested much effort into ending religion in the country: by persecutions, by dismantling church structure, by education and antireligious propaganda. But they underestimated the resilience of folk

---

[11] In September 1937, an information bulletin about preparation for the elections informed M. I. Kalinin about 30,000 religious organizations in the USSR with 600,000 members.

religion. After closing the churches and persecuting institutional religion, popular religiosity did not disappear. The Cults Commission noted that religious feeling, responding to repression, took on modified forms. Besides legal religious groups and communes (*dvadtsatki*) (1735 in Gorky *krai* in 1935), secret circles of former nuns and Christian communes (like Tolstoy's commune) functioned and prayed in homes or groves (Kulakov et al. 2005, p. 954; Torstensen 1999, pp. 46–7; GARF f. 5263, op. 1, d. 32, l. 11). Deprived of traditional services, many believers, especially in the countryside, converted to less visible alternatives to Orthodoxy. Pagan practices and superstitions covertly lingered in rural Christianity for centuries. Now many peasants turned to habitual underground rituals of magic and paganism. Another form of escape and adaptation was the resort to various sects, which proliferated due to the state's ambivalent attitude in the 1920s, and to other Christian denominations. Being less visible and institutionalized, Adventists and Baptists, for example, gained followers, though it does not mean they were not persecuted (GARF f. 5263, op. 1, d. 32, l. 103). Besides the psychological need for a spiritual, transcendental outlet, the need for protection and consolation found its expression in alternative religious practices: religious rumors, numerous "renovations of icons," pronouncements of miracles and signs (omens), and pilgrimages to holy sites and springs. Rumors of the Apocalypse and the emergence of "holy letters" from the Mother of God or Jerusalem[12] affirmed divine control and validated the peasants' religious worldview. The rural public sphere of rumors, however, inevitably acquired political colorations when calling Stalin an Antichrist, *kolkhozes* a creation of the Antichrist, and discussed the persecution of religion in the USSR (RGASPI f. 89, op. 4, d. 121, ll. 1–2, 6, 9, 11; GARF f. 5263, op. 1, d. 32, l. 111). In the 1930s, the authorities won in the public space, forcing rituals to become invisible, but failed at the grassroots level: popular, everyday religiosity took on noninstitutionalized, often improvised forms and retreated underground where it was out of government control. Peasants found new ways to preserve their faith: they adjusted to conditions without places of worship or priests (for example, joining *bespopovtsy*, a sect in Old Belief without priests); invented new ersatz wedding and funeral rituals with remote

---

[12] A kind of (chain) letter, found or fallen from the sky, instructing the reader to go to church and believe in Christ, and promising divine protection and remission of sins after copying the letter and sending it further (see Smith 2005, pp. 285–90).

consecration of the rings or grave earth by priests. People traveled long distances to find a priest who could perform a funeral service on a handful of earth from the grave, and when this consecrated earth was scattered back onto the grave, the deceased was considered to have been buried in a Christian way. Three hundred priests whose churches were closed wandered in Voronezh *oblast'* and now served secretly in homes and sometimes in caves; 26 saints and healers of all kinds clandestinely practiced in Voronezh *oblast'*. The Cults Commission concluded: "Folk religiosity is forced underground by the administrative measures. There it takes the form of secret illegal organizations" (GARF f. 5263, op. 1, d. 32, ll. 103–4, 110).

The antifranchise and anticlerical discourse in the discussion, as opposed to loyalty to faith demonstrated in the census, reflected the diversity of the political culture. Obviously, we hear the voices of different groups. But sometimes contradictory allegiances entwined in one personality, reflecting a conflict between informal norms operating in reality and officially declared norms. In an interview after the war, a young woman, 30 years old and a believer, endorsed the government's controls on religion: "In the Soviet Union, it is said that church and state are entirely separate, have nothing in common. In the democratic world, the church must be connected with the government. The church should receive aid from the government, and the government must exercise control over the church to see to it that it does not carry on propaganda against the government" (HPSSS Schedule A, Vol. 12, Case 145, pp. 60–1). We observe such contradictory allegiances in a former Soviet believer, who witnessed the harassment of the religious, but justified the state's actions in this conflict.

What motivated the anticlerical demands? The abrupt shift in the official line—from persecution of religion to a declaration of conciliation—could produce confusion and defensive reactions from the activists—the Communists, Komsomol, and members of the Godless League. This *aktiv* was probably especially vocal in the discussion because they profited from the social changes, defended their benefits, and were often responsible for the campaign organization. We cannot exclude the probability that members of the Godless League, a state-sponsored antireligious organization, a constituency up from 3.5 to 7 million in CC estimates (RGASPI f. 89, op. 4, d. 80, l. 36), previously involved in numerous harassments and now frightened of revenge, were disproportionally represented in the discussion and contributed to a discourse of resentment against the priests. Their antireligious comments could be read as a sycophantic echo of the previous bellicose campaigns.

Besides the Godless League members, the younger generation—Soviet-trained, which internalized the official secular and class-war rhetoric and made it their own—could resist a rapid shift in politics and defend their convictions. Being atheists for them was to be modern and Soviet. The antireligion stance was seen as an important part of the new Soviet identity. The little man, uprooted and vulnerable, like a kulak son Stepan Podlubnyi, in his diary, strove for mimicry, a new identity, and integration in order to survive in a modern urban world (Garros et al. 1997; Hellbeck 2009b). As many as 877 comments on Article 1, "The USSR is a socialist state of workers and peasants," debated who belonged there and who did not—showing how sensitive the question of identity was (GARF f. 3316, op. 8, d. 222, l. 160; d. 225, l. 2). Most numerous were suggestions to change the formula to "the state of the toilers", thus approving Stalin's dictum about the new homogeneity of society. Fitzpatrick explains the psychological undercurrents: "In many individuals the experience of discrimination [or fear of it—OV] produced a particularly intense and anxious form of Soviet patriotism, expressive of a longing to belong to the community" (Fitzpatrick 2009, pp. 21–2). For many who sought a new identity, discussion of the constitution was an excellent chance to develop a sense of belonging, demonstrate a new persona, and formally and publicly secede from an old identity and "hysterically embrace Soviet values."[13]

On top of the growing indifference to religion in the younger generation,[14] the poor image of priests as moneymakers in Russian popular lore before and after the Revolution may have contributed to negativity in 1936 (Danilov et al. 2002, pp. 859–61; Fitzpatrick 1994, pp. 35, 205; Kosheleva 2014). Democratic propaganda in nineteenth-century Russia created the image of greedy and deceptive churchmen who allegedly used baptisms, weddings, and funerals to extract money from believers (Panchenko 2012, p. 328). This image was cultivated after 1917 and found fertile ground in the public mind. The diarist Lubov' Shtange overheard a conversation on the train in September 1937:

---

[13] This complicated process is discussed in the scholarship on Soviet subjectivity by Sheila Fitzpatrick, Anna Krylova, Jochen Hellbeck, and others.

[14] The census of 1937 showed that 45% of people in their twenties considered themselves believers, in contrast to 78% of people in their fifties.

> They have a priest who goes to see them, he speaks and writes books in 12 languages, you think that he just goes there to pass the time of day? No, he's spreading his propaganda. He'll tell people, "Let me marry you," to others he'll say, "Let me christen your children." And it works. ... [Another voice]: Do you know that church on Mariinskaia Street? That church donated 25 thousand rubles to the Spaniards [Republicans in Spanish Civil War—OV]. I wonder where they got their hands on that kind of money? [First voice]: People go to church and there's your money. And of course they have to prove that they are not against Soviet government, so they make these donations.

The worker Arzhilovsky also counted the kopeks in the pocket of the priest who had just given him alms: "Nevertheless, the phantom of religion is still alive; even the clergy can make a living" (Garros et al. 1997, pp. 132, 199). The vision of a priest-moneymaker, however, gradually receded in the public imagination in the mid-1930s. Because of persecutions, common people gradually sympathized with the clergy (Krapivin 1997, p. 237; Freeze 1998, p. 212).

The people's comments of indignation against the church and priests expressed hostility toward groups of sanctioned outcasts, indicating the authoritarian elements in the popular culture and the split in society. The Revolution let the genie of hatred out of the bottle. The coals of a latent civil war smoldered behind the façade of a socialist society.

Another conclusion to this story concerns Stalin's possible reevaluation of the society's condition. Numerous popular anticlerical and antifranchise amendments were rejected by Stalin at the 8th Congress of Soviets.

> Next follows an amendment ... demanding that the article be changed to provide for the prohibition of religious rites. I think that this amendment should be rejected as running counter to the spirit of our Constitution. ... It is said that this is dangerous, as elements hostile to the Soviet government, some of the former White Guards, kulaks, priests, and so forth, may worm their way into the supreme governing bodies of the country. But what is there to be afraid of? If you are afraid of wolves, keep out of the woods (Laughter and loud applause). (Stalin 1936)

If Stalin had an impression of weakened and shrinking religious beliefs, the revival of religious activities in 1936, reported to him and confirmed in the census, could have convinced him that he was mistaken in his evaluation of secularization, that the *tserkovniki* (as the clergy and religious communities were labeled in NKVD and party jargon) conspired underground and still presented a threat at the elections. Though in his speech he rejected popular opposition to the new liberties, the alarming reports on religious activation likely sank into his mind and influenced the decision to resume oppression on the church as a final blow to the "vestiges of the past," on other enemies, and to finally cancel contested elections.

The consequent wave of arrests of clergy and the closing of churches followed in 1937–1938. The returned kulak-deportees, church people, and sectarians became the major groups of the repressed in villages during the Great Terror. If Stalinists sincerely believed in the advent of socialism and social harmony, the realization of their mistake in their evaluation of progress made them reconsider and revise their previous ideas. In particular, the case of the clergy—its self-mobilization in the aftermath of the constitution and on the eve of elections to the Supreme Soviet—impressed the officeholders, triggered fears of their defeat in elections, and contributed to a new wave of repression in June 1937. F. Sinitsyn believes that church people had a strong chance of being elected into soviets, more so if they actively demonstrated a desire to utilize their constitutional rights (Sinitsyn 2010, p. 89).

The Godless League of Gorky *oblast'* responded to the suspicions among officials by reporting a revival of local religious associations in 1937 that they interpreted as counterrevolutionary: the dissemination of holy Jerusalem letters intimidating collective farmers, spreading rumors of war and the end of the world, "Bartholomew nights" (threatening a massacre of Communists and *kolkhozniks*), the organization of "miracles" (the appearance of an icon in the spring in Ardatovsky *raion*), religious processions in the fields and cemeteries, and charity to the needy forbidden by the 1929 law. Counterrevolutionary activities also included the organization of "good church choirs," entertainment for children—for example, dances, games, and making and distributing toys. According to the Godless League, the church people used "holy fools" for their purposes ("Saint" Vasiana in Apraksino of Boldino *raion*). Some priests wandered as petty traders and sold religious objects together with other goods; others helped illiterate peasants to read and understand the constitution (village of Lapshanga, Varnavinsky *raion*) and helped women in the field (village of Rozhdestveno, Chernukhinskii *raion*); Sergachi's episcope collected donations for Spaniards, and mullahs—for the repair of mosques. They celebrated religious holidays and spoke against *kolkhozes*. As a result of these activities, "the priests raise their authority to be prepared for the coming elections to the Supreme Soviet," concluded the report (Kulakov et al. 2005, pp. 323–5).[15]

In 1937, the NKVD repetitively reported the consolidation of church people determined to use the constitution to open the churches and prepare for elections: in Pavlov, Gagin, Naruksa *raions* of Gorky *oblast'*, in Liadsk, Novgorod, Podporozhie *raions* of Leningrad *oblast'*, Chubarevsky, Soloniansky *raion* of Dnepropetrovsk *oblast'*. Meetings of the clergy and believers were reported as collusion (Berelowich and Danilov 2012, pp. 347, 357, 365). Officeholders reacted with a new wave of propaganda under the slogans "No place for priests in the soviets!" "Priests—spies," and similar. Yaroslavsky, the chair of the Godless League, made it clear: "We can't imagine that Soviet masses would vote for a priest and elect him to a soviet!" Article 141 was the judicial instrument to block the nomination of church people: "The right to nominate candidates is secured to public organizations and societies of the working people: Communist Party organizations, trade unions, cooperatives, youth organizations, and cultural societies." This article discriminated against religious associations. Manipulation of nominations was a common practice in preelection campaigns (RGASPI f. 17, op. 2, d. 625, l. 7),[16] but the most effective tool was repression. At the February–March CC Plenum of 1937, A. A. Zhdanov reported the revival and consolidation of churchmen and suggested using pressure (*nazhim*) against their attempts to enter the soviets. Thereafter, on 27 March 1937, the NKVD sent a secret circular to local departments urging them to take all measures to prevent church and sectarian people from penetrating into the lower soviet apparatus and to stop their propaganda, and suggesting the NKVD infiltrate their ranks with agents (Kurliandsky 2011, p. 512; Khaustov and Samuelson 2010, p. 68). On 8 June, the NKVD ordered the liquidation of church people and sectarians. In 1937, 8000 churches were closed, 136,000 people arrested in "church cases," with

---

[15] Information from the Godless League of Gorky *oblast'* about the facts of counterrevolutionary and wrecking work of religious associations, July 1937.

[16] As revealed in Molotov's speech about the nomination of candidates at the October 1937 CC Plenum.

85,000 among them shot; in 1938, 28,000 were arrested and 21,000 shot (Yakovlev 1995, pp. 94–5).[17]

Stalin's wishful view of society as successfully sovietized changed after the discussion of the constitution and census. This contributed to his renewal of violence.

10.2 THE DUTY TO HATE: BRUTALIZATION ON THE GROUND

Another powerful narrative in the popular comments was a request to tighten control and strengthen punishments: 5% in Leningrad comments according to Getty (1991) (GARF f. 3316, op. 8, d. 225, l. 75). S. Yekelchyk, in his study of the interaction between Soviet citizens and the state in postwar Kiev, noted that "typical of … the exclusionary vision of the world, hatred of enemies emerged in Stalin's time as a core component of the ideal Soviet identity, on par with love of and gratitude to the leader" (Yekelchyk 2014, p. 11). The mid- and late 1930s witnessed an official judicial trend toward significantly more severe punishments applied to criminals: longer terms of confinement and a rise in sentences leading to imprisonment, indirectly encouraged by Stalin (Solomon 1996, pp. 221–7). In 1936 and 1937, *Pravda* never tired of reminding readers that vigilance was a trait of any true Soviet citizen. Historians trace the origin of this divisive worldview to the Revolution and Civil War. The mobilizational potential of such emotions as hatred and suspicion was fully exploited by Stalinism. A few suggestions to abandon the death penalty in the discussion materials contrasted with numerous requirements to expand capital punishment to include such crimes as theft of socialist (state) property (94 suggestions, TsIK) and to other anti-Soviet crimes established under Article 58 of the Criminal Code (RGASPI f. 17, op. 120, d. 232, ll. 83–4; GARF f. 3316, op. 41, d. 85, l. 32). The preoccupation with theft and capital punishment was a long-lasting echo of the harsh decree of 7 August 1932, introducing the death penalty for the theft of socialist property. The decree had been already reversed by the TsIK in March 1933, and convictions were revised, liberating 32% of the convicted (Khlevniuk 2010, p. 243), but

---

[17] Other estimates: in 1937–1938, 150,000 were arrested "for faith," among them 80,000 shot.

the masses continued demanding death for thieves, as that cruel decree probably strongly mirrored the public psyche.

The same animosity revealed itself in rural show trials of 1937 when, according to local newspapers' reports, peasants had frequently called for death sentences for the accused officials, even though the prosecutor had not asked for that penalty or the judge had handed down a lesser sentence. Fitzpatrick cautions that this cannot necessarily be taken at face value, since such expressions of vox populi were often stage-managed by the Soviet authorities, but it may well have been true in local cases of this type, where the peasants knew the defendants and might have genuine grievances against them (Fitzpatrick 1994, p. 301). The general context, however, of widespread animosity in society makes us believe in the authenticity of these emotions. Article 131, which labeled thieves of socialist property as enemies of the people, thereby politicizing a crime, found favor in an alert population. The TsIK registered 118 suggestions to extend the designation of "enemies of the people" to speculators, beggars, thieves, and idlers, and 60 suggestions to relatives who "harbored" lawbreakers (GARF f. 3316, op. 41, d. 85, ll. 38, 55, 60; d. 147, l. 67; f. 3316, op. 40, d. 40, ll. 49, 101–2). The latter implies acceptance of political loyalties over family loyalties. Moreover—these 60 people demanding persecution of wives and relatives believed that the work and party collective, as well as family members, were responsible for the "crime" of the offender. This attitude reverberated with the traditional peasant community system of mutual responsibility (*krugovaia poruka*). Five proposals to make denunciation of enemies a civic duty in reality only followed current practice: people already received punishment because they failed to denounce an alleged conspiracy (Rittersporn 2014, p. 139). One citizen wanted to ban changes of workplace (actually restricted in practice), and some peasant women suggested imprisonment of women for having an abortion (recently outlawed), and men who had too many marriages (GARF f. 3316, op. 41, d. 82, ll. 13–5).

People took it as their civic duty to hate.[18] The words "to punish severely" and "to sue" were favorites in the popular lexicon of the national discussion, unlike the word "mercy," which would imply conciliation. Even *Pravda* noted the aggressive vocabulary of the regional newspaper: "The word 'to press' [*zastavit'*] is the most often used word. 'To punish', to 'sue', to 'take action', to fire—these are the main demands of

---

[18] Serhy Yekelchyk's expression.

most publications. In six months, the newspaper called for punishing 229 persons" (*Pravda* 27 October 1936). Popular comments suggested introducing criminal punishment for parents who kept children out of school, killing thieves at the scene of the crime without the benefit of court, and "strengthening punishments for the criminal and political crimes." Authors of restricting, banning, and toughening recommendations saw the world as full of enemies who designed insidious plans to ruin the country. Such a worldview, together with the acceptance of violence, belongs to the authoritarian type of personality as defined in sociopsychological literature. But before Adorno and Arendt, Georgy Efron, a 16-year-old boy, wrote in his 1941 Moscow diary: "All these people stand and will stand strong like a mountain for Stalin—those who despise such things as freedom of speech, human rights, the value of human life, tolerance, leniency, respect for other opinions. There are always a lot of such people. Maybe there exists a special authoritarian type, a totalitarian man? Maybe they do not become Stalinists, they are born?"[19]

The Soviet population was well trained in hatred. The expressions of ruthlessness typical of the constitution comments followed the exercises of anger during the dekulakization campaign, after S. Kirov's murder, in the show trials, and in August 1936 in the trial of the United Trotskyist-Zinovievist Center. The constitution's reconciling stance was in sharp contrast with the aggressive rhetoric of the trial, giving contradictory signals to the public. One day in August, citizens attended a meeting discussing the constitution and reconciliation with "former people," and the next day at another meeting, they yelled, "Hang these reptiles!" demanding the death penalty without "legal niceties" for the defendants. When in September 1936, N. Bukharin and A. Rykov were spared from trial and persecution, a letter with unidentifiable signatures addressed to S. Ordzhonikidze demanded their death: "Those who go or speak against Stalin, all should be killed. Hammer a wooden stake into their throats and other places!" (Livshin et al. 2002, p. 311). The confrontational and consolidational types of mobilization coincided in 1936, with the confrontational gaining more support. There was no shortage of approval for state violence and discrimination.

In periodic exercises of hatred, the regime cultivated the violent elements of traditional culture, with its tendency to attribute failures to

[19] Diary of Georgy Efron.

other people's malevolent actions, rather than to miscalculations, fortuity, and impersonal forces (Bailey 1987, p. 314). Revolutionary violence was justified in the official class struggle discourse, which stirred up revolutionary zeal and the common people's old social suspicions of the aristocracy, nobility, and intelligentsia. The witch-hunting atmosphere around the August trial encouraged discussants to disapprove of the reconciling message of the constitution as a sudden retreat from class-hatred norms. We hear the aggressive vocabulary exploited by newspapers during the trial campaign parroted in discussion materials and in the letters to authorities. In September, party member G. Vanenko wrote a letter to Molotov with the following recommendations: "In connection with the [future 8th] Congress of Soviet ... and new work procedures (initiated by Stalin's new Constitution) it is necessary to vet all soviet and party managerial apparat and to purge the Trotskyists and suspects." Vanenko meticulously listed almost all branches of government and the military to be checked (Livshin et al. 2002, pp. 302–11). This "recommendation" was actually brought to reality by the government during the Great Terror of 1937–1938. The degree of mass support for political repressions is impossible to measure, but the degree of vindictiveness was high: a significant portion of demands for and approvals of purges were accompanied by suggesting savage methods of execution of enemies and thieves: to impale on a pike, to skin, to try slowly by red-hot iron, or to dismember day by day. The mobilization campaign around the August trial contributed to aggressive discourse in the discussion.

The popular culture of violence was fueled by the deadly experience of wars (1914–1922) and famines and resulted in placing a low price on human life, brutalization of norms, and criminalization of society (Buldakov 1997). A high level of anxiety among the population, along with fear about their surroundings and future, a feeling of insecurity and helplessness, and a lack of confidence in their own powers produced a psychological foundation of inner aggressiveness in the citizenry. It became a psychological backdrop for the future Great Terror. Mass repressions and the experience and consequences of World War II encouraged an acceptance of violence in society, evidenced in the crime rise after the war. The history of state and criminal violence in Russia's twentieth century has had a long-lasting effect. Modern surveys from 1999 show that about 25% of Russians had taken part in fights, had been victims of robbery and family violence. Fifty-eight per cent of the young men who served in the armed forces had been the victims of physical abuse by their fellow soldiers. In 2007, almost half of Russians were in favor of reinstituting and expanding the death penalty, which corresponds generally to the world level (Dubin 2010, pp. 76, 85–6).

10.3 THE STATIST CODE OF POLITICAL CULTURE

Hatred of enemies was motivated by patriotism and love for the Soviet state and leader. Such a belief—that the state should control the life of the country even at the cost of individual interests and rights—permeated the comments. Direct and indirect statements in both public and informal settings showed a close association of individual interests with the state, respect for authority, or even readiness to sacrifice one's life for the sake of the state and beloved leader. Sometimes, publicly and privately, Soviet citizens metaphorically regretted their inability to offer their own lives in exchange for the lives of deceased leaders—Lenin, Kirov, or Ordzhonikidze (TsGAIPD SPb f. 24, op. 2v, d. 2659, l. 109). The narrative of sacrificing one's life in the name of revolution and socialism was a part of the official canon, imposed, among other things, by newspapers and socialist realism. The model was promoted in a cult novel *How the Steel Was Tempered* by N. Ostrovsky, published serially between 1932 and 1936. The protagonist ruined his health, was paralyzed, and then died after working heroically for years round the clock in terrible conditions for the good of the society. In August 1936, reports about the Spanish Civil War reignited the theme of death for revolution. The ethic of self-sacrifice, so deeply rooted in the Orthodox mentality, the rejection of individuality, and reliance on the might of the state saturated the historical-cultural traditions.

Numerous expressions of the public's prioritizing the state and collective good over individual and family values included mass indignation against the theft of socialist (meaning the state's) property, the ranking of treason as the most intolerable crime, demands to review and censor private correspondence, and the punishment of parents whose children do not attend school (usually religious families) (GARF f. 3316, op. 41, d. 207, l. 163; d. 126, l. 46; d. 136, ll. 12, 21). Such comments were naturally provoked by the official trope of paternalism, always cultivated by the Bolsheviks and so intensely embodied in the constitution. *Pravda* educated its readers: "The unity of interests of society and the individual person, of the state and each citizen, is one of the most remarkable characteristics of the soviet order" (*Pravda* 3 December 1936). The granting of voting rights and the expansion of welfare announced by the constitution invited appropriate gratitude from the recipients. A *kolkhoz* woman wrote: "Stalin is taking care of us, but we do not justify [his trust]: we work badly, private property [and interests] overwhelm us, we give too much attention to our households and private plots instead of to *kolkhoz* work" (GARF f. 3316, op. 41, d. 136, l. 5).

We can, of course, question the sincerity of the strong statist emotions displayed by many participants in the campaign. A good share of statism could be amplified by the celebratory format of the discussion, which framed the response, but also by more material reasons. As soon as the Soviet government closed almost all opportunities for private initiative, the state remained the only source of good and now presented itself as a benevolent provider. Paternalism, as Katherine Verdery showed, was at the center of both the party's official ideology and its efforts to secure popular support. It "emphasized a quasi-family dependency" and "posited a moral tie linking subjects with the state through their rights to a share in the redistributed social product" (Verdery 1996, p. 63). Lewis Siegelbaum particularly stressed the disciplinary function of paternalism when, in their access to goods, people depended "on the degree to which individuals conformed to their expected roles of supplicants and grateful recipients" (Siegelbaum 1998, p. 108). The scholars writing about paternalism as a mode of power in the USSR mostly examined the official self-representation of the party—for example, in the press, as with Jeffrey Brooks. However, they all recognized its acceptance in society, especially those authors who worked with the individual letters and analyzed their vocabulary. A 30-year-old Russian woman, a student, pronounced a strong reliance on the state in her postwar interview:

> I think that the government must be in everything and it must be everywhere—in the press, in the theater, in the school—everywhere. There is no area of life in which it does not have a right to interfere. A citizen must have many obligations toward his government: patriotism, help for the government in all aspects of its situation. There are many ties that the government and its citizens have in common. A citizen must be a patriot and he must keep an eye on [*sledit'*] those people who are trying to harm the government, even put them away [*ubrat'*]. In short, every citizen must be vigilant.

Forty-year-old Avar from the Caucasus, a tractor driver, expressed the same view in his interview:

> The government must have censorship so that it will not allow any antinational criticism or harmful criticism of any branch of government. The government must not be allowed to split its people into several parts [nationalities]. It should permit censorship to be carried on in the language of each nationality. If one of these nationalities starts to carry on propaganda directed against some of the others, this would be harmful. (Respondent thought for a very long time before answering.) If people (*narod*) are living under the direction of a government, there is no area of life in which the government should not interfere. A good father interferes in every affair of his children. If he is an indifferent father, then he will not care what his children do. But a good father will know everything his children do and interfere in everything, except when they want to choose a wife to marry. But in the affairs of the state, there are no such examples. (Therefore you believe that a good government should be like a good father?) Yes. (HPSSS Schedule A, Vol. 12, Case 145, p. 60; Schedule A, Vol. 13, Case 159, pp. 74–6)

Note here the opposition of the correspondents' views to the democratic mainstream in the Western environment where the respondents now lived, such disagreement indicating the relative independence of their opinions. The family metaphor strongly points to the roots of this statist narrative in the traditional patriarchal peasant mentality. The researchers in the Harvard Project deduced that Soviet refugees had little understanding of the institutional foundations of the political regime and felt little need "for the strictly constitutional apparatus of guarantees, rights and safeguards" of democracy. They would rather accept a good, kind, and compassionate ruler, who "cared" for people and did not oppress them (Inkeles and Bauer 1959, p. 381). People agreed to weak institutions and venerated the leader at the top.

With postwar interviews, comments about the constitution provide ample confirmation of statist views. A paternalistic posture of the government found strong resonance in the popular worldview as evidenced in the cult of the leader and expectations of welfare (Velikanova 2001, pp. 215–25). Besides materialistic reasons, the Weberian charismatic mode of legitimation imposed from above found fertile soil in the traditional patriarchal relations, which transformed in the USSR into relations of the "moral economy of the gift" (Mauss 2011).[20] The Soviet people, especially beneficiaries of the regime, willingly accepted the recipients' roles assigned them by the press, ready for repayment of the gift (Brooks 2000, pp. xvi, 97, 105; Siegelbaum 1998). A common theme in numerous affirmative comments was gratitude to Great Stalin for the constitution. We hear this gratitude, prioritization of state over individual, adoration of strong power and a strong leader in seven recommendations (TsIK estimates) to rename Moscow "Stalin", an idea to commemorate the constitution with a monument (28 suggestions, my estimates) or with marble slabs with golden script, and in calling plagues upon the heads of traitors and terrorists plotting against the life of the leader (*Kommuna* [Voronezh] 2 July 1936). Preoccupation with the design of a national emblem (90 comments collected by TsIK) reflected the hyperactivism of the masses, who hardly understood the convolutions of state and law functioning, but understood well the simple symbols of the hammer and sickle. They were eager to realize their right to speak and demonstrate loyalty to the state in an act of self-identification with the general will. Moshe Lewin saw this relation originating from the historical-cultural traditions of the country, in particular those represented by the peasantry: "The authoritarian impulses in the party and state administration from above … [were] met by those emanating from below … from the lower classes, still deeply ensconced in patriarchalism" (Lewin 1985, pp. 43, 256, 274). He referred to the old national tradition of acceptance of authority and submission and withdrawal of initiative coined in the Russian saying "The chief knows better (*Nachal'stvu vidnee*)". This particular Soviet popular reliance on the state as benefactor was the source of cyclic waves of hope in the masses and the following inevitable disillusionment: be it with the results of the Constitution of 1936, the October Revolution itself, or later, with unrealized dreams about decollectivization after the World War II victory, and then finally perestroika.

---

[20] A type of economy based on the informal exchange of services, favors, or goods, in contrast with a barter economy or a market economy. Theoretical foundations are introduced in Mauss, *The Gift*, first published in 1925. Soviet and post-Soviet practice are discussed in Ledeneva, *Russia's Economy of Favours*.

10.4 MILITARISM, DEFEATISM, AND REGIMENTATION

Expressions of love to the Red Army were a part of this statist disposition. Such statements reflected not only a high degree of militarization but also the status of this institution in society—a stepladder to upward mobility. The soldier Bespalov, from Archangelsk, wrote: "The Red Army reincarnated me like many others and made me a full-fledged Soviet citizen" (GARF f. 3316, op. 41, d. 207, l. 68). Readiness to spill blood on future battlefields was a way to prove loyalty. Demands for universal air defense training, armament of the whole nation, military education for both genders (90 comments, TsIK), and an astonishing number of voices in favor of military duty for women (281) revealed the statist code of the political culture and significant success in militarizing society.

The last-mentioned gender factor is open to more than one interpretation—according to statist, modernization, socialist, or militarist terms. It may be evidence of women's broadening inclusion in the public sphere—a feature of modernity, or socialist gender egalitarianism, or, as Roger Reese believes, a result of the historical precedents of women's participation in Russia's past wars (Reese 2011, pp. 312–3).[21] Of course, the Soviet press, literature, and cinema actively contributed to the image of the valorous New Soviet Woman, ready and happy to fight for the Motherland. All of this resulted in "Soviet women['s] unprecedented entrance into combat" during World War II (Krylova 2004, p. 627; Petrone 2000).[22] The number of 281 voices calling for women's military service signals the major shift in traditional patriarchal gender values that society, especially the younger generation, underwent in the 1930s.

In the 1920s, enormous state efforts to inculcate bellicose and patriotic values into mass culture through propaganda, education, military training, and the Society of Friends of Aviation and Chemical Defense had not yet borne fruit. The War Scare of 1927 produced a huge wave of defeatism in the postrevolutionary generation, especially among peasants (Velikanova 2013, pp. 89–106). They en masse refused to defend the country in case of war. Yet in the middle of the 1930s, with the coming of a new generation, we see aggressive patriotism well implanted.

---

[21] Reese noted, "Without the war, women would not have served in the armed forces in large numbers," but at least they expressed this desire in 1936.
[22] The cultural impact of women pilots is discussed by Karen Petrone.

Photo 10.1 Pioneers in gas masks participating in a military training march. Leningrad *oblast'*. 1935. V. Bulla. Courtesy of the Central State Archives of Documentary Films, Photographs, and Sound Recordings, Saint-Petersburg (TsGAKFFD SPb)

Brandenberger found "national Bolshevism to be appealing and persuasive" in the late interwar period (Brandenberger 2002, p. 112). Defeatism declined but did not totally recede.

Militarization was a cornerstone of the Stalinist economy, ideology, and social mobilization (Photo 10.1). The emergency mode of the whole Soviet project had at its very foundation the thesis of "capitalist encirclement." The official myth of a besieged fortress was promoted for decades to heighten patriotic willingness to defend the achievements of socialism. While the capitalist threat inspired the loyalty of the Soviet true believers, this reported readiness of the capitalist countries to intervene was, nevertheless, often perverted into a positive, liberating factor in the mass consciousness. Opposite the cult of the Red Army and patriotism presented in the constitution discussion, the common trope in conversations was anticipation of liberation by means of foreign intervention. Veselovsky in 1918 and Shaporina in August 1941 wrote that people wait for the Germans: "They say that Germans are better than Georgians and Jews" (Shaporina 2012, p. 249; Veselovsky 2000, p. 103; RGASPI f. 17, op. 85, d. 289, l. 56).[23] The duty to defend the socialist Motherland written in the constitution was not accepted by everybody. In NKVD jargon, centered on the super value of the state, this mood was labeled as "defeatism," while in peasant vernacular, centered on the human dimension, it did not so much mean the "defeat" of the Red Army but rather the salvation of the people from the yoke of the Soviet regime. People not only passively expected the liberation but were ready to act—if we believe the numerous NKVD records about rebellious (*povstancheskie*) moods among Cossacks and peasants. These moods included expectations of foreign intervention and alleged preparations for military actions behind the front lines to help the invaders (Pokrovsky et al. 2006, pp. 498, 507; TsGAIPD SPb f. 24, op. 2v, d. 2065, ll. 8, 63, 197; d. 2064, l. 46; Danilov et al. 2002, pp. 752–3; Berelowitch and Danilov 2012, pp. 299, 304, 313–4, 323, 333, 337–8, 360–1, 365; Prishvin 2010, p. 538).[24] This "intervention" narrative flourished among the disillusioned for whom anticipation of the inner reformation of the regime had been exhausted. Some threats promised that 50–60% of future draftees would turn their weapons against the government. The rise of the hopes in the constitution temporarily pushed back the hopes for foreign intervention, but still the impression of British diplomats reported in October 1936 was that "the general morals of the people are not good enough for the Government to be able to count with certainty on their loyalty in a prolonged war" (British F.O. 371, 1936, Vol. 20351, p. 86 verso). Stalin's panic in June 1941 proves that he took such warnings very seriously.

Related to the militarization tendency, many discussants advocated a total regimentation of life. They suggested in their comments the introduction of censorship, universal mandatory physical exercises, a loyalty

---

[23] This echoed the historian Veselovsky's entry in his diary in February 1918: "People of very different ranks, despite shame, instability, and possible oppression, do not conceal their joy concerning the forthcoming entry of the German troops [into Petrograd]. The Bolshevik terror, anarchy, and famine brought such despair that foreign enslavement is regarded as liberation from slavery, hunger, and so on" (Veselovsky 2000, p. 103). We hear the same in 1927: "It couldn't be worse under the power of a Polish or English government" (RGASPI f. 17, op. 85, d. 289, l. 56).

[24] Comments are from 1930 to 1936.

oath both in the army and in civil institutions, mandatory permits for public meetings and demonstrations, and even "childbirth duty for women" (two recommendations, TsIK) (Sokolov 1998, p. 158; GARF f. 3316, op. 41, d. 82, l. 3). Pregnancy and maternity at that period were treated by the state like a production activity along with other kinds of work, implied inter alia in the abortion ban (Yarskaia-Smirnova and Romanov 2009, p. 10). The inclination to obey the regulations of the central authority connects such values as respect for authority and striving for simplification—all the elements, in fact, of the totalitarian consciousness, as well as the indirect consequences of a rapid "shift from local parochialism to centralized authority" (Almond and Verba 1989, p. 22; Gozman and Etkind 1992, p. 41). The tendency toward uniformity, as described by Kazimierz Dobrowolski, was essentially conservative and stabilizing, and manifested a close kinship to a traditional peasant culture, as noted by another connoisseur of village culture: "The Russian peasant was obsessed by a fear of defying the numerous prohibitions, rules, and demands of the village world" (Mironov 1994, pp. 66–7; Ellis 2009, pp. 243–55, 321; Dobrowolski 1987, p. 291). A craving for regulated forms of conduct compensated for the loss of the old peasant world with its stability.

Articles about basic human rights, like the inviolability of correspondence, home, and the person, provoked as much criticism as endorsement. Remarkable was the number of 21 proposals to introduce the surveillance of private correspondence. Unaware that this unlawful practice had been in operation since 1918, vigilant citizens wanted to prevent enemies from conspiring and sending Soviet secrets abroad (GARF f. 3316, op. 8, d. 226, l. 135; op. 40, d. 40, ll. 3, 101; op. 41, d. 136, ll. 12, 69; f. 1235, op. 76, d. 153, l. 136; TsGAIPD SPb f. 24, op. 2v, d. 1772, ll. 205–6; British F.O. 371, 1936, vol. 20351, p. 146).[25] In contrast, 3 comments approved the inviolability of correspondence, 4 suggested expanding inviolability to telephone and telegraph communications, and 11, to bank information (GARF f. 3316, op. 8, d. 225, ll. 79, 137; d. 226, l. 136; op. 41, d. 207, l. 165). Others worried that the inviolability of the home would give a free hand to the wreckers and conspirators; or that those letting rooms could gain illegal profits; some sought confiscation of dwellings not maintained properly (GARF f. 3316, op. 41,

---

[25] British diplomats were aware that their private correspondence was "clumsily opened in the post."

d. 85, l. 28; d. 207, ll. 3, 66; op. 40, d. 40, l. 38; f. 1235, op. 76, d. 153, l. 102). Privacy was not a subject of concern; there is no such word in the Russian language and so there was no discourse on privacy. Ordinary citizens often accepted state intervention at the expense of individual rights. In all probability, citizens striving for normalization and security associated regimentation with order and stability. Uniformity imposed by the official culture found resonance with elements of traditional representations in the popular mind as soon as simplification helped unsophisticated minds understand the chaotic modern world.

The comments and recommendations against new liberties were in line with the conclusions made by Hellbeck on the basis of the diaries studied—that illiberal attitudes were universal and prominent in society and not confined only to specific social groups such as the disenfranchised or former outcasts (Hellbeck 2009a, p. 54). Discussion comments showed that the totalitarian regime responded to the aspirations of those multitudes of small men, who believed in and benefited from the Revolution, offering them, if not wealth, at least recognition, meaning of life, opportunities for upward mobility, the social benefits of socialism (concentrated in the hands of the state), and relieving them of the "burden of freedom." When in 1936 freedom, plurality, diversity, and rights for minorities were suggested by the constitution (at least in the format of discourse), the beneficiaries, activists, and young true believers (like Lev Kopelev) (Kopelev 1980) rejected them, and defended the illiberal status quo—their own newly acquired social assets and/or their loot—but for others (perceived as enemies), they reserved segregation, censorship, and repression. These citizens merged with the state with delight and clung to a revolutionary ideology that justified the redistribution of wealth and social capital, but only in their favor. They did not want a new round of redistribution of material and social assets.

REFERENCES

Almond, Gabriel A., and Sidney Verba. 1989. *The Civic Culture: Political Attitudes and Democracy in Five Nations*. Newbury Park: Sage.

Bailey, F. G. 1987. "The Peasant View of the Bad Life." In *Peasants and Peasant Societies: Selected Readings*, edited by Teodor Shanin, 286–91. New York: Blackwell.

Berelowitch, Alexei, and Victor Danilov, eds. 2012. *Sovetskaia derevnia glazami VChK-OGPU-NKVD: Dokumenty i materialy*. Vol. 4. Moscow: ROSSPEN.

Brandenberger, David. 2002. *National Bolshevism: Stalinist Mass Culture and the Formation of Modern Russian National Identity, 1931–1956*. Cambridge, MA: Harvard University Press.
British Foreign Office—Russia Correspondence, 1781–1945. 1975. Wilmington, DE: Scholarly Resources.
Brooks, Jeffery. 2000. *Thank You, Comrade Stalin! Soviet Public Culture from Revolution to Cold War*. Princeton, NJ: Princeton University Press.
Buldakov, V. P. 1997. *Krasnaia smuta: Priroda i posledstviia revolutsionnogo nasiliia*. Moscow: ROSSPEN.
Danilov, Viktor Petrovich, Roberta Thompson Manning, and Lynne Viola. 2002. *Tragediia sovestskoi derevni: Kollektivizatsiia I raskulachivanie: dokumenty i materialy*. Vol. 4. Moscow: ROSSPEN.
Dobrowolski, Kazimierz. 1987. "Peasant Traditional Culture." In *Peasants and Peasant Societies: Selected Readings*, edited by Teodor Shanin, 286–91. New York: Blackwell.
Dubin, Boris. 2010. "The Worth of Life and the Limits of Law: Russian Opinions on the Death Penalty, Russian Laws, and the System of Justice." *Russian Social Sciences Review* 51 (3): 69–88.
Efron, Georgy. 2004. "Diary of Georgy Efron." 1001.ru. http://1001.ru/books/item/dnevniki-52. Accessed June 25, 2017.
Ellis, E. 2009. "Svidetelei net. Vospominania." In *Rossiiskaia i sovetskaia derevnia pervoi poloviny XX veka glazami krestian*, 243–354. Moscow: Russkii Put.
Fitzpatrick, Sheila. 1994. *Stalin's Peasants: Resistance and Survival in the Russian Village After Collectivization*. Oxford: Oxford University Press.
———. 1999. *Everyday Stalinism*. Oxford: Oxford University Press.
———. 2009. "Popular Opinion in Russia Under Prewar Stalinism." In *Popular Opinion in Totalitarian Regimes: Fascism, Nazism, and Communism*, edited by Paul Corner, 17–32. Oxford: Oxford University Press.
Freeze, Gregory L. 1998. "The Stalinist Assault on the Parish, 1929–1941." In *Stalinismus vor dem Zweiten Weltkrieg: Neue Wege der Forschung*, edited by Manfred Hildermeier, 208–32. Munich: Oldenburg Verlag.
Garros, Véronique, Natalia Korenevskaya, and Thomas Lahusen. 1997. *Intimacy and Terror: Soviet Diaries of the 1930s*. New York: New Press.
Getty, A. 1991. "State and Society Under Stalin: Constitutions and Elections in the 1930s." *Slavic Review* 50 (1): 18–35.
———. 2013. *Practicing Stalinism: Bolsheviks, Boyars, and the Persistence of Tradition*. New Haven, CT: Yale University Press.
Gosudarstvenny Arkhiv Rossiiskoi Federatsii (GARF) [State Archives of Russian Federation].

Gozman, Leonid, and Alexander Etkind. 1992. *The Psychology of Post-totalitarianism in Russia*. London: Centre for Research into Communist Economies.
"Harvard Project on the Soviet Social System" (HPSSS). *Harvard College Library*. http://hcl.harvard.edu/collections/hpsss/index.html.
Hellbeck, Jochen. 2009a. "Liberation from Autonomy: Mapping Self-understandings in Stalin's Time." In *Popular Opinion in Totalitarian Regimes: Fascism, Nazism, and Communism*, edited by Paul Corner, 49–63. Oxford: Oxford University Press.
———. 2009b. *Revolution on My Mind: Writing a Diary Under Stalin*. Cambridge, MA: Harvard University Press.
Inkeles, Alex, and Raymond Bauer. 1959. *The Soviet Citizen: Daily Life in a Totalitarian Society*. Cambridge, MA: Harvard University Press.
Khaustov, V. N., and L. Samuelson. 2010. *Stalin, NKVD I repressii, 1936–1938 gg*. Moscow: ROSSPEN.
Khlevniuk, Oleg. 2010. *Khoziain: Stalin i utverzhdenie stalinskoi diktatury*. Moscow: ROSSPEN.
Kopelev, Lev. 1980. *The Education of a True Believer*. New York: Harper & Row.
Kosheleva, A. I. 2014. "Obraz pravoslavnyh sviaschennosluzhitelei v svetskoi I tzerkovnoi periodicheskoi literature vo vtoroi polovine XIX veka." *Izvestia vysshih uchebnyh zavedenii. Povolzhskii region: Gumanitarnye nauki* (2): 14–21.
Krapivin, M. Yu. 1997. *Nepridumannaia tzerkovnaia istoriia: vlast' I tserkov' v Sovetskoi Rossii (octiabr' 1917– konetz 1930 godov)*. Volgograd: Peremena.
Krylova, Anna. 2004. "Stalinist Identity from the Viewpoint of Gender: Rearing a Generation of Professionally Violent Women-Fighters in 1930s Stalinist Russia." *Gender and History* 16 (3): 626–53.
Kulakov, A. A., V. V. Smirnov, and L. P. Kolodnikova, eds. 2005. *Obshchestvo I vlast': Rossiiskaia provintsiia*. Vol. 2. Moscow: Institute Rossiiskoi Istorii RAN.
Kurliandsky, Igor. 2011. *Stalin, Vlast', Religia*. Moscow: Kuchkovo Pole.
"Law on Religious Organizations." 8 April 1929. *Seventeen Moments in Soviet History*. http://soviethistory.msu.edu/1929-2/churches-closed/churches-closed-texts/law-on-religious-organizations/. Accessed May 29, 2016.
Ledeneva, Alena V. 1998. *Russia's Economy of Favours: Blat, Networking and Informal Exchange*. Cambridge: Cambridge University Press
Lewin, Moshe. 1985. *The Making of the Soviet System: Essays in the Social History of Interwar Russia*. London: Methuen.
Livshin, A. Y., I. B. Orlov, and O. V. Khlevniuk, eds. 2002. *Pis'ma vo Vlast', 1928–1939*. Moscow: ROSSPEN.
Mauss, Marcel. 2011. *The Gift: Forms and Functions of Exchange in Archaic Societies*. Eastford, CT: Martino Fine Books.

Medushevsky, A. N. 2010. "Stalinism kak model' sotsial'nogo konstruirovania." *Rossiiskaia Istoria* (6): 3–29.
Mironov, Boris. 1994. "Peasant Popular Culture and the Origins of Soviet Authoritarianism." In *Cultures in Flux: Lower-Class Values, Practices, and Resistance in Late Imperial Russia*, edited by Stephen Frank and Mark D. Steinberg, 54–73. Princeton, NJ: Princeton University Press.
Odintsov, Mikhail. 2014. *Russkaia pravoslavnaia tserkov' nakanune i v èpokhu stalinskogo sotsializma, 1917–1953*. Moscow: ROSSPEN.
Panchenko, Alexander. 2012. "'Popular Orthodoxy' and Identity in Soviet and Post-Soviet Russia: Ideology, Consumption and Competition." In *Soviet and Post-Soviet Identities*, edited by Mark Bassin and Catriona Kelly, 321–40. Cambridge: Cambridge University Press.
Petrone, Karen. 2000. *Life Has Become More Joyous, Comrades: Celebrations in the Time of Stalin*. Bloomington: Indiana University Press.
Pokrovsky, N. N., V. P. Danilov, S. A. Krassil'nikov, and L. Viola, eds. 2006. *Politburo and Krestianstvo: Vysylka, Spetsposelenie, 1930–1940*. Moscow: ROSSPEN.
Priestland, David. 2007. *Stalinism and the Politics of Mobilization: Ideas, Power, and Terror in Inter-War Russia*. Oxford: Oxford University Press.
Prishvin, M. M. 2010. *Dnevniki, 1936–1937*. Saint-Petersburg: Rostok.
Reese, Roger. 2011. *Why Stalin's Soldiers Fought: The Red Army Military Effectiveness in World War II*. Lawrence: University Press of Kansas.
Rittersporn, Gábor. 2014. *Anguish, Anger, and Folkways in Soviet Russia*. Pittsburgh: University of Pittsburgh Press.
Rittersporn, Gábor, Malte Rolf, and Jan C. Behrends. 2003. *Sphären von Öffentlichkeit in Gesellschaften sowjetischen Typs: Zwischen partei-staatlicher Selbstinszenierung und kirchlichen Gegenwelten*. Frankfurt am Main: P. Lang.
Rossiisky Gosudarstvenny Archiv Sotsial'noy Politicheskoy Istorii (RGASPI) [Russian State Archives of Social and Political History].
Schloegel, Karl. 2012. *Moscow, 1937*. Cambridge, UK: Polity.
Shaporina, Liubov'. 2012. *Dnevnik*. Vol. 1. Moscow: NLO.
———. 2017. *Dnevnik*. Vol. 2. Moscow: NLO.
Siegelbaum, Lewis H. 1998. "'Dear Comrade, You Ask What We Need': Socialist Paternalism and Soviet Rural 'Notables' in the Mid-1930s." *Slavic Review* 57 (1): 107–32.
Sinitsyn, F. L. 2010. "Konstitutsionnye printsipy svobody sovesti I vseobschego izbiratel'noogo prava v SSSR: popytka realizatsii I protivodeistvie (1936–1939)." *Rossiiskaia Istoriia* (1): 81–92.
Smith, Stephen. 2005. "Nebesnye pis'ma I rasskazy o lese: "sueveria" protiv Bolshevisma." *Antropologicjesky Forum* (3): 280–306.
Sokolov, A. 1998. *Obshchestvo i vlast', 1930-e gody: Povestvovanie v dokumentakh*. Moscow: ROSSPEN.

Solomon, Peter H. 1996. *Soviet Criminal Justice Under Stalin.* Cambridge: Cambridge University Press.

Stalin, I. V. 1936. "On the Draft Constitution of the U.S.S.R.: Report Delivered at the Extraordinary Eighth Congress of Soviets of the U.S.S.R." https://www.marxists.org/reference/archive/stalin/works/1936/11/25.htm. Accessed May 31, 2016.

———. 1947. *Doklad o proekte konstitutsii SSSR.* Moscow: OGIZ.

Torstensen, Tatiana V. 1999. *Elder Sebastian of Optina.* Platina, CA: St. Herman of Alaska Brotherhood.

Tsentral'ny Gosudarstvenny Arkhiv Istoriko–Politicheskikh Dokumentov Sankt-Peterburga (TsGAIPD SPb) [Central State Archives of Historical–Political Documents in Saint-Petersburg].

Velikanova, Olga. 2001. *The Public Perception of the Cult of Lenin Based on Archival Materials.* Lewiston: Edwin Mellen.

———. 2013. *Popular Perceptions of Soviet Politics in the 1920s: Disenchantment of the Dreamers.* Basingstoke, UK: Palgrave Macmillan.

Verdery, Katherine. 1996. *What Was Socialism and What Comes Next?* Princeton, NJ: Princeton University Press.

Veselovsky, S. V. 2000. "Dnevniki, 1915–23, 1944." *Voprosy Istorii* (3): 93–112.

Yakovlev, A. N. 1995. *Po moscham I Elei.* Moscow: Evrazia.

Yarskaia-Smirnova, E., and P. Romanov. 2009. "The Rhetoric and Practice of Modernization: Soviet Social Policy, 1917–1930s." In *Amid Social Contradictions: Towards a History of Social Work in Europe*, edited by Gisela Hauss and Dagmar Schulte, 149–64. Opladen, Germany: Barbara Budrich.

Yekelchyk, Serhy. 2014. *Stalin's Citizens: Everyday Politics in the Wake of Total War.* Oxford: Oxford University Press.

CHAPTER 11

Other Comments and Recommendations

11.1 Demands for Welfare Benefits

The segment of welfare comments was premier in the list of popular concerns. Chapter X, "The Core Rights and Duties of Citizens," which received 53% of all comments in the discussion (23,428 out of 43,427) claimed, "Citizens of the U.S.S.R. have the right to work, ... annual vacations with full pay *for workers and employees*, care in old age and in case of sickness, ... ensured by social insurance of *workers and employees* at state expense, ... education, including higher education, being free of charge" [my italics—OV]. The expansion of social benefits to *all* workers and employees, and the revoking of previous restrictions (see below) was the great attainment of socialism and showed the leaders' faith in the expected social harmony. Articles 120 and 119 about the right to pensions and the right to vacations got respectively 4966 and 4060 comments. Both articles got 31.9% in Leningrad, 21.9% in Smolensk, and 6.5% in Gorky *krai* (GARF f. 3316, op. 8, d. 222, l. 160; Getty 1991, p. 25; GARF f. 3316, op. 41, dd. 127–9).[1] Such an explosion of comments had its primary source in the noticeable exclusion of peasants from state social benefits. The state provision of pension, vacation, medical, maternity benefits, and days off was still available only to urbanites, enraging the deprived villagers, who comprised two-thirds of the

---

[1] Getty reviewed 2,627 and 474 letters from Leningrad *oblast'* and Smolensk *oblast'*.

© The Author(s) 2018
O. Velikanova, *Mass Political Culture Under Stalinism*,
https://doi.org/10.1007/978-3-319-78443-4_11

population. The collective farms' elders and sick were to be supported by the scarce public funds of the *kolkhozes*.

The history of soviet welfare deserves further research (Madison 1968; Caroli 2003; Hoffmann 2011; Yarskaia-Smirnova and Romanov 2009, pp. 150–64; George and Manning 1980). In theory, the socialist project, as understood by the leaders, included the state provision of social benefits to the population. While historically, the first attempts to organize public aid in different forms were undertaken in Great Britain and Germany, the principle of social assistance was written on the banner of the first socialist state. After seizing power, the Bolsheviks decreed comprehensive social insurance (unemployment, sickness, free medical care) for all waged workers and the village poor, but scarcity did not permit introducing these benefits to all and at once. With the introduction of the New Economic Policy (NEP), scarce social benefits were reserved for industrial workers only (Kotkin 2001, pp. 145–6; Madison 1968). This privileged class of workers received higher rations, priority in housing, subsidized living quarters, and free health care. Industrial workers were the first group in 1929 to get old-age pensions, which were paid to 70,000 individuals who had worked for 25 years—women over the age of 55, and men over 60. Before that, only the disabled could apply for meager pensions (Hoffmann 2011, pp. 57–8, 62; Caroli 2003, p. 46). During the 1930s, the number of urbanites eligible for insurance increased from 10.8 million in 1928 to 25.6 million in 1936, and 31.2 million in 1940 (George and Manning 1980, p. 41). The class principle prioritizing industrial workers was used to allocate scarce state resources. With the transition of social insurance from the Commissariat of Labor to the All-Union Council of Trade Unions during the reforms in 1931 and 1933, benefits for workers included pay for maternity leave, health spas and resorts, education stipends, and funeral assistance. But, as Caroli concluded, these reforms turned the welfare provision into a kind of privilege reserved for the most productive workers (Caroli 2003, pp. 29, 48).

The class and political approaches defined social policy toward the disabled. In this group, too, the social benefits became a political tool to discriminate against the socially alien. The journal *Sotsial'noe strakhovanie* wrote in 1929: "The social security law must be a tool of the proletarian class; it must serve the interests of the proletariat and be directed against our enemies." A regulation from 25 November 1929 initiated a purge of social aliens among the disabled. Job vacancies reserved for people with disabilities discriminated against "former" people (Caroli 2003, p. 47; Yarskaia-Smirnova and Romanov 2009, p. 6). Behind the façade of the welfare state, millions of disabled veterans of World War I and the Civil War lived in horrible conditions. A government decree from 16 November 1918 granted only feeble support—15 rubles per month in 1924 (Caroli 2003, p. 39). The disabled of the tsar's army were excluded from welfare, as World War I was considered imperialist and tsarist.[2] In the mid–1920s, only 145,000 out of 634,000 wounded and disabled veterans were covered by social security, including 21,000 who lived in shelters and 105,000 who drew pensions (in 1927) that were considerably lower than the living minimum. Others were left to the mercy of fate. Mandates for the 1927 law to raise pensions to 40% of the minimum wage were not fulfilled. Negligible privileges for active Red Army soldiers' families, such as tax relief, failed to be realized on the local level. The Manifesto of 1927 announced a doubling of social funding for disabled war veterans. State support for this group, however, was so anemic that even this twofold increase (if fulfilled) was barely a weak gesture.

As the People's Commissar of Social Security, I. A. Nagovitsyn, stated in 1927, the total social security funds in the Russian Federation (RSFSR) comprised only 0.67% of the entire budget, while it was 11.5% in France, 37.7% in Germany and 8.64% in England. At this time, only 45,198,000 rubles in total were spent on veterans, while the Russian Empire in 1913—before the disastrous world and civil wars—had spent more than 40 million rubles (TsGAIPD SPb f. 16, op. 1, d. 8485, ll. 164–5, verso).[3]

Constitution Articles 119 and 120 addressed vacations and pensions for workers and employees but left the other two-thirds of the population in limbo. Attempts by the state to transfer responsibility for social security onto public organizations like village mutual aid associations (similar to relief during the famine of 1921–1922 being made the responsibility of the village commune) were no more than demagogic, as the latter had insufficient resources. The Kolkhoz Statute accepted in February 1935 put the duty of caring for sick, elderly, and disabled peasants on *kolkhoz* funds: "To create, in accordance with the decision of

---

[2] Decree, 28 April 1919, *Dekrety* (1957, pp. 118–22).
[3] Information from I. A. Nagovitsyn to Secretary of Leningrad *Gubernia* party committee, N. K. Antipov, 6 August 1927.

the [*kolkhoz*] general meeting, funds to assist disabled, old, or sick people, poor families of Red Army soldiers, and to maintain nursery schools and waifs; all these funds should not exceed 2% of the total annual production" (Kolkhoz Statute 1935). When maternity leave was discussed at the Second Congress of Outstanding Kolkhozniks in February 1935, Stalin personally intervened, suggesting two months of maternity leave with half of a woman's earnings [again, from *kolkhoz* funds—OV].

The problem was that under the ineffective conditions of the collective farm system, most *kolkhozes* were unable to allocate enough funds for these purposes. Particularly in the summer and fall of 1936, under dismal drought conditions, the elderly as well as laboring members of the collective were threatened by famine. The chair of the Lomonosovo *kolhoz*, Northern *krai*, Morgun, knew the dearth of local funds too well (see Chapter 8) and expressed in his recommendations for the constitution a typical demand: to cover the collective farmers by "centralized" resources, meaning state provisions (Danilov et al. 2002, pp. 806–7). Since *kolkhozniks* saw too little support from the *kolkhoz* or from mutual aid societies,[4] they rarely mentioned them in the discussion (Danilov et al. 2002, p. 938, n. 150). Nevertheless, *Pravda* presented praise from peasants: "The article about the support of elders and the sick gladdens me as an elder." These phony publications could only confuse the readers and evidenced very little concrete support received by the collective farmers: "When I became a member of a collective farm, I injured myself one day and could not work for a month. The *kolkhoz* council took care of me, provided food, and brought me a doctor" (*Pravda* 14 June 1936).

Responding to overwhelming demands for the equal treatment of villagers and urbanites at the state's expense, *Pravda* framed the vernacular by careful editing in line with official norms. On 3 July, the newspaper published a speech made by the chair of the Shapki village soviet, Bogoroditsky *raion*, Gorky *krai*, Ekaterina Mitriakhina, at the local meeting of village activists organized by the party committee. Major points of her speech corresponded to thousands of similar demands that paid vacations should be granted to "*kolkhozniks* who work all year round without any rest", but with the sly addition "from the account of *kolkhoz* funds," probably inserted by the editor. "The second recommendation

---

[4]The funds of the peasant committee of mutual aid (KKOV) comprised *kolkhoz* shares and individual fees.

is for Article 120, which said that citizens of the USSR have the right for support in old age and sickness. ... It says 'citizens of the USSR', but not only workers and employees; correspondingly, *kolkhozniki* have [the right] too. For that, we need to add a few words about widely developing *kolkhoz* mutual aid funds and reserves for disabled members. Without that addition, the foreign peasants wouldn't see that the Constitution takes care of sick and disabled *kolkhozniks*" (*Pravda* 3 July 1936). This demand for the development of *kolkhoz* funds was a timid request for state contributions. In practice, it was the chair of the village soviet's responsibility to accumulate these funds out of members' deductions.

The propagandists, whose duty was to deliver lectures and explain the constitution, had a hard time accommodating the phony declarations with the popular demands and peasants' complaints. According to the testimony of a teacher-propagandist, the *kolkhozniks* often asked him:

"You say that the Constitution gives [people] the right to labor and to rest. How about us? We do not have any rest; we work every day. No one cares about us." What could I say to them? I could only say: "This is nature of your occupation." I could not tell them anything else. Or perhaps an old invalid would ask: "What kind of pension do they give me, I who have broken legs?" If I said something else, someone might inform on me. These were very good questions, but I had no right to answer [with the truth]. (HPSSS Schedule A, Vol. 9, Case 111, p. 2)

Demands followed to provide pensions for orphans, veterans, and other miserable groups.

The Commissar of Social Security, I. A. Nagovitsyn, supported these massive demands on 2 October 1936: "I see it necessary to expand Article 120 ... to include [in the system of social benefits] besides workers and employees, also disabled veterans who defended their socialist motherland, *kolkhozniks*, artisans in cooperatives, and invalids" (Danilov et al. 2002, pp. 839–40). His letter went to the party Central Committee (CC) and the Soviet Central Executive Committee (TsIK) through public channels like any other outsider complaints, which makes it possible the commissar probably lacked internal working channels to bring his opinion to the attention of the government. The commissar of social welfare was probably excluded from the government conversation on the constitution—an assumption suggesting that his office was overlooked.

The glaring inequality of workers and peasants, contrasted with the socialist rhetoric of equality and fraternity, produced an overarching discourse in the peasants' complaints: serious social conflict between the city and the countryside began surfacing in the mid-1920s. This conflict originated in the grain requisitions of War Communism and was intensified by overtaxation of the countryside, the massive rural–urban migration, and urban unemployment in the 1920s. The narrative of inequality grew during the decade as peasants felt deceived by the Bolsheviks for providing no rewards to villages after their sacrifices in the Civil War. Their dissatisfaction culminated in 1927 with the introduction of the TsIK Manifesto on the 10th Anniversary of the Revolution. It caused an explosion of protests and grievances from deprived peasants upset that the manifesto gave workers many privileges at their expense (Danilov et al. 1999, pp. 124–5, 131, 134). The symbolic gift to the peasantry was the manifesto's promise to start deliberations on a law to grant state social care for the elderly over 60 in poor families. These promises were dependent on the capabilities of the state budget, and took almost 40 years to gradually fulfill (*Pravda* 16, 18, 19 October; 3, 5 November 1927).

The infringement of peasants' interests and their exclusion from social benefits resulted in their longing to find an agency to protect and advocate their interests to the state. Demands for a Peasant Union—a kind of political party or trade union—proliferated through the 1920s until collectivization and dekulakization. Attempts to organize local Peasant Unions were undertaken by villagers, the intelligentsia, and students between 1923 and 1928, but under the OGPU surveillance and repressions, the movement existed mostly as discourse. How deeply the idea of a Peasant Union was entrenched in an awakened peasant consciousness shows the revival of the idea during the constitution discussion: "It is necessary to give to all *kolkhozes* and individual peasants the right to organize a local Peasant Union under every rural soviet" (Sokolov 1998, p. 149).[5] While the constitution satisfied the decade-long political demand for equal voting and representation in the government, material inequality remained a hot subject. The 1936 debate still centered on the issue of inequality between workers and peasants. The widow K. F. Shestakova, Sverdlovsk *oblast'*, complained about overtaxation

---

[5] Letter from I. A. Tushin, Yaroslav *oblast'*.

and the misery of life. Her two sons could not have milk from their cow because she had to take it away from them and gave it to the state as a state duty: "Why in the USSR have we ended up with two classes—one liberated, and one oppressed? The state buys from us cheaply, and sells to us at great cost. ... Workers, employees, farmers—we are all toilers; a *kolkhoznik* is also a human being: he also needs to eat well." The letter is signed "Collective farmer, a widow, half hungry, I weep as I write" (Sokolov 1998, p. 134).

In the 1936 discussion of Stalin's constitution, the demand for social benefits for *kolkhozniks* constituted the largest section of all demands, together with access to resorts, a seven-hour working day, and paid vacations. *Kolkhozniks* only acquired the right to pensions in 1964. The constitution's articles on the social welfare system showed that they remained class–based and discriminatory in opposition to the articles on universal voting rights. Peasants felt the discrepancy and used this moment to negotiate and protest.

Analyzing the vocabulary of the welfare comments, we can distinguish two main discourses. The flood of peasants' demands for social benefits used the terms of civil rights and the social equality of citizens—evidence of a growing civic culture. "We collective farmers [should] enjoy no lesser rights than city workers" (RGASPI f. 17, op. 120, d. 232, l. 74). They employed the socialist rhetoric of equality when comparing their second-class status with the privileges of the workers—a continuing topic since the 1920s when the narrative developed into open conflict or "anti-worker" moods, as *chekists* defined them. The Peasant Union's idea to defend their economic and political rights, vocalized among the most entrepreneurial villagers, was an important sign of political maturing. Political language was commonly used to question the socialist and just nature of the regime, thus remaining within the frames of the political discourse.

Many welfare demands, however, lacked political coloration and focused on everyday deprivations. They could be generated by participants, whom Sidney Verba and Norman Nie called parochial: generally apolitical, they willingly contact officials about their very specific, often personal, problems. The engine could be misery and hardships or simple envy of a more successful counterpart as peasants en masse demanded the social benefits they believed the workers enjoyed. Of course, this feeling of injustice reflected very dire conditions in the countryside. Besides objective economic inequality, psychological factors influenced the welfare demands of the peasantry: the old antagonism between city and village, and social ressentiment. Additionally, as Fitzpatrick noted, these demands echoed the century-old patriarchal relations between the nobility and serfs. Villagers extrapolated the old pattern of client–patron relations typical of serfdom to the Soviet state and saw it as natural that "the state had welfare obligations" toward them (Fitzpatrick 1994, pp. 130, 151). These factors all combined and contributed to the extraordinary popularity of the constitution's articles about social benefits. Despite that, Stalin dismissed them in his final report as not relevant to the constitution but rather to current legal practice. Articles remained unchanged, peasants' demands ignored. The referendum was not binding on the organizers; they chose whatever they wanted to accept as amendments.

11.2 Distrust

Previous chapters have already shown that skepticism and disbelief accompanied almost every theme of the popular discourse—the talks about democratic elections, religious freedom, free speech, and other subjects. Whichever article of the constitution was discussed, distrust was a major theme—popular pessimism about improvement of life, declarations of the authorities, and officialdom as a whole. "There would be nothing better for us. Freedoms exist only on paper." "There is no sense in discussing the constitution and suggesting amendments. At any rate, they won't do it our way. The government works in its own interests." "Freedom of speech exists only on paper. It's a trap: if you say something inappropriate, they will arrest you" (Berelowitch and Danilov 2012, pp. 356–7).

Generalized social distrust was characteristic of Soviet society throughout the 1920s and 1930s. It resulted from unrealized promises, the rapid reversals of state policy, insecurity, and the discrepancies between official declarations and Soviet reality. How was this combined with the statist tendency in the political culture and the cult of leader? A "culture of distrust" does not exclude a "culture of trust," as A. Tikhomirov showed (Tikhomirov 2013, pp. 84, 86). The relations between these dispositions were complicated and entwined. The gullible relied on the state, while more critically minded citizens refused to accept the new promises. Trust in the personalities in power was accompanied by mistrust of the institutions. Sociologists recently discovered that a high level of mistrust persists in the population: modern Russians are least likely to trust political parties, the judicial system, the police, trade unions, the State Duma, the press—the main institutions of democratic societies—and they have the greatest trust in the president, the government, governors, the Federal Security Service, and the armed forces—the pillars of a centralized regime and authoritarianism (Gorshkov 2010, pp. 44–51).

As personal letters evidence, disbelief was articulated by Soviet dreamers soon after the Revolution, and continued to accumulate into 1927. The major crisis of faith became massively articulated when the country celebrated the tenth anniversary of the October Revolution. Rejecting official claims about the achievements of socialism in the USSR, a huge part of the urban and rural population denied socialism as a reality or an attainable goal, and openly refused to defend these false accomplishments in the event of war. Disillusionment and distrust were the major themes of popular discourse in 1927. A mobilization campaign promoting the counter–story of success was futile then, as Bolsheviks failed to gain the support of the population in transforming the country and creating a new Soviet identity (Velikanova 2013, pp. 160–87). The industrialization crusade raised new hopes, mostly among the youth and urbanites, but collectivization and famine shattered them again, especially in the countryside. The major reason for the growing social mistrust was the failed promise of prosperity after the first Five–Year Plan. In the cities, real wages fell, working and housing conditions deteriorated, and rationing was canceled only two years later, while death and hunger ruled the countryside. Mistrust was another side of the mobilizations, with cycles of enthusiasm and disillusionment.

A leaflet found in the Rubezhansky Institute of Chemical Technology, Donetsk region, in 1935 denounced the deprivations of students and workers, and unfulfilled Five-Year Plan promises: "Have the economic conditions of the working class improved?" The leaflet compared prices and wages of 1930 and 1935: prices for basic goods grew from 400 to 2,500%, but the average wage grew only 300% (Getty and Naumov 1999, p. 215). "What have we gained?" was the common narrative of anti-Soviet leaflets through the interwar period, especially numerous during the 1927 anniversary of the October Revolution. Another underground leaflet, from the Western area of the USSR, signed "The National Workers Union," echoed this question in 1939: "A huge lie, treacherous promises, terror and a desolate life. … We received a good constitution, but how has it been put into practice? It all remained on paper and we have been cheated in the most unheard of manner. Where were the secret elections? Who was elected as members of the Supreme Council? Only puppets [*Van'ki-Vstan'ki*], but not our deputies. They are appointed by Stalin's supporters. We dare not believe any of their promises. We must fight again for freedom" (Reynolds 1984, Reel RX. Report 31, October 1939).

Another reason for mistrust was the rapid turns of state policy common during Stalinism. Such events as the introduction of the NEP, the German–Soviet Nonaggression Pact of 1939, reversing of the Doctors' Plot Affair in 1953, and denouncing Stalin's cult in 1956 produced waves of confusion and disappointment among militant party men and true believers who followed the official line. The democratic nature of the constitution, canceling previous policies, belonged to these reversals. Discontent with the shifts in politics starkly revealed the inertia of the mass consciousness: for example, world revolution rhetoric persisted in popular discourse long after it ceased in the official narrative after 1925 (Velikanova 2013, p. 93). Authors such as Dostoevsky, Fromm, Etkind, and Kotkin showed that sharing the authorities' myth and merging with power—voluntarily and gratefully—provides security and comfort to the little man, who in certain circumstances grew into a totalitarian personality. "Even when those in power themselves reject it [the state myth], the bearer of mythology, like addicts ... cling to their customary conceptions of the world" (Gozman and Etkind 1992, p. 17). Unexpected shifts produced confusion and mistrust, and "undermined the credibility of the state as a producer of ideological discourse" (Yekelchyk 2014, p. 33). While the sudden introduction of democracy puzzled the Stalinist true believers and beneficiaries of the dictatorship, in the next turn, the hopes associated with the constitution were dashed again as the Great Terror ravaged the population. As the political and cultural elite was decimated, distrust of the party leadership was continually voiced. The reaction of the population to the purges of the elite reflected the fragility of the "forced trust" and legitimacy. In 1937, newspapers almost daily announced arrests at the top, which undermined confidence: "Now I don't trust any member of the CC. Today Gamarnik shot himself and tomorrow they'll arrest Kalinin." "It is difficult to trust the Politburo, when the leading figures in the Red Army have turned out to be spies." "We should disband the entire CC and elect a new government"

(TsGAIPD SPb f. 24, op. 2v, d. 2664, ll. 2, 7, 207–9, 217). Finally, Stalin had to dismiss and scapegoat Yezhov to restore a kind of legitimacy, which had been severely damaged by the repression (Hosking 2013).

Disorientation and fear in society found its reflection in the decline of the Red Army's general morale in the second part of the 1930s when conscription rapidly grew to 5.5 million by mid-1941. Defeatism and distrust were reported by political workers. The purges in the military in 1937 and the arrests of field marshals Tukhachevsky and Yakir were the first that caused a lack of respect for officers. "Whom to trust then? How can I know, when a commander gives an order, whether it is good or bad?" asked disoriented soldiers. Another reason, as Mark von Hagen concluded, was the ever-widening social gap between the top officers, who enjoyed certain privileges, and soldiers and junior officers. Excessive secrecy in the Red Army added to the confusion. All of this led to a decline in discipline and an increase in extraordinary accidents, including suicides—up to 400,000 in four months of 1937. The spread of defeatist sentiments and distrust of officers were reported by the political workers along with expressions of patriotism, with its chauvinistic overtones and common belittling of enemy strength (von Hagen 2000, pp. 189–97).

Together with vertical distrust in relations between society and the rulers, horizontal mistrust weakened the cohesiveness of society from within. "People have completely stopped trusting each other. They go about their work and do not even whisper to one another," one diary says (Prishvin 2010, p. 762). Party member Y. A. Zaretsky in Leningrad, afraid of a party purge, committed suicide in 1935: "For me, the situation of distrust was becoming such that I could no longer even conceive of living and working," he wrote in his last letter (Getty and Naumov 1999, p. 217). Mobilizations, with their slogans and promises, ignited new cycles of hope in the population, resulting finally in disillusionment, especially in the adult generation who lived through the NEP and its curtailment, promises of the "socialist offensive," and resulting famine. Here, we see the roots of cynicism that characterized the generation of the 1970s, called by Alexander Zinoviev *Homo sovieticus*, which finally eroded the soviet system from within. It was the discrepancies between official declarations and Soviet reality that recruited new Russian democrats to confront the Soviet political system in the 1980s (Lukin 2000, p. 137).

Summarizing the "trust studies," Alexei Tikhomirov shows that trust is a characteristic of social relations of modernity, usually associated with democratic Western countries. In contrast, distrust is a feature of undemocratic regimes and the main obstacle to the development of democracy. Distrust prevented the development of interconnectedness in society as a whole and—because of that—formation of a public sphere and civil society. Confidence in other people is an important component of civic culture (Almond and Verba 1965, p. 366). The relationship of trust/mistrust is a two-way communication involving both government and society. In the case of Soviet Russia, it was only logical that the Bolshevik party, seizing power in a coup and throwing the country into a civil war, mistrusted and feared the population. The party behaved as an aggressor in the occupied territory and a colonizer in the countryside. As we have seen, the population—at least a significant part—answered with the same suspicion. Mistrust is destructive and, according to sociologists, it leads to paralysis of human agency in social relationships, erosion of social capital, mobilization of defensive attitudes, hostile stereotypes and rumors, and renunciation of individualism to seek alternative identities (Sztompka 1997). Lack of confidence in the ineffective political institutions generated a compensatory practice when people seeking security and stability relied on personalized client–patron networks or grassroots cooperativeness, traditionally powerful in Russia. Tikhomirov concluded, "Distrust became a cultural frame in forming Communist modernity" (Tikhomirov 2013).

Distrust continued to accumulate in popular opinion during the discussion of the constitution, then again after the elections of 1937, which turned out to be a sham, and then during the repressions (TsGAIPD SPb f. 24, op. 2v, d. 2664, ll. 2, 200, 202, 207, 217; Brandenberger 2011, pp. 184–8, 192). Diaries and especially interviews with Soviet refugees after the war repeat the theme of mistrust and disillusionment in the constitution. "The 1936 constitution was awaited with great expectation. Many thought the time had come to pass into real socialism. The people were all for it. But in the end, the constitution was another fine piece of paper that was never realized. Nothing changed, and the people were greatly disillusioned" (HPSSS Schedule A, Case 433 p. 50; Vol. 12, Case 149; Shaporina 2012, p. 219). Political participation in the discussion, however, showed at least the temporary success of the regime's attempts to gain legitimacy. Soviet enthusiasts celebrated the constitution. For those who hesitated, the democratic nature of the constitution awakened their hopes. As one worker expressed: "I was basically skeptical, yet I felt that perhaps there might be a change. Yet it must be said that my hopes were weak" (HPSSS Schedule A, Vol. 28, Case 540. p. 45). Always skeptical and critical, Lubov' Shaporina, curious about the new voting rules, participated in elections with interest.

A significant portion of society, especially those in relatively privileged positions—young workers in major cities—eagerly took the principles of the constitution at face value. If any group believed in the achievements of socialism (besides the *apparatchiki*), it was the youth. The Leningrad worker M. Gerasimov in 1941 became a volunteer militiaman (*opolchenets*). On the night of 15–16 July 1941, he wrote a letter entitled "Address to All Toilers of Foreign Countries of the Entire World" and at 6 a.m. delivered it to the political commissar for publication in the newspaper. In the address, he called on the foreign toilers to join the Soviet workers in their fight against fascism. He praised the rights of the Soviet workers: "We have a system in which there is no difference between nationalities ... all have full rights who are for the liquidation of exploiters." All have the right to work, vacations, education, and the guarantee of equal well-being. "Such is our constitution." Belonging to a privileged group, he saw no contradiction between the reality and the constitution. Though his address was met by his superiors with sympathy, the political commissar did not publish the letter as its calls for international revolution were in conflict with new relations with the European countries, on which military aid depended. This letter, written in the front trenches, sounds sincere in its expressions of patriotism and proletarian internationalism and corresponded to the feelings of thousands of young soldiers (Dzeniskevich 2000, pp. 79–80).

Another young man, after losing his elder brother and father in the repressions in 1927 and 1929, and, as "socially alien," his own job as well, blamed Communists and the collective tragedy of collectivization for his misfortunes. But later he became an economic engineer with a good salary and married. The Constitution of 1936 was a contributing factor to his reconciliation to the regime; he believed it heralded the beginning of a new era. He even considered joining the party. Then came a terrible shock—13 March 1937 (the respondent said he would remember this date as long as he lived)—his father-in-law, a Communist, who was like a father to him, was arrested. This event again changed his ideology (HPSSS Schedule A, Vol. 35, Case 96, p. 60).

The testimonies of mistrust are copious. During the elections to the Supreme Soviet in December 1937, nearly all government automobiles in Moscow were requisitioned in order to bring the aged and infirm to the polling places. In each automobile, a team of two young, well-educated and extremely polite election commissioners was sent to escort old people and invalids to polling stations and then return them home. The solicitude of these young men seemed extreme. The old, illiterate people received the unheard-of attention and care with the greatest suspicion and fear, taking the young commissioners for NKVD men. The state-owned automobiles, colloquially called "Black Ravens," were so closely associated with the NKVD and arrests (Velikanova 2002, p. 4) that people thought they were being driven not to polling stations but to the secret police. When nothing adverse happened after casting their votes, suspicion turned into wonder and amazement. People did disbelieve and fear unusually polite officials in government cars (Reynolds 1984, Reel RX, Report 1077, 14 December 1937). They remembered the precedents: a common practice of the OGPU during the NEP and later years was to wring valuables from the wealthy in favor of the state, using torture by heat in a small cell (called by the populace *parilka*). The victims reported that "the OGPU [staff] were very polite. Thanked them nicely" when victims delivered the valuables afterwards (Bullard 2000, p. 88; Shaporina 2012, p. 129).

In the long run, unrealized promises eroded the legitimacy of the regime, at least in the eyes of an adult generation who endured repeated cycles of hope and disillusionment. While many citizens relied on the state, the more critically minded succumbed to skepticism and cynicism.

REFERENCES

Almond, Gabriel A., and Sydney Verba. 1965. *Civic Culture*. Boston, MA: Little, Brown.

Berelowitch, Alexei, and Victor Danilov, eds. 2012. *Sovetskaia derevnia glazami VChK-OGPU-NKVD: Dokumenty i materialy*. Vol. 4. Moscow: ROSSPEN.

Brandenberger, David. 2011. *Propaganda State in Crisis: Soviet Ideology, Indoctrination, and Terror under Stalin, 1927–1941*. New Haven: Yale University Press.

Bullard, Reader W. 2000. *Inside Stalin's Russia: The Diaries of Reader Bullard, 1930–1934*. Charlbury, UK: Day Books.

Caroli, Dorena. 2003. "Bolshevism, Stalinism, and Social Welfare (1917–1936)." *International Review of Social History* 48 (1): 27–54.
Danilov, Viktor Petrovich et al., eds. 1999. *Tragediia sovestskoi derevni: Kollektivizatsiia i raskulachivanie: dokumenty i materialy*. Vol. 1. Moscow: ROSSPEN.
Danilov, Viktor Petrovich, Roberta Thompson Manning, and Lynne Viola, eds. 2002. *Tragediia sovestskoi derevni: Kollektivizatsiia i raskulachivanie: dokumenty i materialy*. Vol. 4. Moscow: ROSSPEN.
Dekrety sovetskoi vlasti. 1957. Vol. 5. Moscow: Izdatel'stvo politicheskoi literatury.
Dzeniskevich, Andrei R. 2000. "The Social and Political Situation in Leningrad in the First Months of the German Invasion: The Social Psychology of the Workers." In *The People's War: Responses to World War II in the Soviet Union*, edited by Robert W. Thurston and Bernd Bonwetsch, 71–84. Urbana: University of Illinois Press.
Fitzpatrick, Sheila. 1994. *Stalin's Peasants: Resistance and Survival in the Russian Village After Collectivization*. Oxford: Oxford University Press.
George, Victor, and Nick Manning. 1980. *Socialism, Social Welfare, and the Soviet Union*. London: Routledge.
Getty, A. 1991. "State and Society Under Stalin: Constitutions and Elections in the 1930s." *Slavic Review* 50 (1): 18–35.
Getty, A., and Oleg V. Naumov. 1999. *The Road to Terror: Stalin and the Self-destruction of the Bolsheviks, 1932–1939*. New Haven, CT: Yale University Press.
Gorshkov, M. K. 2010. "The Sociological Measurement of the Russian Mentality." *Russian Social Science Review* 51 (2): 32–57.
Gosudarstvenny Arkhiv Rossiiskoi Federatsii (GARF) [State Archives of Russian Federation].
Gozman, Leonid, and Alexander Etkind. 1992. *The Psychology of Post-totalitarianism in Russia*. London: Centre for Research into Communist Economies.
Hagen, Mark von. 2000. "Soviet Soldiers and Officers on the Eve of the German Invasion: Toward a Description of Social Psychology and Political Attitudes." In *The People's War: Responses to World War II in the Soviet Union*, edited by Robert W. Thurston and Bernd Bonwetsch, 189–97. Urbana: University of Illinois Press.
"Harvard Project on the Soviet Social System." *Harvard College Library*. http://hcl.harvard.edu/collections/hpsss/index.html.
Hoffmann, David L. 2011. *Cultivating the Masses: Modern State Practices and Soviet Socialism, 1914–1939*. Ithaca, NY: Cornell University Press.
Hosking, Geoffrey. 2013. "Trust and Distrust in the USSR: An Overview." *The Slavonic and East European Review* 91 (1): 1–25.

"The Kolkhoz Statute." 17 February 1935. *Seventeen Moments in Soviet History.* http://soviethistory.msu.edu/1936-2/second-kolkhoz-charter/second-kolkhoz-charter-texts/kolkhoz-statute/. Accessed July 29, 2016.

Kotkin, Steven. 2001. "Modern Times. The Soviet Union and the Interwar Conjuncture." *Kritika: Explorations in Russian and Eurasian History* 2 (1): pp. 111–64.

Lukin, Alexander. 2000. *The Political Culture of the Russian "Democrats".* Oxford: Oxford University Press.

Madison, Bernice A. 1968. *Social Welfare in the Soviet Union.* Stanford, CA: Stanford University Press.

Prishvin, M. M. 2010. *Dnevniki, 1936–1937.* Saint-Petersburg: Rostok.

Reynolds, Dale, ed. 1984. *U. S. Military Intelligence Reports: Soviet Union, 1919–1941.* Frederick, MD: University Publications of America.

Rossiisky Gosudarstvenny Archiv Sotsial'noi Politicheskoi Istorii (RGASPI) [Russian State Archives of Social and Political History].

Shaporina, Liubov'. 2012. *Dnevnik*, Vol. 1. Moscow: NLO.

Sokolov, A. 1998. *Obshchestvo i vlast' 1930–e gody: Povestvovanie v dokumentakh.* Moscow: ROSSPEN.

Sztompka, Piotr. 1997. *Trust, Distrust and the Paradox of Democracy.* Berlin: WZB.

Tikhomirov, Alexei. 2013. "The Regime of Forced Trust: Making and Breaking Emotional Bonds Between People and State in Soviet Russia, 1917–1941." *The Slavonic and East European Review* 91 (1): 78–118.

Tsentral'ny Gosudarstvenny Arkhiv Istoriko–Politicheskikh Dokumentov Sankt-Peterburga (TsGAIPD SPb) [Central State Archives of Historical–Political Documents in Saint-Petersburg].

Velikanova, Olga. 2002. *The Myth of the Besieged Fortress: Soviet Mass Perception in the 1920s–1930s.* Working Paper No. 7, Stalin-Era Research and Archives Project. Toronto: CREES.

———. 2013. *Popular Perceptions of Soviet Politics in the 1920s: Disenchantment of the Dreamers.* Basingstoke: Palgrave Macmillan.

Yarskaia-Smirnova, E., and P. Romanov. 2009. "The Rhetoric and Practice of Modernization: Soviet Social Policy, 1917–1930s." In *Amid Social Contradictions: Towards a History of Social Work in Europe,* edited by Gisela Hauss and Dagmar Schulte, 149–64. Opladen, Germany: Barbara Budrich.

Yekelchyk, Serhy. 2014. *Stalin's Citizens: Everyday Politics in the Wake of Total War.* Oxford: Oxford University Press.

CHAPTER 12

Outcome of the Discussion: From Relaxation to Repression

In November 1936, the Central Executive Committee of the Soviets (TsIK) summarized the popular suggestions and sent their results to the Editorial Commission. Forty-three thousand comments were collected by the TsIK, copious reports directed to party leaders from the newspapers, localities, and the NKVD—how were these materials read and used by the leaders?

If the leaders of the USSR were interested in popular recommendations, they did not intend to follow them. Analysis of the discussion's outcome was not made public. Only one review presented the main trends of the received suggestions, in *Izvestia* by I. A. Akulov, the secretary of the TsIK and a former procurator general of the USSR. After reading his article, British intelligence analysts concluded: "Akulov would have us believe that the bulk of public opinion is unwilling to accept so 'liberal' a constitution, and would prefer to see the paternal government endowed with more effective powers for the suppression of dangerous thoughts" (British F.O. 371, 1936, Vol. 20351, p. 117).[1] Akulov reviewed the compendium of comments with necessary details, but almost without quantification. He acknowledged that the chapter dealing with citizens' rights and duties provoked more interest than any other, accounting for 23,000 out of 43,000 comments. He did not bother to explain the real reasons for the discussants' agitation, namely

---

[1] Dispatch from 24 November 1936.

© The Author(s) 2018
O. Velikanova, *Mass Political Culture Under Stalinism*,
https://doi.org/10.1007/978-3-319-78443-4_12

the omission of peasants from the system of social security and benefits, but stated: "the constitution should confine itself to fundamental principles, details to be worked out in special legislative measures." This same subterfuge was used by Stalin in his final speech at the 8th Congress of Soviets. It was a vague promise, predictably not realized. Akulov's review outlined with unexpected openness the discussion's major themes: the voices for expanding the notion "enemy of the people;" people's trepidation about the use of constitutional liberties by such enemies, the right of every republic to secede freely from the USSR; and finally, the popular rejection of the enfranchisement of the "former" people. What was the reason, in an atmosphere dense with the ideological vigilance of those days, for publicizing the strong illiberal trend against the major message of the constitution? It could hardly have been objective coverage of popular opinion. Was it a quiet acknowledgment of popular support for the illiberal reality? Ellen Wimberg (1992) believes that the personal position of N. Bukharin, the chief editor of *Izvestia*, distinguished his newspaper in its coverage of the discussion. Akulov's review, though lacking numbers of the respective comments, reflected the collected data more accurately than Stalin's report to the congress.

The popular discussion did not presuppose voting. Only a small number of constitutional amendments, those concerned with relatively unimportant points, were taken into consideration by the leaders, who simply pretended that the views of the population had been respected. Stalin reviewed selected suggestions in his report on 25 November and gave his feedback on the popular discussion.[2] He announced that *all* suggestions were published in the press but most of the materials were buried in archives. Stalin avoided any evaluation of the popularity of the articles. At the congress, the hottest issue of the popular discussion—welfare benefits for the peasantry—was silenced and dismissed by the dictator as a subject under the jurisdiction of future legislative bodies, not the constitution. These most numerous demands were not implemented. The trick used to sidestep the popular comments was Stalin's artificial subdivision of the proposals into three categories: those dealing with "matters of current legislation" and therefore inappropriate in the constitution; those comments with historical references thought to be excessive for the document; and finally, those essential matters worth discussing.

---

[2] See Stalin's comments on the respective articles in earlier chapters.

After speaking about several articles with low response rates, evidently unappealing to the public, Stalin mentioned very popular Articles 124 and 135—the suggestions demanding banning religious rites and voting rights for "former" people. Without deliberation or arguments, he recommended rejecting these amendments "as being in disaccord with the spirit of our constitution" and "stamped" this with a quotation from Lenin. The speaker granted his approval of the comments to mostly procedural articles and on the formation of the Defense Industry Ministry.[3]

Stalin returned to the results of the discussion at the 5 December meeting of the congress. As a chair of the Editorial Commission, he reported that it had included 43 amendments to the final text of the constitution (only 20 were deemed essential, the others—of an editorial nature). They altered 32 articles, while another 114 remained intact. Stalin considered it worthwhile to explain to the congress only seven accepted amendments to Articles 8, 10, 35, 40, 48, 49, and 77 (all discussing politically safe themes). The new constitution was passed by the congress with a unanimous show of hands. The final announcement—"The all-nation discussion was extremely useful in working out and the final editing of the constitution" (*Pravda* 6 December 1936)—was an exaggeration. The number of accepted proposals was in sharp contradiction to the propagandistic storm that had electrified the media for five months. The mountain gave birth to a mouse.

Whatever the vox populi said, it did not seriously affect the final version of the constitution. Chapter X, "Basic Civil Rights and Duties," which received 53.7% of all comments, was not acknowledged, and the champions among comments—Articles 120 about pensions and 135 about universal voting rights—were rejected by Stalin. The rationale of the discussion was a process per se—an orchestrated exercise in political conformity, not a promised adjustment of the constitution to the people's demands. The organizers worked to mold cultural discourse, not to satisfy the public (Tables 12.1 and 12.2).

Nevertheless, the participants brought the rulers their opinions, and their voices were heard. What Stalin had heard—differed from his idea of harmony. Ridiculing the "bourgeois critique of the constitution" in the report, Stalin actually repeated the major themes of domestic skeptics too: distrust in new freedoms, and fear of democratization and dissolution of the Bolsheviks' principles. Now the dictator learned that, despite

---

[3] Article 77, which received 630 comments.

Table 12.1 Proposed amendments according to article (table compiled by TsIK summarizing typical comments, 17 November 1936. GARF f. 3316, op. 8, d. 222, l. 160)

Article no.	Number of comments
120 Right to material protection in old age, illness	4966
135 Universal electoral rights	4716
119 Right to rest	4060
121 Right to education	3400
127 Inviolability of personality	3218
132 Universal military duty	2416
109 Formation of people's courts	1551
142 Deputies' reports and the right to recall them	1048
8 Land bound to *kolkhozes* for ever	1026
131 Citizens' duty to respect socialist property	942
122 Equal rights of women and men	888
1 Definition of the USSR	877
143 State emblem	675
133 Defense of motherland and treason	654
77 Formation of all-union ministries	630
118 Right to labor	581
12 Duty to work and right to compensation	475
95 Soviets' terms of service	395
78 Formation of republican ministries	366
130 Citizens' duties	332
Others	10,211
Total	43,427

his expectations, society was still divided, that discontent was high, but he also learned that the repressive state policy did not antagonize many. What implication did this outcome have for high politics? It moved Stalin to reevaluate the Sovietization of society.

Stalin received information about the popular reaction from the TsIK, NKVD and other sources. His report shows his mental swing back and forth between his attachment to expectations of social harmony and warnings from the grassroots about numerous enemies. These warnings gradually sank into his mind:

> 13. An amendment to Article 135 ... proposes that ministers of religion, former White Guards, all the former rich, and persons not engaged in socially useful occupations be disfranchised, or, at all events, that the franchise of people in this category be restricted to the right to vote but not

Table 12.2 Proposed amendments according to chapter (table compiled by TsIK summarizing typical comments, 17 November 1936. GARF f. 3316, op. 8, d. 222, l. 159)

Chapter no.	Number of comments	Percent
10 Basic rights/duties of citizen	23,098	53.0
11 Electoral system	6369	14.2
1 Social order	3412	7.9
9 Court and procuracy	3210	7.9
5 Organs of state, USSR	1243	2.9
3 Higher organs of state power, USSR	1214	2.8
8 Local organs of state power	953	2.2
12 Emblem, flag, capital	903	2.1
2 State order	675	1.6
4 Higher organs of power, republics	145	0.3
13 Order of changing the constitution	70	0.16
6 Organs of state government, republics	39	0.09
7 Higher organs of state power, autonomous republics	22	0.05
Other	2074	4.8

to be elected. I think that this amendment should likewise be rejected. The Soviet government disfranchised the nonworking and exploiting elements, not for all time, but temporarily, up to a certain period. There was a time when these elements waged open war against the people and actively resisted Soviet laws. The Soviet law depriving them of the franchise was the Soviet government's reply to this resistance. Quite some time has elapsed since then. During this period we have succeeded in abolishing the exploiting classes, and the Soviet government has become an invincible force. Has not the time arrived for us to revise this law? I think the time has arrived.

From past expectations the speaker moved to received warnings: "It is said that this is dangerous [to grant them the franchise], as elements hostile to the Soviet government, some of the former White Guards, kulaks, priests, and so forth, may worm their way into the supreme governing bodies of the country" (Stalin 1947).

What was Stalin's response? "In the first place, not all the former kulaks, White Guards and priests are hostile to the Soviet government." Here, Stalin clung to his thesis about the new social condition. But next, he recognized the existence of "hostile persons" and their threat: "Secondly, if the people in some places do elect hostile persons, that will show that our propaganda work was very badly organized." It was a threatening hint to the bad organizers. "If, however, our propaganda work is conducted in a Bolshevik way, *the people will not let hostile persons* [my italics—OV] slip into the supreme governing bodies." This phrase could be read by the officials in only one way—"Do not let hostile persons gain power." Then, Stalin addressed the officials: "This means that we must work and not whine ..."—an ominous hint to bureaucrats responsible for blocking enemies from attaining power (Priestland 2007, p. 346). Getty noted this change in Stalin's mind: "For a long time Stalin minimized the threat [of the anti-Soviet elements] in the countryside ... By July 1937, though, he had become convinced of the danger, changed his mind, and personally triggered the mass terror" (Getty 2013, p. 224).[4] Getty focuses mostly on the sabotage of constitutional liberties by the regional elites, but popular hostility itself, reported by them and internalized by Stalin, made him expand repressions from the elite and bureaucrats to the ordinary masses—believers, kulaks, nationals.[5]

Let us imagine how Stalin could react to popular and *chekists'* warnings provided to him by the TsIK and the NKVD. He regularly received admonitions about enemies from the NKVD.[6] He knew that *chekists* had a tendency to overemphasize the danger: "*Chekists* exaggerate some things—it is a specific of their job, but I do not doubt their honesty" (February–March Plenum, pp. 33–4), but the same warnings came from the party and soviet officials, nervous about the contested elections. Now, on top of that, popular comments recorded by the TsIK about omnipresent enemies confirmed NKVD reports and raised his feeling of insecurity. At the plenum, Stalin urged delegates to listen to the "voices

---

[4] Leonid Maksimenkov (2017) analyzed recently declassified "Journals of registration of outgoing documents with Stalin's resolutions." He noted the change in character of Stalin's resolutions in mid-1936 from slack and irresolute toward energetic and punitive. Khlevniuk noticed heightened incoherence, awkwardness, and confusion in Stalin's resolutions in 1937, accompanied by "explosions of fury" (Khlevniuk 2010, p. 300).

[5] In 1937–1938, 767,000 of 1,344,923 people were convicted in operations against anti-Soviet elements (Khlevniuk 2010, p. 320).

[6] Among many, in October 1936 the leadership received information from North Caucasus UNKVD about protests in connection with the constitution against *kolkhozes*, unjust taxes, and demands for opening the churches, welfare provisions, and calls "to study the constitution and prepare for elections" to crash the Bolsheviks (Khaustov et al. 2003, pp. 773–6).

of little people" (probably those warning about enemies) (*Pravda* 29 March 1937).

Finally, the discouraging census results were received on 25 January and 14 March 1937 and confirmed his misapprehension about the new condition of society—for example, persistent religiosity (see Chapter 10.1). It is probable that the incongruity of progress in society with the leadership's projections, as revealed in the discussion commentaries, led the government to classify the census data in advance—in December 1936, a directive to local census workers demanded, "*Not one figure from the census can be published.*" With the task of the census to quantify the social changes of the last decade, including "elimination of the hostile classes" (*Pradva* 2 January 1937), two campaigns—the census and the constitution discussion—had a function in common: to monitor society, initially simultaneously (Merridale 1996, pp. 226, 232). Both campaigns showed society altered, "fixed structures and social barriers dissolved," and elements of internal modernization newly formed, but not as uniform and homogeneous, not as Soviet as the leadership may have imagined (Schloegel 2012, pp. 118–9).

How could Stalin conceptualize the social situation revealed in 1936 and the beginning of 1937 with a mind as suspicious as his, with his wishful thinking and disrespect of Soviet citizens? The social conciliation declared in the constitution was premature; enemies were still numerous and active, society was against conciliation, the fight was not ended, a final purge necessary. The infamous order 00447 from 30 July 1937 called for the elimination of the anti-Soviet elements "once and for all." At the February–March Plenum, Stalin emphasized: "We need to end the opportunistic complacency [*blagodushie*] and philistine carelessness" and returned to rhetoric about "exasperation of the remnants of the broken exploiting classes," available as a resource for Trotskyist wreckers (Khaustov et al. 2004, pp. 96, 104, 106). Before the plenum, on 15 February, Stalin received the secret note with inventories of "anti-Soviet elements," which included 18 categories: "former" people, kulaks, former members of the socialist parties, more than 1.5 million expelled members of the Communist Party,[7] and around 100,000 "alien" and "socially harmful" people. Stalin carefully underlined the figures in the note. Stephen Kotkin noted: "Suddenly the number of punitive enemies

---

[7] The Communist Party numbered 2 million active members.

were colossal and they were everywhere" (Kotkin 2017, pp. 383, 391 cites RGASPI, f. 17, op. 71, d. 43, 44, 45, 46). When the plenum delegates discussed the threats in view of the coming elections, they reproduced the same personages from the discussion commentaries and NKVD reports—now emphasizing the believers and kulaks returning from exile, "former people", former Communist Party and prerevolutionary parties' members—and often referred to the results of the census. Society's reactions to the constitution ruined Stalin's "complacency." He read the comments through watchful lenses and formed the impression that society was not yet sufficiently Sovietized. The boomerang of social schism returned to the thrower.

In December 1936 and January 1937, Stalin's conceptualization of the popular commentaries and census results could provide a missing piece in the puzzle of why relative "moderation" ended and the state violence expanded to the wider population. Stephen Kotkin wondered: "There was no 'dynamic' forcing him to do so, no 'factional' fighting, no heightened threat abroad. The terror was not spiraling out of his control. He just decided, himself, to approve quota-driven eradication of entire categories of people in a *planned* indiscriminate terror" (emphasis in original) Khlevniuk noticed the signals of a shift from elite to mass purges at the beginning of 1937 (Kotkin 2017, p. 433; Khlevniuk 2010, p. 307). Fitzpatrick detected that something changed in the period from December 1936 to February 1937. "There had been a genuine impulse toward democratization at an earlier point, but this impulse had disappeared almost completely by … the February–March plenum" (Fitzpatrick 1994, p. 281). Getty came close to explaining the turn to mass operations: it was "precipitated by the unexpected dangers posed by the new constitution" (Getty 2013, p. 234). Stalin's December report, taken in the context of the dictator's disappointment with the January 1937 census results and consequent expansion of repressions, speaks in favor of his reevaluation of conditions in society. The granting of voting rights to the "enemies" and "exes" in 1936 grew from the Marxist maxim that new socialist relations of production (combined with appropriate "cleansings" of society) should define a new consciousness and a new Soviet unity of "friendly classes." But with popular and activists' comments warning against conciliation, high numbers of believers showed him this was not the case. Society should be purged more to reach desired purity. Such a trajectory in Stalin's thinking seems plausible, supported by his rhetorical switch from earlier "friendly classes" and "transformed former people" to the plenum's "exasperation of broken classes," and the cancellation of contested elections in October 1937 and other post-Terror events: the reintroduction of the social unity thesis after the Great Terror; the elimination in 1939 of admission class quotas in the Communist Party statute (though not realized); and the dropping of the term "socially alien elements" (for example, in the laws regulating distribution of housing) (Meerovich 2008, p. 208).[8]

Events of the Spanish Civil War in August–October 1936 may have also contributed to Stalin's reevaluation of conditions in Soviet society and the growth of his insecurity. The term "the fifth column," born in Spain to define the wartime internal opposition's insurgency, was eagerly adopted by official Soviet discourse because it corresponded to Stalinists' intrinsic fear of traitors inside the besieged fortress of the USSR. Reports of domestic hostile elements could sound especially frightening in the context of the Spanish insurgency.

Disregard of the proposed amendments demonstrated a pattern of controlled democracy—common for the Stalinist mode of relations with society. Democratic elements in discussion were used by the Stalinists to meet their pragmatic needs—as a tool to mobilize the people and apparatus, to purge intermediate cadres, but not to limit the dictatorship. Flexibility with election procedures, manipulation of nominations (quotas), intimidation, and sheer force (the arrests of the people's candidates, shown earlier, or entire unreliable constituencies, as with priests in 1937) were utilized to make democracy comfortable for the government. The base nature of dictatorship precluded sharing power with the populace. The dictator's arrogant disrespect of the political potential of the Soviet population (recall Stalin's famous utterance, "They need a tsar") and his use of manipulation as a tool of government structured his exploitation of democracy.

As early as 1927, for example, the All-Union forum on the pages of *Krestianskaia Gazeta* was a part of the tenth anniversary of the Revolution celebrations. Similar to the mobilization campaign in 1936, it invited readers to express their thoughts about Soviet policies and achievements. They responded with hundreds of letters, including critical ones. It was within the power of Kalinin, the chair of the

---

[8] However, the propaganda state failed to inculcate the socialist identity in general and the heroic and patriotic trope among youth specifically as a result of the Great Terror's desecration of Soviet Olympus (Brandenberger 2011, p. 197).

forum, to publicize or neglect the letters. Kalinin published a letter from the peasant N. F. Elichev with a thoughtful critique of Soviet economic policy, provoking a campaign of damnation against the dissident on the pages of the newspaper, with scornful peasants objecting to his arguments: "Nobody complains about the taxes" (Velikanova 2013, pp. 173–5). This forum exemplified controlled participation and shaped the prescribed Soviet identity. Another example of controlled democracy was the Second Congress of Outstanding Kolkhozniks in 1935 adopting the new Kolkhoz Statute (see Chapter 9), which provided a forum for the upward transmission of information and the expression of local concerns (Fitzpatrick 1994, p. 118). The all-nation discussion of 1936 belongs to such a pattern, called controlled or sham democracy.

The mobilization campaign around the constitution continued during the congress. Stalin's speech at the congress was broadcast all over the Soviet Union by radio, a major source of news, yielding only to the newspapers (Inkeles and Bauer 1959, pp. 162–3).[9] A technology that brought Stalin's voice to the distant corners of the huge country produced a formidable impression on the population—both intellectuals and average people. Almost all diarists of the decade noted this broadcast speech in their entries. Journalist-repatriate Nikolai Ustrialov provides us with the emotional record of the broadcast:

> Listening to the radio. I hear the inviting sounds of "The Internationale", but in such an extraordinary, unique performance: the Eighth Congress of the Soviets is joined in song. Kalinin has already given his introductory speech. Stalin is just about to speak! ... A large amount of time is taken up with greetings — that's probably how it has to be. Comrades Ordzhonikidze, Petrovsky, Postyshev, Rudzutak. Comrade Stalin? A renewed storm of applause, shouts, outbursts of enthusiasm, cheering, never-ending ovations. One would like to think and live amid such a din, such excitement. One would even like to join in the shouting.

The author continues with the detailed account of the main points of Stalin's speech (Schloegel 2012, pp. 225–6). The speaker announced that the first phase of Communism—socialism—had been achieved; social structure transformed—a proletariat became the liberated working

---

[9] Half of respondents of the Harvard Project mentioned radio as a source of information and 35% as the most important source.

class, peasantry became integrated in the socialist economy, the new Soviet-trained intelligentsia was formed and class war ceased.

We can learn how people reacted in private settings. A repatriate, Prince D. S. Svyatopolk-Mirsky, a Guard officer in tsarist Russia, an officer in World War I and the Civil War, emigrated, became a literary critic and historian, lectured at London University, wrote the unsurpassed *History of Russian Literature*, became a Communist in 1931, returned to Moscow the following year, was arrested in 1937, and died in a camp in 1939. He contributed to the campaign with an article, "On the Great Charter of the Peoples: The Constitution of Victory," published on 20 July in *Literaturnaia Gazeta*. But Vera Suvchinskaia recalled Mirsky's quite revealing private reaction to Stalin's speech: "I remember sitting on the floor at my friend's place and listening to that Georgian voice on the radio for an hour and a half explaining about all sorts of freedoms, democratic rights, and so on. ... I had dinner with Mirsky and his face was completely distorted and he said: 'Surely you understand that it's a *diabolical* lie!' I was a Communist, remember, and naïve, and a complete idiot. I told him he should be ashamed, that he was demoralized" (Smith 2000, p. 286; emphasis in original).

This solemn occasion was an incentive to expand the radio network. In 1935, there were 50 receivers per 1000 population in the cities and only about 4 receivers per 1000 in the rural areas (still only 8 in 1941)—a very poor scale of *radiofication* in comparison with the US and Western Europe. The entire network was inadequate: by 1937, there were 2,946,000 wired speakers and 650,000 ordinary radio-receiving sets in the largest country in the world. By the end of 1936, the Radio Committee claimed that 500,000 new sets[10] were ready to broadcast Stalin's address, but in practice many were idle for lack of current, repairs, or technical support (Inkeles 1950, pp. 247, 250–1). The quality of the connection was often very poor—static made the voice totally incomprehensible in many places, but the public assembled in clubs patiently listened to the noise, afraid to disrupt the political tone of the moment (TsGAIPD SPb f. 24, op. 5, d. 3195, l. 19). In one case, when static interrupted the speech, a joyful young listener exclaimed "Stalin started singing!" causing general laughter. His name was written down as a disrupter and reported by a vigilant informer to the NKVD.

---

[10] In August 1936, the equipment and materials for radio were bought in the US (Khlevniuk et al. 2001, p. 629).

Collective listening to the speech was well organized, as in Chudov *raion* in Leningrad *oblast'*, where party officials arranged for workers to march under banners with revolutionary songs to the radio club. During the sessions of group listening at clubs and conference halls, listeners spontaneously joined the delegates singing the party hymn, "the Internationale", and the ovation in the congress hall that lasted several minutes (TsGAIPD SPb f. 24, op. 5, d. 3195, ll. 18–26). In this pre-television era, the dictator's live voice broadcast all over the USSR had a strong bonding effect and showcased Soviet technological achievement. A special newsreel of the speech was produced and contained footage of Soviet achievements.

The "historical" significance of the event was emphasized by making 5 December, when the constitution was ratified, a national holiday. While the 8th Congress celebrated the constitution, people in the provinces stood in lines for six to eight hours to buy bread. The NKVD reported 300 people lines in Kirov *krai* and other regions. "Just before 6 a.m. I went out and got in line for bread. My happy fellow countrymen were already standing there, getting used to socialism," wrote Arzhilovsky on 4 December 1936 (TsGAIPD SPb f. 24, op. 2v, d. 1860, l. 79; Garros et al. 1997, pp. 130, 144).

He referred, of course, to the famous Stalin motto, "Life has become better, comrades!"

REFERENCES

Brandenberger, David. 2011. *Propaganda State in Crisis: Soviet Ideology, Indoctrination, and Terror Under Stalin, 1927–1941*. New Haven, CT: Yale University Press.
British Foreign Office—Russia Correspondence, 1781–1945. 1975. Wilmington, DE: Scholarly Resources.
February–March Plenum TsK VKPb, 23 February 1937. 1992. *Voprosy Istorii* (4–5).
Fitzpatrick, Sheila. 1994. *Stalin's Peasants: Resistance and Survival in the Russian Village After Collectivization*. Oxford: Oxford University Press.
Garros, Véronique, Natalia Korenevskaya, and Thomas Lahusen, eds. 1997. *Intimacy and Terror: Soviet Diaries of the 1930s*. New York: New Press.
Getty, J. Arch. 2013. "Pre-election Fever: The Origins of the 1937 Mass Operations." In *The Anatomy of Terror. Political Violence Under Stalin*, edited by James Harris, 216–35. Oxford: Oxford University Press.

Inkeles, Alex. 1950. *Public Opinion in Soviet Russia: A Study in Mass Persuasion*. Cambridge, MA: Harvard University Press.
Inkeles, Alex, and Raymond Bauer. 1959. *The Soviet Citizen: Daily Life in a Totalitarian Society*. Cambridge, MA: Harvard University Press.
Khaustov, V. N., V. P. Naumov, and N. S. Plotnikova, eds. 2003. *Lubianka: Stalin i VChK- GPU-OGPU-NKVD, 1922–1936*. Moscow: Demokratiia.
Khaustov, V. N., V. P. Naumov, and N. S. Plotnikova, eds. 2004. *Lubianka: Stalin i Glavnoe Upravlenie Gosbezopasnosti NKVD, 1937–1938*. Moscow: Demokratiia.
Khlevniuk, Oleg. 2010. *Khoziain: Stalin i utverzhdenie stalinskoi diktatury*. Moscow: ROSSPEN.
Khlevniuk, O. V., R. W. Davies, L. P. Kosheleva, E. A. Rees, L. A. Rogovaia, eds. 2001. *Stalin i Kaganovich. Perepiska. 1931–36 gg*. Moscow: ROSSPEN.
Kotkin, Stephen. 2017. *Stalin: Waiting for Hitler, 1929–1941*. New York: Penguin Press.
Maksimenkov, Leonid. 2017. Kommersant.ru. 03.07.2017. https://www.kommersant.ru/doc/3336286?from=doc_vrez. Accessed January 16, 2018.
Meerovich, Mark. 2008. *Nakazanie zhilischem: Zhilischnaia politika v SSSR, 1917–1937*. Moscow: ROSSPEN.
Merridale, Catherine. 1996. "The 1937 Census and the Limits of Stalinist Rule." *The Historical Journal* 39 (1): 225–40.
Priestland, David. 2007. *Stalinism and the Politics of Mobilization: Ideas, Power, and Terror in Inter-War Russia*. Oxford: Oxford University Press.
Schloegel, Karl. 2012. *Moscow, 1937*. Cambridge: Polity.
Smith, G. S. 2000. *D. S. Mirsky: A Russian-English Life, 1890–1939*. Oxford: Oxford University Press.
Stalin, I. V. 1947. *Doklad o proekte konstitutsii SSSR*. Moscow: OGIZ.
Tsentral'ny Gosudarstvenny Arkhiv Istoriko–Politicheskikh Dokumentov Sankt-Peterburga (TsGAIPD SPb) [Central State Archives of Historical–Political Documents in Saint-Petersburg].
Velikanova, Olga. 2013. *Popular Perceptions of Soviet Politics in the 1920s: Disenchantment of the Dreamers*. Basingstoke: Palgrave Macmillan.
Wimberg, Ellen. 1992. "Socialism, Democratism and Criticism: The Soviet Press and the National Discussion of the 1936 Draft Constitution." *Soviet Studies* 44 (2): 313–32.

CHAPTER 13

On Russian Political Culture in the Twentieth Century

Having reviewed the major characteristics of Soviet political culture in 1936, I will place them briefly alongside the recent research on the Russian-Soviet political culture, especially those studies based on sociological data. In fact, modern sociological surveys often refer to studies of late Soviet attitudes, dispositions, values, and stereotypes typical of *Homo sovieticus*, no matter how controlled and biased these Soviet studies were. The different nature of any evaluations of the political culture of the 1930s versus the later periods is emphasized in this book by the term of *popular* opinion rather than the established sociological term *public* opinion. The term *popular* opinion stresses the peculiarities of our sources, which preclude quantification and reflect political, not scientific, methods of gathering information in the 1930s. Saying that, we cannot neglect an opportunity to relate the qualitative attributes of political culture under Stalinism with data collected under the less repressive ideological conditions of the late Soviet period and freer post-Soviet studies.

Sociological studies in the USSR started only in the 1960s—isolated from the world, controlled and directed by party ideologists. They were conducted under conditions of control and an ideologically framed agenda similar to those in the 1930s, though less repressive. As such, they were used in the more reliable and freer post-Soviet studies as a reference point (Slapentokh 1986).[1] Modern sociologists often

---

[1] An example is the works of Soviet-American sociologist V. Slapentokh.

conclude that the basic values of Russian citizens in the 1990s–2000s did not differ much from the late Soviet past (Zorkaia 2010, p. 6; Gorshkov 2010, pp. 32, 34). The Stalinist period, when sociology was declared a "bourgeois" science, lacks reliable empirical studies on the political culture of the Soviet people. In this chapter, I will compare my findings about the 1930s with the main conclusions made by selected but representative sociological and historical studies regarding the postwar Soviet period and modern Russia. Sociological surveys, even with their limitations, are valuable because of their measurability and precise data. Recent historical writings debating the postwar period are augmented by using a modern methodological research arsenal. The outcomes of my study generally support their conclusions.

Even when we study such a huge country during a social transformation, some hypotheses can be made. An empirical study of the political culture, based on popular comments about the constitution and other sources and placed in the context of modern research, opens the opportunity to review the Soviet/Russian political culture over a longer timeline. The periods reviewed here are, first, the postrevolutionary decade of the 1920s, studied by the author earlier; second, the postwar era as reflected in compendiums of opinions of a later origin: the postwar sources similar to those used in this study, examined by Elena Zubkova (1945–1957) and Serhy Yekelchyk, the interviews of the Harvard Project (1950–1951), and late Soviet and post-Soviet sociological data. The questions asked by modern sociologists, however, do not always directly match the topics discussed by the participants in the constitution campaign. The analysis of 1936 popular comments in a wider historical context reflects the evolution of political culture over time. It is beyond the scope of this book to examine in detail the studies of popular opinions in the second half of the twentieth century in Russia, but we can review how the major characteristics of political culture in 1936 evolved in other periods.

Some general patterns of the Soviet popular mind have remained reasonably constant through all periods: lack of social solidarity, high levels of dissatisfaction with material conditions and the inability of the regime to fulfill its promises, us–them thinking, favor for the welfare provisions, veneration of the leader, and the myth of a besieged fortress in relation to foreign affairs.

Discussion in the literature about the general outlines of the political culture runs along a traditional–modern divide. In the twentieth century, forces of modernization launched the shift of Russian society toward economic and political independence, individual rights, and diversity. The characteristics of a modern worldview existed in society during all periods, though never prevalent. One example was the Peasant Union movement of 1922–1929, which exposed the growth of a nascent political consciousness among the more active, entrepreneurial peasants. Parts of the Russian countryside ceased to be a mere crowd of submissive subjects and instead became political agents who quickly learned to articulate their interests in political terms. They strived for their class organization and demanded their appropriate place in a system of power relations. Though the majority was still traditional, the strata of active peasants held the potential for modernization as embodied in an orientation toward the market, profit, and representation. Such attainment could be actualized under favorable conditions, or at least without massive state repressions (Velikanova 2013, p. 159). Elements of civic culture emerging among peasants in the 1920s were, as we have seen, well articulated in the repressive 1930s, especially in concerns in discussions about judicial, voting, administrative, and individual rights.

The continuity of the modernization influences is reflected in refugees' comments in 1950–1951, presenting a gradual shift of social values and attitudes from traditional peasant beliefs to those common in urban and industrial societies. Though the interview questions pertained to the correspondents' experiences in the prewar USSR, their comments were recorded a decade later and thus colored by their war and postwar experiences. The Harvard Project analytics revealed that in the 1950s the values of the peasant family, rooted in the local community and religious values, suffered enormous attrition, while the urban values associated with the dominance of work in a man's life, a consumption ethic, and the drive for success became more prominent. Former Soviet professionals criticized the treatment of failures in Stalin's Russia, ascribed officially to political defiance or the criminal negligence of the cadres (typical for a traditional worldview), and showed more understanding of impersonal and other factors (Inkeles and Bauer 1959, p. 381). As the authors concluded, these changes developed as in any industrial society and had more in common with American society than not.

Igor Orlov analyzed the trajectory of liberal elements in political culture in the post-Soviet period. He argues that liberal discourse was most expressed in society in the mid-1990s. According to the Institute of Sociological Analysis, 40% of respondents between 1991 and 1995 prioritized "social justice" (a quite moderate number for a period of economic collapse, deprivation, and the emergence of new Russian oligarchs), while more than 30% stood for "radical-liberal" values (more in the megalopolises, and fewer in the provinces). At the end of the 1990s, surveys showed disillusionment with democratic ideals and the rise of paternalistic expectations. Orlov argues that the old "submissive" culture prioritizing the state's role remains the basis of Russian political culture (Orlov and Dolgova 2008, pp. 208–10).

All students of Russia highlight the traditional elements of political culture. Findings in the 1980s revealed illiberal attitudes and traditional, prerevolutionary modes of citizen–state interactions. They were reinforced by a pattern of Soviet socioeconomic development and by a highly centralized and hierarchical administrative structure, itself a continuation of tsarist patterns (DiFranceisco and Gitelman 1984, p. 603; Fitzpatrick 2014, p. 378). Twenty years later, the sociological study conducted by the Institute for Sociological Research from 2004 to 2007 emphasized the continuity of attitudes between Soviet and post-Soviet society and the resilience of traditional values. The traditionalist and paternalistically oriented portion of society still prevailed, and even increased in the three years under survey from 41 to 47%, while the proportion of modernists (defined as those "who favor individual freedoms, personal responsibility, and human rights and are carriers of the modernist, innovative type of thinking") declined from 26 to 20%. According to other parameters, the traditions of paternalism still dominate the consciousness of most Russians (62%), connected primarily with the low income status of 60% of the Russian population, those most dependent on the state (Gorshkov 2010, pp. 44, 49).

Besides these general attributes of political culture, some specific cultural patterns were persistent in the 1920s, 1930s, 1950s, and 2000s. Social integration, so eagerly envisioned by the Stalinists, appears deficient throughout all periods of Soviet and post-Soviet history. The deeply split postrevolutionary generation did not successfully heal the trauma of the Civil War (Velikanova 2013, pp. 129–36). While comments on the constitution showed a continuing fragmentation and social hostility during the 1930s, World War II unsurprisingly produced a semblance of unity of the society and state in the face of a deadly threat. This consolidation, however, survived only temporarily, quickly dissipating as the popular postwar hopes went unrealized. This transient feeling of unity marked the comments of the refugees isolated from the USSR since 1945 and led Inkeles and Bauer to conclude that in the 1950s the Soviet system seemed to enjoy support by popular consensus, though people continued to separate themselves from the Communist Party officials (Inkeles and Bauer 1959, pp. 301, 397).

The mindset of USSR residents from the wider period of 1945–1957, analyzed by historian Elena Zubkova, demonstrated a lack of unity. Society was divided both within and against the party-state. Seeking a new national integrity after the wartime mobilization ended, the party-state launched new mobilization campaigns against the external enemy (the US in the context of the Cold War) and the internal enemy (the Jews ostracized and attacked in the Doctors' Plot affair). To fill the spiritual vacuum, the government promoted the grand goals of reconstruction, and in 1947 "building communism." Just as in 1936 the party mobilized society with the idea of attaining socialism, the party program in 1947 set the goal of building a communist society in the USSR over the course of the next twenty years, though it met more limited recognition in society. In social discord, as Zubkova argues, the major link uniting the higher and the lower orders was Stalin's cult. Unlike Inkeles and Bauer, who found that a measure of trust increased in postwar society, Zubkova argues that general distrust was common: the public was skeptical about the results of elections, and authorities saw veterans and repatriates as a potential threat (Zubkova 1998, pp. 25, 75, 107, 141, 204). Social tensions within classes—the conflict between party and non-party members, and the hostility of workers to Stakhanovites—persisted after the war (Inkeles and Bauer 1959, p. 307). Social strain was manifest in the reemergence of disadvantaged groups larger than in the 1930s: the stigma of inferior citizens branded repatriates, prisoners of war, and residents of occupied territories suspected of Nazi collaboration or distrusted by the government as witnesses of Western life. Millions of deportees were partially or wholly disenfranchised. The electoral and legal status of these groups was questioned by the public (Zubkova 1998, pp. 76, 106). The official image of a harmonious, consolidated society of the new supranational entity of the Soviet people was in truth a hollow shell in the period between the 1930s and 1950s. The 1980s study—the Soviet Interview Project among the emigrant Soviet Jews—confirms the continuing divide among the party elite and the population, and a growing irritation about the inability of the party-state to fulfill its promises (Millar 1987). Even in the most prosperous years in Russian history, 2004–2007, sociologists observed a "fragmentation of society …

split up into smaller and smaller closed communities that are built on relations just 'among themselves'" (Dubin 2010, p. 82). Thus, social solidarity and consensus have measured low throughout the last hundred years of Russian history.

After the war, a statist code, expressed by discussants in 1936, lingered in the political culture. Many refugees, newly acquainted with pluralistic and democratic capitalism in the US, still demonstrated devotion to government control of the economy and its right to intrude in any other spheres of life. Soviet immigrants to the US in the 1950s felt pride in the industrial, military, and cultural achievements of the Soviet state and emphasized its strength—an important factor in the acceptance of power in the Russian mind (Zubkova 1998, p. 86; Johnston 2011, pp. 160–5; Inkeles and Bauer 1959, p. 382). Most of the refugees believed that the common interests should prevail over individual rights, and favored some limitations on freedom of speech, assembly, and the press (Inkeles and Bauer 1959, pp. 248, 461). A late 1980s survey supports the tendency to limit personal freedoms in favor of the interests of society (Gibson and Duch 1993, pp. 87–8). Soviet Jewish emigrants in the late 1970s and early 1980s and the Russian population in the 1990s, 2004, and 2007 showed the same attachment to the established statist model favoring the state's domination of the economy, especially heavy industry (Millar 1987, p. 105; Gorshkov 2010, p. 46; Dubin 2010, p. 74; Orlov and Dolgova 2008, p. 209).[2]

Recent sociological studies demonstrate citizens' aspirations for freedoms and individual independence; although willing to claim rights for themselves, they often did not grant the same rights to others, a distinctive feature of the Russian/Soviet understanding of democracy that was already evident in the constitution campaign. The assessments by Gibson and Duch and also by the All-Union Center for the Study of Public Opinion (VTsIOM) in November 1989 confirmed that the population regarded political freedoms and rights as less important goals than improving material conditions (Levada 1993, pp. 280–1).

Lukin claimed that the subculture of Soviet democrats in the period 1985–1991, who then led the 1990s reforms, inherited some features of the Marxist and traditionally uncompromising Russian stance: a vision of democracy as a moral and social ideal close to Marxist utopianism, rather

---

[2] "Prestige of the state in mass consciousness turned out to be quite high (almost 70 percent of respondents)," according to Orlov and Dolgova.

than a system of political institutions. The democrats illustrated their radicalism in seeing the Soviet state as an absolute evil counterposed to the ideal of Western democracy. They showed a weak commitment to democratic procedures and laws, seen by them as instrumental to better attain the ideal model. The inability of democrats to forge a unified political party shows the lack of a will to compromise. Lukin's conclusion is that Gorbachev's Russia lacked the necessary cultural preconditions for successful democratization (Lukin 2000, pp. 274, 277, 298). Thus, the weaknesses of the democratic movement in post-Soviet Russian society reflected the fragile democratic elements in Soviet political culture.

Another characteristic entrenched in Soviet and post-Soviet citizens' minds was the image of foreign relations colored by the enduring idea of a besieged fortress and an "imperialist conspiracy" against the USSR (Velikanova 2002). When this narrative emerged in official discourse in the 1920s, the public as a whole did not share the feeling. Official xenophobia and cosmopolitan popular culture coexisted and overlapped in the 1920s. After eight years of wars, people were exhausted and did not accept the theme of an international threat. In the War Scare of 1927, they showed an unwillingness to fight, turned to defeatism, and even expected liberation by foreign countries (Velikanova 2013, p. 117). In the 1930s, with the coming of a new generation, defeatism receded but remained well articulated in talk of a future war. Without access to travel and direct firsthand experience, the image of the outside world strongly depended on the party's representation of it. The official narrative of international and internal conspiracy with dark forces behind the scenes reverberated in the mass consciousness in the 1930s and during the Cold War (Inkeles and Bauer 1959, p. 382; Johnston 2011, pp. 160–5; Velikanova 2002). Young patriots accepted the official picture of a hostile world, though self-regulating narratives permeated society: pro-German and pro-Hitler feelings were not rare. Many did not see any difference between Hitler and Stalin; others valued Hitler's strong leadership and antiSemitism. People said in 1941: "The Russians should not be afraid of the Nazis. They will destroy only the Communists and Jews" (TsGAIPD SPb f. 25, op. 5, d. 180, l. 134; d. 74, l. 75; f. 24, op. 2v, d. 2704, l. 120; d. 2487, l. 58; d. 2486, l. 182; d. 1772, l. 265; Barber 1991, pp. 10–11).

Stalinist society's aggression and mercilessness was understandably produced by the ordeal of the Civil War, the attack on peasants in 1930, and the feeling of ontological danger and insecurity in the face of continued repressions that provoked retributive reactions in the population. The post-Civil War society remained fractured by hatred and anxiety exemplified by hostility between workers and peasants, animosity to the new Soviet businessmen (*nepmen*), and an "us–them" mentality (Velikanova 2013, pp. 129–36). Discussing constitutional conciliation in 1936, those who spoke out rejected peace with the clergy, rehabilitated kulaks, individual farmers, and mercy to "criminals." Both Serhy Yekelchyk and the Harvard Project studies confirm the high level of general hostility in postwar society. In the 1950s, for example, 40–60% of the refugees expressed the opinion that in the event of a change of the Communist regime, its leaders should be executed (Inkeles and Bauer 1959, p. 433; Yekelchyk 2014, Chapter 1). Refusal to forgive criminals is notably prevalent in all strata of modern Russian respondents. A moratorium on capital punishment in Russia in August 1996 did not find strong support in society. Modern sociological surveys show only a moderate decline in the number of adherents of executions—from two-thirds at the end of the 1980s to almost half of surveyed Russians in 2007, this however, corresponds to the 52% worldwide average (Dubin 2010, pp. 80, 85; Gallup 2000). Tolerance, conciliation, and compromise do not belong among prevalent Russian values. Poet and thinker Olga Sedakova says, "Forgiveness, conciliation now is absolutely a rare thing in people of soviet and post-Soviet formation ... [who see] the world as evil and unfriendly by its nature" (Sedakova 2017).

Thus, the studies of the postwar period and much more quantifiable modern sociological data support the major findings revealed by analysis of the constitution comments. Liberal (in our categorization) or democratic/modern (in the sociological surveys' terms) values and attitudes were always represented in the Soviet/Russian mass political culture, despite an authoritarian regime which fueled illiberal values. Despite the limitations inherent in generalizing about so diverse and complex subject as Soviet and Russian political culture, literature shows that such characteristics as statism, an uncompromising stance, lack of social solidarity, and distrust persisted through the twentieth century in Russia.

References

Barber, John. 1991. "Popular Reactions in Moscow to the German Invasion of June 22, 1941." *Soviet Union/Union Sovietique* 18 (1–3): 5–18.

DiFranceisco, Wayne, and Zvi Gitelman. 1984. "Soviet Political Culture and 'Covert Participation' in Policy Implementation." *The American Political Science Review* 78 (3): 603–21.

Dubin, Boris. 2010. "The Worth of Life and the Limits of Law: Russian Opinions on the Death Penalty, Russian Laws, and the System of Justice." *Russian Social Sciences Review* 51 (3): 69–88.

Fitzpatrick, Sheila. 2014. "Popular Opinion Under Communist Regimes." In *The Oxford Handbook of the History of Communism*, edited by Stephen A. Smith, 371–86. New York: Oxford University Press.

"Gallup Organization International Opinion Poll." 2000. Gallup. Available at: http://www.gallup.com/poll/1606/death-penalty.aspx. Accessed September 10, 2017.

Gibson, James L., and Raymond M. Duch. 1993. "Emerging Democratic Values in Soviet Political Culture." In *Public Opinion and Regime Change: The New Politics of Post-Soviet Societies*, edited by Arthur H. Miller, William M. Reisinger, and Vicki L. Hesli. Boulder, CO: Westview.

Gorshkov, M. K. 2010. "The Sociological Measurement of the Russian Mentality." *Russian Social Science Review* 51 (2): 32–57.

Inkeles, Alex, and Raymond Bauer. 1959. *The Soviet Citizen: Daily Life in a Totalitarian Society*. Cambridge, MA: Harvard University Press.

Johnston, Timothy. 2011. *Identity, Rumour, and Everyday Life Under Stalin, 1939–1953*. New York: Oxford University Press.

Levada, Yu A., ed. 1993. *Sovetskii prostoi chelovek*. Moscow: Mirovoi Okean.

Lukin, Alexander. 2000. *The Political Culture of the Russian "Democrats"*. Oxford: Oxford University Press.

Millar, James R., ed. 1987. *Politics, Work and Daily Life in the USSR: A Survey of Former Soviet Citizens*. Cambridge: Cambridge University Press.

Orlov, I. B., and E. O. Dolgova. 2008. *Politicheskaia kul'tura rossiian v XX veke: Preemstvennost' i razryvy*. Sergiev Posad: SPGI.

Sedakova, Olga. Interview. 2017. Available at: https://philologist.livejournal.com/8987803.html?utm_source=fbsharing&utm_medium=social. Accessed December 28, 2017.

Slapentokh, V. 1986. *Soviet Public Opinion and Ideology: The Interaction Between Mythology and Pragmatism*. New York: Praeger.

Tsentral'nyi Gosudarstvennyi Arkhiv Istoriko-politicheskikh Dokumentov Sankt-Peterburga (TsGAIPD SPb) [Central State Archives of Historical–Political Documents in Saint-Petersburg].

Velikanova, Olga. 2002. *The Myth of the Besieged Fortress: Soviet Mass Perception in the 1920s–1930s*. Working Paper No. 7. Stalin-Era Research and Archives Project. Toronto: CREES.

———. 2013. *Popular Perceptions of Soviet Politics in the 1920s: Disenchantment of the Dreamers*. Basingstoke, UK: Palgrave Macmillan.

Yekelchyk, Serhy. 2014. *Stalin's Citizens: Everyday Politics in the Wake of Total War*. Oxford: Oxford University Press.

Zorkaia, Natalia. 2010. "'Nostalgia for the Past', or What Lessons Young People Could Have Learned and Did Learn." *Russian Social Science Review* 51 (2): 4–31.

Zubkova, Elena. 1998. *Russia After the War: Hopes, Illusions, and Disappointments, 1945–1957*. Armonk, NY: M. E. Sharpe.

CHAPTER 14

Conclusion

Stalin's Constitution of 1936 was a key moment in relations between society and the party-state. What do the constitution and related discussion tell us about politics and society?

New knowledge about the origins of constitutional reform shifts our understanding of the entire project. The centrality of election reform undermines the conventional interpretation of the constitution as a cynical trick mostly for international consumption. Rather, it moves the internal ideological and political goals to the forefront. When the constitution announced to the people that socialism had been achieved, it had propagandistic and legitimization value. But it also reflected the dogmatic belief of Stalinists that the economic, political, and social transformations they conducted would automatically bring about socialism and transform society. The discussion campaign showed Stalin that society had failed to sufficiently Sovietize. The voices in the discussion were not unanimous in their approvals and conformity as expected.[1] To the leaders' disappointment, this society did not fit into an ideological template. It had not *yet* lived in the prescribed way, but remained religious, divided, unmanageable, parochial, an inhibitor of socialism.

---

[1] Prishvin, a writer, thought the discussion was a kind of a test for Sovietness after which freedom would be allowed. "[The government] … expects real hosannas [praise] … from the people, and then, after they [the government] are confident of the genuineness of the hosannas, [they will] say: … speak, write whatever you want freely" (Prishvin 2010, pp. 298, 382).

In launching the constitution, the ideological motives (accomplishment of socialism) intertwined with the political and managerial goals of improving the effectiveness of government through a new election law—to use democratic procedures to motivate, revitalize, outvote, or purge the sluggish, corrupt, or unreliable elites and enemies on all levels. Afraid of being dismissed in democratic elections, the cadres obstructed its implementation. In Stalin's logic, both anti-Soviet elements in a population encouraged by new freedoms and reluctant officials needed a final purge ("once and for all") to reach success in the socialist transformation. This logic can explain the political shift from relative relaxation in 1933–1936 to the Great Terror.

The wide range of opinions voiced in the constitution discussion provides evidence that society was not a passive recipient but an active negotiator of politics, shaping Soviet culture with grassroots interpretations. Nonconformist opinions demonstrated that average citizens longed for expression and were eager to share their thoughts with their countrymen and with the government, even under conditions of dictatorship. It means that pockets of alternative public spaces as nongovernment communication channels did exist in the 1930s and found expression in the national discussion of the constitution as autonomous, and sometimes liberal, voices in the *staged* public sphere.

The lessons of the constitution were learned by the citizens: its principles had been hammered into their minds, educating those who had never heard of civil rights. On the one hand, many embraced the necessary Soviet skills of survival: mimicry and obedience, for instance, when they parroted officialese at meetings. But on the other, the population learned a new vocabulary of democracy and problematized areas that until then had not been considered. For example, we know of two cases—high school students in Leningrad and Moscow had created constitutions for their classes in 1937 based on the USSR constitution, as well as drafts of the Students' Rights Declaration—thus demonstrating an internalization of the norms and language of the law (Petrone 2000, p. 200). The constitution provided a reference point for the powerless population to appeal for the implementation of individual rights.

Another lesson learned in 1936 was of mistrust—another side of the mobilizations, with cycles of enthusiasm and disillusionment. The discrepancy between the law and practice led to a moment of truth for many on the way to a critical assessment of the regime. But the main outcome of the constitution was the distrust and skepticism that its sham nature produced in citizens, contributing to the growth of cynicism in society, which in the long run eroded the foundation of the political system.

The studied testimonials for the first time give us an opportunity to empirically check assumptions made in the literature about Soviet mass political culture. Foremost, discussion of the constitution, designed as a mobilization campaign to shape the public's attitudes and to consolidate society around Soviet values, failed in its major goal. We see no consensus, no unity, no settled identity, but instead a fragmented, multilayered population torn apart by dissimilar values and a civil war mentality. The social peace message of the constitution found limited support among the masses. Society remained fractured by hatred and anxiety. This heterogeneity found in 1936 society was confirmed in the 1937 census. "A society that had lost its grip, its structure, its cohesion, or had not yet found it, a city [Moscow] that was composed of millions of people whose lives have been disrupted and who had nowhere where they could feel at home, such a society was fragile in the extreme, [and] also in dire need of a sense of belonging" (Schloegel 2012, pp. 51, 53, 118–9). The voices in the discussion demonstrated social tensions that manifested as hatred: of *kolkhozniks* for the *edinolichniki*; nonparty population for party members; freshly minted atheists for priests; kulaks and deportees for villagers who dispossessed them and now lived in their homes; workers for managers and Stakhanovites; peasants for workers; suspicion of the *lishentsy*; and, overarching, a general distrust of high authorities. This rivalry and envy "fueled the political culture of repression" (Goldman 2007, p. 7).

Besides the pressure to participate, the unexpectedly democratic character of the constitution and a shift in official discourse provoked the citizens to voice their political views and allowed them to express an entire spectrum of both liberal and illiberal perspectives. In their comments, we found liberal, democratic, and conciliatory discourse coexisting with revolutionary, confrontational, and intolerant—and elements of traditionalist—modes of world perception. Liberal values were well articulated in the discussion and contemporary personal documents. The concern of many citizens about individual and civil rights, the effective work of the soviets, election reform, and the rule of law, as well as their political engagement—all point to the existence of a liberal political subculture with democratic components. This was an important characteristic of

Stalinist society, influenced by the energies of modernity and prerevolutionary liberal traditions.

The liberal character of the new constitution, however, opposed the aspirations of another segment of the discussants. Innovations such as pluralism, the extension of electoral rights to previously disenfranchised classes, and the democratic judicial process—including the right to a defense, and individual freedoms for former outcasts—often met with cultural discomfort, criticism, and disapproval. Whatever its genesis—the legacy of the Civil War, imprints of catastrophic experiences during collectivization and a religious war, the influence of the Bolsheviks' antagonistic class ideology, or the predispositions of the peasants' traditional psychology—this confrontational pattern of thought represented a strong element of mass reactions.

The sources display much intolerance, hostility, radicalism, little compassion, and acceptance of violence. Such features of communal thinking as envy, egalitarianism, leveling tendencies, and commitment to collective values over individualism were well delineated. Traditional tropes of piety and patrimonialism, and the cult of the leader articulated in the summer of 1936, indicate that Stalin's society inherited some centuries-old habits of political behavior (Mironov 1994; Kollman 2009, p. 99; Daniels 1987). These "deep and old structures" of the popular mentality got an endorsement in the Bolsheviks' revolutionary class ideology and authoritarian policies that ensured proliferation of this worldview (Medushevsky 2010, pp. 6–7).

This illiberal trope could be an indirect product of the involuntary nature of participation, which brought to the political arena a cohort only recently literate and largely unsophisticated in politics. Social scientists consider this politically indifferent population group as usually uneducated, unstable in its inclinations, more vulnerable to manipulation, inclined to conformist voting and welfare measures, and in general, more susceptible to populist appeals. When this normally silent and passive majority is pressed to participate, they can bring parochial, illiberal views to polity. History knows two examples: the introduction of universal male suffrage in Germany in 1871, and almost-universal male suffrage in Great Britain in 1882, both introduced by authorities expressly to facilitate manipulation of the masses to outvote the liberals. Previously, the limited franchise helped elect urban liberals who criticized the monarchies (Zakaria 2003, pp. 61–2). This argument is supported from another angle: "A mass public recently introduced to literacy is particularly susceptible to manipulation by the printed word" (Lovell 2000, p. 13). The citizenry with such a background comprised the social basis of Stalinism and predetermined the phony nature of constitutionalism in twentieth-century Russia.

Despite the authoritarian and traditional dispositions in the discussion comments, elements of civic culture indicate much greater flexibility of political culture, evolving under the pressures of modernization. Scholar-optimists emphasize the variability and flexibility of political culture responsive to the core process of modernization: "Change the system, and *homo sovieticus* would soon die out" (Sakwa 2002, pp. 191, 344; Almond and Verba 1965, p. 373). In the mid-1930s, Soviet people were not unremittingly antidemocratic. Along with the desire to regulate life and with the love of the "little man" for power, evident in abundant praises to the leaders, popular sentiment in 1936 showed the development of individual subjectivity and civic consciousness shaped by social mobility, mass education, mass communication, and urbanization. Alongside archaic political relations and social development, communist societies did achieve individual modernization, suggesting a person who is mentally open, cognitively flexible and creative, with a definite sense of individual efficacy (Smith 2008, p. 235; Inkeles and Smith 1974). Even peasant culture, generally unfavorable to democracy (Moore 1966, p. 420), developed, under the stresses of modernization, the basics of civic consciousness as voiced in demands for a peasants' party and civic rights. In the modernization process, however, the conditions of crisis and emergency do not work in favor of the successful formation of a civic culture, which "is a culture of moderation" and requires gradual development, with the fusing rather than excision of various cultural elements (Almond and Verba 1965, pp. 368–70).[2] It means that the catastrophic course of Russian modernization might impede the nurturing of civic culture, with its strong participatory and democratic elements.

The discussion of the Constitution of 1936 showed the culture in a state of flux, with elements of the old and modern, liberal and illiberal. Because the transition to modernity, by definition a disruptive process, occurred in Russia through a sequence of catastrophes and political

---

[2] "First, the civic culture emerged in the West as a result of a gradual political development—relatively crisis-free, untroubled, and unforced. Second, it developed by fusion: new patterns of attitudes did not replace old ones, but merged with them" (Almond and Verba 1965, pp. 368–70).

violence, it produced extraordinary disorientation in the population, crises of identity, and shifting paradigms.

The forces of modernity, the archetypical elements of Russian traditional culture, a dictatorial regime, and the catastrophic nature of social life—all contributed to the political culture of Stalinism.

REFERENCES

Almond, Gabriel A., and Sidney Verba. 1965. *The Civic Culture: Political Attitudes and Democracy in Five Nations.* Boston: Little, Brown.
Daniels, Robert V. 1987. "Russian Political Culture and the Post-revolutionary Impasse." *The Russian Review* 46 (2): 165–75.
Goldman, Wendy Z. 2007. *Terror and Democracy in the Age of Stalin.* Cambridge: Cambridge University Press.
Inkeles, Alex, and D. H. Smith. 1974. *Becoming Modern: Individual Change in Six Developing Countries.* Cambridge: Cambridge University Press.
Kollman, Nancy Shields. 2009. "Muscovite Political Culture." In *A Companion to Russian History*, edited by Abbott Gleason, 89–104. Chichester, UK: Wiley-Blackwell.
Lovell, Stephen. 2000. *The Russian Reading Revolution: Print Culture in the Soviet and Post-Soviet Eras.* Basingstoke: Palgrave Macmillan.
Medushevsky, A. N. 2010. "'Stalinism kak model' sotsial'nogo konstruirovania." *Rossiiskaia Istoria* (6): 3–29.
Mironov, Boris. 1994. "Peasant Popular Culture and the Origins of Soviet Authoritarianism." In *Cultures in Flux: Lower-Class Values, Practices, and Resistance in Late Imperial Russia*, edited by Stephen Frank and Mark D. Steinberg, 54–73. Princeton, NJ: Princeton University Press.
Moore, Barrington. 1966. *Social Origins of Dictatorship and Democracy: Lord and Peasant in the Making of the Modern World.* Boston: Beacon.
Petrone, Karen. 2000. *Life Has Become More Joyous, Comrades: Celebrations in the Time of Stalin.* Bloomington: Indiana University Press.
Prishvin, M. M. 2010. *Dnevniki, 1936–1937.* Saint-Petersburg: Rostok.
Sakwa, Richard. 2002. *Russian Politics and Society.* 3rd ed. London: Routledge.
Schloegel, Karl. 2012. *Moscow, 1937.* Cambridge: Polity.
Smith, S. A. 2008. *Revolution and the People in Russia and China: A Comparative History.* New York: Cambridge University Press.
Zakaria, Fareed. 2003. *The Future of Freedom: Illiberal Democracy at Home and Abroad.* New York: W. W. Norton.

Glossary

CC VKPb	Central Committee of All-Union Communist Party (Bolsheviks)
chekists	Officers of the NKVD
Comintern	Communist International
edinolichniki	Individual out-*kolkhoz* farmers
ispolkom	Executive committee of provincial or county soviet
lishentsy	Disenfranchised people
kolkhoz	Collective farm
kolkhoznik	Collective farmer
Komsomol	Communist Young League
krai, oblast', raion	Administrative units: region, province, county
kulak	An entrepreneurial peasant
MTS	Machine and tractor stations in countryside
NEP	New Economic Policy
NKVD	People's Commissariat for Internal Affairs—secret police, formerly OGPU and Cheka
partcom	Party committee of the enterprise
Politburo	Political Bureau of Communist Party
raznariadka	Quota system in elections
samizdat	Self-published typescripts
SNK, Sovnarkom	Soviet of People's Commissars
svodki	Regular reports of the Soviet security police and Communist Party

troikas	Emergency-style three-member boards working as extralegal courts
TsIK	Soviet Central Executive Committee
VKPb	All-Union Communist Party (Bolsheviks)

Archives

British F.O.	British Foreign Office—Russia Correspondence, 1781–1945
GARF	State Archives of Russian Federation (Gosudarstvenny Arkhiv Rossiiskoi Federatsii)
HPSSS	Harvard Project on the Soviet Social System
RGASPI	Russian State Archives of Social and Political History (Rossiisky Gosudarstvenny Arkhiv Sotsial'noi i Politicheskoi Istorii)
TsGAIPD SPb	Central State Archives of Historical–Political Documents in Saint-Petersburg (Tsentral'ny Gosudarstvenny Arkhiv Istoriko–Politicheskikh Dokumentov Sankt-Peterburga)
TsGAKFFD SPb	Central State Archives of Documentary Films, Photographs, and Sound Recordings of Saint-Petersburg (Tsentral'ny Gosudarstvenny Arkhiv Kinofoto-fonodokumentov Sankt-Peterburga)

US Military Intelligence Reports: Soviet Union, 1919–1941

Index

A
Absenteeism, 79, 81, 130
Activists, 82, 90, 95, 140, 164–166, 168, 174, 176, 182, 199, 208, 228
Almond, Gabriel A., 11, 12, 80, 159, 198, 216, 249
Amendments, 33, 34, 36, 72, 105, 184, 212, 222–225, 229
Anti-*kolkhoz* protests, 86
Antimachinery (anticombine) mood, 119
Antireligious campaign, 86, 172, 178
Anti-Semitism, 86, 241
Anti-Soviet activities, 17
Apparatus, 63–66, 77, 82, 87, 186, 193, 229
  party and soviet bureaucracy, 64, 226
  purges of, 66, 67, 214
Arrests, 42, 43, 51, 127, 214, 215
Arzhilovsky, Andrei, 5, 81, 91, 105, 111
Associations, public, 81, 149
Attendance at the meetings, 79, 83, 90, 121. *See also* Participation, political
Authoritarian regime, 1, 2, 9, 91, 242

B
Believers, churchgoers, 17, 75, 136, 147, 173–179, 183
Belomor Canal, 53
Belorussia, 2, 43, 73, 74, 124, 143
Beria, L.P., 42
British Foreign Office, the, 18, 111
Bukharin, N., 58, 100, 189, 222
  death letter, 58

C
Census, 1937, 18, 177, 183, 227, 228, 247
Central Committee Plenum, 29, 33, 44, 54, 59, 64, 66, 67, 115, 133, 146
  February 1935, 34, 170
  February–March, 1937, 62, 147, 186

December 1936, 67
June 1935, 29, 34, 42, 54
June 1936, 59, 66, 115
June 1937, 133, 147
Charity, 4, 93, 94, 172, 185
Churches, 75, 86, 93, 133, 136, 152, 172–176, 178–182, 185, 186, 226
Citizenship, 60, 91, 92, 121, 123, 134, 136, 138, 151, 155
Civil culture, 4, 11
Civil rights, 11, 23, 40, 41, 88, 123, 124, 139, 140, 142, 144, 158, 163, 166, 211, 223, 246, 247
Civil values. *See* Civil culture
Civil war, 3, 32, 63, 79, 90, 102, 107, 128, 164, 166, 172, 184, 187, 191, 207, 210, 216, 229, 231, 238, 241, 242, 247, 248
Clergy, 17, 164, 171, 172, 175, 178, 184–186
priests. *See* Clergy
Collectivism, 3, 123, 124, 170
Collectivization, 30, 31, 35, 42, 44, 45, 56, 80, 118, 119, 125, 127, 135, 137–139, 141, 151, 166, 169, 170, 194, 210, 213, 217, 248
Comintern, 44, 51
Communist International. *See* Comintern
Commissariat of Justice, 43, 126
Committees of Mutual Help, the, 81
Communism building, 106, 239
Complaints, 60, 88, 92, 141, 142, 155, 175, 209, 210
Compromise, 3, 23, 41, 241, 242
Confiscation, 173, 198
Congress of Outstanding *Kolkhozniks*, the, 1935, 140, 170, 208, 230
Constitutional commission, 29, 33, 49
Correspondence, secrecy of, 89

secret scanning of, 100
Corruption, 67, 78, 157
Cossacks, 41, 197
Criminals, 43, 44, 53, 94, 168, 176, 187, 242
Criticism, 16, 21–23, 63, 64, 71, 73–76, 88, 105, 131, 132, 145, 193, 198, 248
Crop failure, 112–115, 117, 118, 121
Cults Commission, the TsIK, 173–175, 179, 181, 182
Cultural revolution, 40, 45, 56
Cursing, insults, 153, 154

D
David-Fox, Michael, 6, 7
Davies, R.W., 16, 112–115, 118
Death penalty, capital punishment, 187, 189, 191
Defeatism, 86, 195–197, 215, 241
Defense, 9, 19, 44, 61, 112, 125–127, 149, 171, 195, 223, 224, 248
Dekulakization, 128, 131, 140, 165, 172, 189, 210
Democratization, 2, 3, 8, 34, 35, 45, 62, 65, 223, 228, 241
Denunciations, 63, 76, 77, 92, 105
Deportations, 79, 128
Diaries, 5, 6, 20, 90–92, 94, 105, 199, 216
Dichotomy of Soviet life, 6, 7, 87
Dignity, 94, 153, 155, 156
Diplomat, 50, 51, 111, 132, 197, 198
Disabled, the, 206, 207
Discontent, 10, 63, 64, 73, 82, 85, 89, 91, 94, 115, 116, 128, 130, 132, 144, 158, 170, 214, 224
Disenfranchised, the, 31, 34, 43, 135, 164, 239
disenfranchisement, 53, 133
outcasts, 61, 155, 199, 248

Dissent, 4, 8, 17, 19, 20
Duality of thinking, 21
Dzerzhinsky, F.E., 17, 94

E

Education, access to, 21
  political, 62, 100
  reeducation, 56, 67, 178, 180
Elections, 2
  to the Constituent Assembly, 80, 102
  contested, 51, 59, 147, 185, 226, 229
  election reform, 29, 31, 34–36, 39, 51, 59, 62, 67, 124, 149, 158, 245, 247
  of the judges, 125
Emergency, mode, 79, 80, 104, 196
Employment, 50, 60, 94
Enfranchisement, 57, 59, 106, 137–139, 144, 165, 222
Enlightenment, the, 55, 100, 153, 168
Extralegal practices, extralegality, 38, 125
Extraordinary 8th Congress of Soviets, the, 1936, 78

F

Family Legislation, 152
Famine, 39
  in 1932, 43, 57
  in 1936, 57, 77, 156
  starvation, 113
Far East, 79, 137, 178
Feuchtwanger, Lion, 51
"Fifth column", 51, 103, 229
Figes, Orlando, 4, 5, 155
Fitzpatrick, Sheila, 6, 7, 16, 19, 21, 40, 41, 45, 56, 62, 64, 77, 78, 92, 95, 96, 100, 116, 120, 131, 135, 138, 140, 141, 158, 165, 166, 169, 170, 173, 174, 179, 183, 188, 212, 228, 230, 238
Five-Year Plan, 52
  the first (1928–1932), 58, 62, 101, 111, 144, 145, 213
  the second (1933–1937), 39, 53, 180
Flight from collective farms, 73, 84, 85, 116, 156
Folklore, 81, 95
Food queues, 93
  food lines, 113
Foreign intervention, fear of, 80, 95, 196, 197
"Former people", 43, 53, 106, 134, 163–165, 168, 169, 172, 189, 207, 222, 223, 227–229
  lishentsy, 134, 166, 247
Freeze, Gregory, 173–175, 179, 180, 184
Friendship of the Peoples, 56

G

Generation, new Soviet, 7
  the older, 40, 61, 79, 100
  postrevolutionary, 131, 195, 236, 238
  the younger, 40, 100, 103, 183, 195
German–Soviet Nonaggression Pact, 38, 214
Germany, 16, 49, 50, 124, 206, 207, 248
Getty, J. Arch, 3, 9–11, 19, 45, 52, 55, 62, 64, 66, 67, 72, 74, 77, 100, 103, 125, 128, 132, 147, 164, 165, 168, 187, 205, 213, 215, 226, 228
Gide, André, 51

Godless League, the, 82, 182, 183, 185, 186
Goldman, Wendy, 10, 62–64, 67, 72, 77, 145, 147, 247
Gorky, A.M., 54
Gorky, a city, 19, 76
Great Terror, the, 42–44, 67, 102, 128, 147, 185, 190, 214, 229, 246
Gulag, 16, 118, 139, 141, 142

H
Hardships, 21, 61, 91, 112, 137, 211
Harvard Project on the Soviet Social System, 20, 84, 88, 95, 102, 193, 230, 236, 237, 242
Hellbeck, Jochen, 6, 20, 54, 89, 92, 183, 199
Hostility, 10, 11, 123, 164, 169, 184, 226, 238, 239, 242, 248
Housing, 9, 104
 distribution of, 156, 157, 229

I
Identity, Soviet, 78, 154, 164, 183, 187, 213, 230
Ideology, 6, 7, 30, 55, 57, 61, 63, 78, 87, 89, 92, 100, 136, 167, 168, 172, 192, 196, 199, 217, 248
Independent peasants. *See* Individual out-*kolkhoz* peasants
Individualism, 3, 23, 123, 153, 216, 248
Individual out-*kolkhoz* peasants, 152, 169
Industrialization, 42, 45, 56, 80, 213
Informers, of OGPU/NKVD, 139, 140
Integration, 53, 78, 86, 106, 107, 154, 183, 238

Intelligence, 17
 American, 17, 18, 144
 British, 17, 221
 culture of, 17
Intelligentsia, 4, 53, 56, 81, 90, 93, 94, 154, 180, 190, 210, 231
International Exhibition in Paris, 1937, 50
Intolerance, 11, 87, 123, 164, 165, 170, 176, 248
Inviolability of the person, the, 127, 153
 of the home, 156
Irreconcilable, the, 168, 169
Italy, 50
Izvestia, 19, 67, 151, 166, 168, 221, 222

J
Judges, 125–127
Judicial system, 1, 67, 125, 213

K
Kaganovich, L.M., 34, 42, 147
Kalinin, M.I., 31, 73, 180
Khlevniuk, O.V., 41, 42, 44, 114, 231
Khrushchev, N.S., 60
Kiev, 66, 79, 94, 174, 187
Kolkhoz Statute, 31, 41, 140, 207, 208, 230
Kolonitsky, Boris, 4, 5, 155
Komsomol, 79, 82, 100, 121, 154, 173, 178, 182
Krasikov, P.A., 173
Krasnodar, 83
Krestianskaia Gazeta, 19, 20, 74, 92, 99, 152, 170, 229
Krylenko, N., 43, 126

L

Law on abortion, the, 99
Legality, 37, 42, 44, 50, 52, 87, 124, 142, 158, 166
Legitimacy, 62
  legitimation, 100, 103, 193
Leningrad, 9, 10, 18, 19, 43, 53, 66, 79, 82, 83, 86, 89, 90, 93, 94, 101, 104, 125, 128, 133, 134, 143, 145–146, 148, 150, 157, 164, 177, 186, 187, 196, 205, 207, 215, 217, 232, 246
Letter writing, 91, 92
Letters, anonymous, 16, 88
Lewin, Moshe, 5, 12, 82, 194
Liberalization, 45, 50, 115, 176
Literacy, 53, 92, 180, 248
Loyalty, 20, 40, 61, 76–78, 81, 85, 91, 102, 103, 124, 127, 139, 163, 166, 182, 194–197

M

Machine-tractor stations (MTS), 30, 120
Market, 1, 55, 56, 92, 93, 115, 137, 169, 194, 237
Marxism, 52, 54, 64
  Marx, 56, 58
  Marxian theory, 53
Mass operations, 41, 43, 79, 135, 136, 147, 228
Mass repressions, 30, 80, 102, 103, 190
Mead, Margaret, 3
Medushevsky, Andrei, 4, 6, 7, 23
Memory, 61, 128
Mensheviks, the, 136, 149, 168
Military, 17, 61, 80, 90, 100, 102, 106, 112, 119, 144, 172, 176, 190, 195–197, 215, 217, 240
  militarization, 195–197
Mimicry practices, 78

Mission, 61, 102
Mobility, 2, 40, 120, 142, 149, 156, 157, 195, 199, 249
Mobilization, mass, 2–5, 7, 8, 10, 11, 15, 30, 41–43, 45, 54, 58, 61, 63, 64, 66, 71, 77–81, 94, 100, 102–105, 116, 118, 124, 125, 128, 130, 135, 136, 138, 143, 145, 147, 151, 154, 163, 165, 171, 172, 176, 177, 186, 188–191, 194–196, 213–216, 226, 228, 229, 230, 239, 240, 242, 246–249
Moderation, 35, 38, 44, 45, 124, 172, 173, 228, 249
Modernization, 2, 3, 4, 7, 92, 155, 172, 178, 195, 227, 237, 249
Molotov, V.M., 30, 33–35, 42, 43, 50, 52, 54, 56, 59, 65, 99, 115, 128, 135, 138, 151, 186, 190
Multiparty system, 150, 151
Mutual aid societies, 208

N

Narod (Soviet people), 53, 56, 107, 124, 193
National issues, 82
  nationalist discourse, 95
Nationalization, 156
New Economic Policy (NEP), 38, 144, 206, 214, 215, 218
New Soviet Man, 6, 92, 156
  Soviet new personality, 54

O

OGPU Collegium, 42
Oppositionists, 43, 44
Orlov, Igor, 237, 238
Orthodox Church, the, 81, 172
  Renovation branch, the, 81

P

Participation, political, 11, 64, 78, 80–82, 85, 87, 89, 91, 92, 100, 123, 216
  meaningful, 78, 79, 123. *See also* Attendance at the meetings
Passports, 41, 120, 131
Paternalism, 191, 192, 238
Patriotism, 22, 37, 56, 183, 191, 192, 195, 196, 215, 217
Peasant Union movement, the, 5, 81, 237
Pensions, 104, 133, 137, 205–207, 209, 211, 223
Petrone, Karen, 9, 75, 195, 246
Pilgrimages, 173, 181
Plots, conspiracies, 3, 67, 103, 112
Pluralism, 3, 23, 151, 248
Podlubny, Stepan, 20, 183
Police (militia), 128
Political thought of Stalin, 64
Popular sovereignty, 11, 63, 101
Praise of Stalin, 61
  gratitude, 89, 103, 187, 192, 194
Pravda, 19, 34, 49, 56, 59, 60, 61, 64–66, 73, 74, 76, 120, 121, 132, 146, 151, 152, 154, 180, 187–189, 191, 208–210, 223, 227
Prince Svyatopolk-Mirsky, D.S., 231
Prishvin, Mikhail, 91, 94, 103, 138, 174, 197, 215, 245
Private sphere, 80, 93, 94, 104
Procuracy, 42, 43, 126, 128, 225
  procurator, 42
Procurements, state, 39, 41, 57, 77, 86, 114–116, 118, 119
Propaganda, 5, 10, 51–53, 55, 56, 59, 84, 86, 95, 100, 114, 123, 156, 164, 166, 167, 172, 176, 178, 180, 182–184, 186, 193, 195, 226, 229
Property, personal, 151
  private, 3, 156
  socialist (state), 32, 34, 39, 187, 188, 224
Public opinion, popular opinion, 1, 10, 22, 51, 67, 105, 221, 235, 240
  unconventional, unorthodox, 88
Public space, sphere, 92, 93, 95, 153, 181, 246

Q

Qualitative research, studies, 8, 22, 23, 235
Quantification, 19, 23, 221, 235

R

Radio, 78, 79, 85, 87, 105, 106, 230–232
Rationing, 39, 111, 213
Red Army, 41, 82, 176, 195–197, 207, 208, 214, 215
Rehabilitation, 66, 124, 139, 142, 143
Relaxation, political, 37. *See also* Moderation
Religiosity, popular, 5
Religious communities, 93, 179, 185
Report campaign in the soviets, 1936, 63, 77, 86, 104
Residence registration, 44, 156
Resistance, 78
Returnees, from exile, 141, 143
Reviews of popular moods, svodki, 17, 18
Rights of minorities, the, 152
Ritual, 78, 79, 85, 176, 177, 179, 181
Rolland, Romain, 51
Rose, Richard, 1, 4, 8, 40, 102
Rumors, 4, 86, 93–95, 152, 181, 185, 216

S

Sabotage, 41, 55, 57, 64, 114, 142, 226
Sakharov, A.D., 94
Sakwa, Richard, 2, 4, 249
School, 20, 61, 84, 88, 89, 100, 106, 128, 150, 189, 191, 192, 208, 246
Scott, James, 154
Sect, religious, 156
Secularization, 174, 177, 179, 185
Security police, 16, 17, 94
  KGB, 16
  NKVD, 16–19
  OGPU, 42, 43
7th Congress of Soviets, the 1935, 31, 34, 35, 50
17th party conference, the, 1932, 53
17th Party Congress the, 1934, 31, 54
Shaporina, Liubov', 20, 82, 87, 88, 94, 148, 149, 154, 178, 197, 216–218
Shaw, Bernard, 51
Shortages, 112–115, 157, 189
Show trial, 51, 77, 78, 104, 165, 188, 189
  of the United Trotskyist–Zinovievist Center, 1936, 59, 104, 189
Siberia, 43, 113, 119, 137, 143, 152
Siegelbaum, Lewis, 10, 19, 62, 63, 83, 140, 192, 194
Skepticism, disbelief, 16, 149
Smolensk, 10, 19, 113, 125, 128, 164, 205
Social benefits, insurance, 121, 136, 199, 205, 206, 209, 210–212
"Social defense campaigns", 44
Socialist realism, 7, 53, 58, 191
Socialists-Revolutionaries, the party of, 149
Socialization, 40, 100, 105

Social origin, 40, 43, 53, 60, 129, 135, 136, 164
Sociological data, surveys, 8, 22, 23, 235, 236, 242
  prognoses, 1
Solomon, Peter H., 9, 43, 67, 102, 125, 126, 187
Solzhenitsyn, A.I., 16, 94
Spanish Civil War, the, 184, 191, 229
Special settlements, 40, 53, 137–141, 143, 165
  settlers, 137, 139–144
Stakhanov's movement, 39
  shock worker, 60, 139
  Stakhanovites, 53, 239
Stalin's revolution from above, "socialist offensive", 53
Stalin's speech about the constitution draft, 78, 222, 230
Statism, 123, 192, 242
Strikes, 81, 116, 118, 119, 155, 176
  agricultural, 119
  labor strikes, 155
Subjectivity, 5, 6, 20, 78, 89, 124, 155, 158, 183, 249
Suicides, 84, 135, 215
Supreme Council, 51, 214
  elections to, 51
Surveillance, 15–17, 80, 86, 93, 104, 198, 210
Svanidze, A.S., 33

T

Taxes, taxation, 77, 130, 131, 135–137, 152, 170, 175, 226, 230
Threat, external, foreign, 103
Tikhomirov, Alexei, 158, 212, 216
Traditionalist peasant culture, 5, 178, 198, 237, 241, 242, 249
Troikas, 43

Trotskyists, 51, 66, 67, 190
Trotsky, L., 54
Trust, 79, 130, 174, 192, 212–216, 239
TsIK, Presidium, 17–19, 29–31, 33, 35, 71–74, 81, 82, 88, 99, 129, 131–133, 135, 136, 139, 140, 142, 144, 146, 153, 156, 157, 166, 167, 171, 173, 175–177, 187, 188, 194, 195, 198, 209, 210, 221, 224–226
Commission on Cults, 17, 19

U
Ukraine, 2, 39, 41, 43, 119, 124, 133
Unions, the, 63
Universal suffrage, voting, 8, 32, 34, 35, 40, 57, 59, 63, 78, 99, 105, 125, 130, 133–138, 141, 142, 144, 146, 148, 149, 165, 171, 192, 210, 211, 217, 222, 223, 228, 237, 248
Urals, the, 111
Ustrialov, Nikolai, 6, 20, 91, 105, 106, 230

V
Vengeance, revenge, 140, 165, 166, 176, 182
Verba, Sidney, 11, 12, 80, 159, 198, 211, 216, 249
Verification of party documents, 1935–1936, 65, 66, 76, 77, 104
Victory of socialism, achievement of socialism, 37, 45, 52, 53, 143, 145
Vigilance, 57, 61, 64, 67, 75, 77, 187, 222
Viola, Lynne, 7, 16, 53, 65, 119, 120, 138, 142, 143
Violence, state, 104, 189, 228
Vladivostok, 79, 106
Vodka, 56, 95
Vyshinsky, A.Y., 43, 127, 143

W
War Scare, 1927, 80, 102, 195, 241
Washington, US, 15, 17, 20, 21, 51, 231, 239, 240
Weber, Max, 6, 102, 103, 151
Welfare, 21, 56–59, 92, 121, 123, 136, 192, 193, 205–207, 209, 211, 212, 222, 226, 236, 248
Western allies, 64
White Guard, the, 90
Wishful thinking, 3, 55, 58, 227
Women, 53, 60, 80, 82, 116, 117, 146, 153, 158, 179, 185, 188, 195, 198, 206, 224
housewives, 82, 133
World revolution, global socialism, 37, 51, 52, 54, 214
World War I, 104, 207, 231
Wrecker, wrecking, 57, 63, 64, 112, 119, 120, 186, 198, 227

X
Xenophobia, 241

Y
Yagoda, G.G., 42, 139
Yenukidze, A.S., 29–35, 52, 56, 59, 62, 71
Youth, 38, 40, 87, 139, 140, 149, 153, 178, 179, 186, 213, 217, 229
Yurchak, Alexei, 7, 78, 87

Z
Zhdanov, A.A., 32, 147, 186
Zhukov, Yury, 31, 35, 62
Zubkova, Elena, 236, 239, 240

Printed by Printforce, the Netherlands